# Rethinking Learning for a Digital Age

## LRC Learning Resource Centre

*Rethinking L*
experiences (
text combine
analysis, inclu
range of strate
their lives. A
book focuses
important cha

*Rethinking Le*

- Moves t
  of e-lear
- Analyse
  and lear
- Reveals
  right, wl
  and lear

Today's learne
shaping their o
researchers an
invaluable for
responses.

**Rhona Sharpe**
for Staff and Le
**Helen Beethar**
**Sara de Freita**
Coventry Technology Park.

# Rethinking Learning for a Digital Age

## How Learners are Shaping their own Experiences

Edited by
**Rhona Sharpe, Helen Beetham
and Sara de Freitas**

 Routledge
Taylor & Francis Group

NEW YORK AND LONDON

First published 2010
by Routledge
270 Madison Ave, New York NY 10016

Simultaneously published in the UK
by Routledge
2 Park Square, Milton Park, Abingdon, Oxon, OX14 4RN

*Routledge is an imprint of the Taylor & Francis Group, an informa business*

Transferred to Digital Printing 2010

© 2010 Taylor and Francis

Typeset in Minion by
HWA Text and Data Management, London

*Library of Congress Cataloging in Publication Data*
Rethinking learning for a digital age : how learners are shaping their own experiences / edited by Rhona Sharpe, Helen Beetham, and Sara de Freitas.
   p. cm.
   Includes bibliographical references and index.
1. Computer-assisted instruction. 2. Education–Effect of
technological innovations on. 3. Digital electronics.
I. Sharpe, Rhona, 1969- II. Beetham, Helen, 1967- III. Freitas, Sara de.
LB1028.5.R438 2010
   371.33'4–dc22                                         2009045553

ISBN 13: 978-0-415-87542-4 (hbk)
ISBN 13: 978-0-415-87543-1 (pbk)
ISBN 13: 978-0-203-85206-4 (ebk)

# Contents

# Tables

# Figures

# Contributors

**Helen Beetham** is an independent consultant, researcher and author in the field of e-learning, with particular expertise in UK Higher Education. Since 2004 she has played a leading role in the Joint Information Systems Committee (JISC) e-learning programme, advising on programmes in curriculum design, learning literacies, open educational resources and learners' experiences of e-learning. She is an experienced workshop leader and a regular speaker at conferences in the UK and abroad. With Rhona Sharpe she co-edited *Rethinking Pedagogy for the Digital Age* (Routledge 2007). She was a member of the expert panel for the Department for Children, Schools and Families (DCSF) funded 'Beyond current horizons' programme.

**Greg Benfield** is an educational developer within the Oxford Centre at Staff and Learning Development at Oxford Brookes University, with particular responsibility for e-learning. He provides internal consultancy on e-learning developments for Brookes' course teams and tutors on the Postgraduate Certificate in Teaching in Higher Education, as well as running workshops and online courses for higher education (HE) staff across the UK.

**Nick Bishop** is a freelance journalist and former university student. He has a BA (Hons) in Modern History and Politics from the University of Southampton and a postgraduate diploma in Journalism Studies from Cardiff University. During his time at Southampton, Nick was a key contributor to the LEXDIS project. LEXDIS is a JISC funded study examining the disabled students' use of technology and e-learning. For Nick, who has cerebral palsy and uses a wheelchair full-time, computers and digital technology have always been crucial learning resources. In his career as a journalist, Nick has written for a variety of publications including *The Guardian, The Bournemouth Echo* and *Media Wales*.

**George R. Bradford** is an instructional designer for the University of Central Florida (UCF). He has provided consulting services to twenty multinational companies on topics of traditional training, e-learning, blended learning and online support systems. For the last few years, he has been working with higher education and their growing practices of teaching and learning online. His current research is focused on the constructs and research designs for studying student satisfaction in distance learning.

**Jay Brophy-Ellison** is an Associate Professor of Psychology at the University of Central Florida (UCF). During Jay's thirty-six-year career at UCF, he has been instrumental in bringing innovative technology into the classroom. He has been involved with course development and web services at UCF since its inception. An early user of WebCT, he has offered courses in traditional, hybrid-reduced seat time, and fully web-based courses since 1996. During the last five years, Jay has been teaching large sections (400+ students) of General Psychology and Physiological Psychology with a heavy emphasis on web-enhanced instruction. Jay has earned numerous teaching awards and is currently a Senior Teaching Fellow with the UCF Faculty Center for Teaching and Learning.

**Cheryl Brown** is a Lecturer in the Centre for Educational Technology (CET) at the University of Cape Town, South Africa. Over the past six years she has been the primary researcher on CET's research projects on higher education students access to and use of information and communication technologies (ICTs). She is currently undertaking her PhD in Information Systems, focusing on discourses of ICTs amongst university students.

**Betty Collis** is a specialist in the application of technology for strategy, learning and change in educational organizations and corporate training. She now works as a consultant but was a member of the Faculty of Education at the University of Victoria, Canada, from 1976–1988, and Professor in the Faculty of Educational Science and Technology (now Behavioural Sciences) at the University of Twente in The Netherlands until she took early retirement in 2005. She is a prolific author and has published approximately 690 scientific publications, is a frequently invited conference speaker and currently works with a number of universities and (inter)national organizations as an advisor, including, during 2007–2008 as a Senior Consultant with the Higher Education Academy in the UK.

**Gráinne Conole** is Professor of E-Learning in the Institute of Educational Technology at the Open University in the UK. Previously she was Professor of Educational Innovation in Post-Compulsory Education at the University of Southampton and before that Director of the Institute for Learning and Research Technology at the University of Bristol. Her research interests include the use, integration and evaluation of information and communication technologies, and e-learning and the impact of technologies on organizational change. Two of her current areas of interest are focusing on the evaluation of students' experiences and perceptions of technologies and how learning design can help in creating more engaging learning activities.

**Linda Creanor** is Development Director for Professional Practice in the Caledonian Academy, a centre for educational research and scholarship at Glasgow Caledonian University. She has been involved in a range of national and European e-learning projects as a researcher, designer, evaluator and consultant, and has presented and published widely. Most recently, she led the UK-wide LEX study, which explored the learner perspective on e-learning across the post-16 sectors, in collaboration with the Open Learning Partnership, London. She is currently a Trustee of the Association for Learning Technology (ALT), having previously served as Vice-Chair, Chair and President. She is a Fellow of the Higher Education Academy.

**Laura Czerniewicz** is Associate Professor at the University of Cape Town, South Africa. Laura is the Director of Centre for Educational Technology (CET) and previously was the Director of the Multimedia Education Group (MEG). She operates at multiple interfaces, and considers the true nature of her job to be that of an interpreter and translator. She is interested in the relationships between policy and practice, as well as the conceptual underpinnings of this emerging domain of enquiry.

**Sara de Freitas** is Director of Research at the Serious Games Institute (SGI) – an international hub of excellence in the area of games, virtual worlds and interactive digital media for serious purposes, including education, health and business applications. Situated on the Technology Park at the University of Coventry, Sara leads an interdisciplinary and cross-university applied research group. Based as part of the largest commercial arm of any UK university, the SGI applied research group – with expertise in artificial intelligence (AI) and games, visualization, mixed reality, augmented reality and location aware technologies – works closely with international industrial and academic research and development partners.

**Maarten de Laat** works at IVLOS, University of Utrecht and at Ruud de Moor Centrum, The Dutch Open University, where he coordinates a long-term research programme on Networked Learning and Communities of Practice in the context of professional development. His research is currently focused on how these social perspectives on learning facilitates teacher learning and how this can be implemented in organizations.

**Lone Dirckinck-Holmfeld** is Dean of the Faculty of Humanities at Aalborg University. She came from a position as Professor of ICT and Learning at Aalborg University, Department of Communication, and was the Scientific

Director of E-learning lab. Her main field of research is computer-supported collaborative learning (CSCL) in distributed environments, participatory design and implementation. She has authored and co-authored several books, articles and reports on ICT and learning.

**Charles D. Dziuban** is Director of the Research Initiative for Teaching Effectiveness at the University of Central Florida (UCF) where he has been a faculty member since 1970 teaching design and statistics. Since 1996, he has directed the impact evaluation of UCF's distributed learning initiative, examining student and faculty outcomes as well as gauging the impact of online courses in the university. In 2005, Chuck received the Sloan Consortium award for Most Outstanding Achievement in Online Learning by an Individual. In 2007, he was appointed to the National Information and Communication Technology Literacy Policy Council.

**Robert A. Ellis** is Associate Professor and Director of eLearning at the University of Sydney. He has been a continuing chief investigator on Australian Research Council Discovery Grants since 2005 with Peter Goodyear of the University of Sydney and Mike Prosser of the University of Hong Kong. He has published over fifty peer reviewed journal articles, books and conference papers in the areas of student experience of learning, educational technologies and academic literacy. His current research is focusing on how key aspects of the university student experience of learning are fundamentally related across physical and virtual contexts.

**Keri Facer** is Professor of Education at the Institute of Education, Manchester Metropolitan University (MMU), where she leads the Create research group in informal learning, digital cultures and educational change. Keri was responsible for leading the UK government's 'Beyond current horizons' research programme, tasked with exploring the future of education beyond 2025. Prior to joining MMU, Keri was Research Director of Futurelab where she led the team responsible for developing a wide range of projects in areas ranging from curriculum innovation, to computer games and mobile learning, to assessment reform. She has published widely in areas of digital cultures and learning, and regularly advises government, non-governmental and private sector organizations on issues relating to socio-technical change, educational futures and social justice.

**Peter Goodyear** is Professor of Education at the University of Sydney and a Senior Fellow of the Australian Learning and Teaching Council. He is co-director of the University's Centre for Research on Computer-Supported Learning and Cognition (CoCo). His research addresses educational implications of technological change. Over the last thirty years he has published widely on learning and teaching with new technology, the design and management of productive learning environments and the capabilities needed for successful participation in a knowledge society – learning to 'think for a living'. His latest book, written with Rob Ellis, is *Students' Experiences of E-learning in Higher Education* (RoutledgeFalmer 2009).

**Amanda T. Groff** is an Instructor of Anthropology at the University of Central Florida (UCF) where she has been both a student and faculty member since 1999. Her current research focuses on the archaeology and bioarchaeology of the Ancient Maya, as well as the application of new communication tools in the online teaching environment.

**Judy Hardy** works at EPCC, a Research Institute within the School of Physics and Astronomy at the University of Edinburgh. She is a member of the Physics Education Research group at Edinburgh and has an active involvement in a range of e-learning projects. These have included a European Community funded project to develop tools for collaborative online learning, investigations into students' use of e-learning resources and a JISC funded project to explore students' experiences of the ways that e-learning resources are used across a variety of academic disciplines. She teaches on a number of courses at both undergraduate and postgraduate level and is Director of Studies for the MSc in High Performance Computing.

**Julie Hughes** works in the School of Education at the University of Wolverhampton. Julie's teaching and research interests focus upon exploring, with her students and colleagues, how e-portfolio-based learning can support the transitions into and out of HE, the development of HE identities and the creation of new learning and teaching cultures and communities.

**Jill Jameson** is Director of Research and Enterprise at Greenwich's School of Education and Training, Fellow of the Institute for Learning (FIfL), with a PhD and MA (Distinction, Kings College London, Computers in Education), MA (Goldsmith's), MA (University of Cambridge), Postgraduate Certificate in Education (PGCE) (Distinction, University of Nottingham). Co-Chair of ALT-C 2008, Guest Editor *British Journal of Educational Technology* (BJET) (2006) and ALT-J (2000), Jill is a 'Critical Friend' for JISC's Users and Innovations Programme and JISC Experts' Group member. Jill was Director of the JISC funded e-learning Independent Design Activities for Collaborative Approaches to the Management of e-Learning (eLIDA CAMEL), Director of the eLearning Independent Study Award (eLISA) Distributed eLearning (DEL) programme, funded by JISC Greenwich lead for JISC infoNet's CAMEL and Higher Education Academy Student Experience of E-learning Laboratory (SEEL) project research lead/survey designer.

**Amanda Jefferies** is a Principal Lecturer and University Teaching Fellow in the School of Computer Science at the University of Hertfordshire, currently seconded to their Blended Learning Unit, a Higher Education Funding Council for England Centre for Excellence in Teaching and Learning, where she leads research on the evaluation of technology-enhanced learning with academics and students. She was Director of the Student Reflections On Lifelong e-Learning (STROLL) project in the JISC 'Learners' experiences of e-learning' programme, developing research through student-constructed video and audio diaries. She is a member of the JISC Learning and Teaching Experts group.

**Jef Moonen** is Emeritus Professor in the Faculty of Behavioural Sciences (formerly the Faculty of Educational Science and Technology) at the University of Twente in The Netherlands. Prior to his retirement he served as Department Chair and Dean of the Faculty. Before this, he was Director of the National Institute for Computers in Education in The Netherlands. His current research includes studying digital portfolios as tools for the contribution-oriented pedagogy. In addition, he continues his long-standing research on return on investment of computer-supported learning. He also works as a consultant for technology supported learning initiatives.

**Patsy D. Moskal** is Associate Director for the Research Initiative for Teaching Effectiveness at the University of Central Florida (UCF) where she has been a faculty member since 1989. Since 1996, she has served as a liaison for faculty research of distributed learning and teaching effectiveness at UCF. She has co-authored a number of book chapters and journal articles on research in online and blended courses.

**Martin Oliver** is a Reader in ICT in Education at the London Knowledge Lab, which is part of the Institute of Education, University of London. He is an editor of the journal *Learning, Media and Technology*. His research focuses on the use of technology in higher education, particularly how the use of technology changes peoples' roles and practices.

**Malcolm Ryan** is a principal lecturer in Education in the School of Education and Training at the University of Greenwich. He is a qualified and experienced teacher and educational technologist and brings these skills to his role as Head of Teaching and Learning Enhancement Team (TALENT). Known for working collaboratively with colleagues, Malcolm has been a team member of several JISC and Higher Education Academy projects including DEL eLISA, CAMEL and Design for Learning eLIDA CAMEL. Malcolm is a member of the Editorial Committee of the *International Journal of E-Learning* (IJEL), on the Steering and Programme Committees of Association for the Advancement of Computing in Education's Ed-Media and a reviewer for ALT-J.

**Thomas Ryberg** is an Assistant Professor at Aalborg University, Department of Communication and Psychology. He is affiliated with the research centre E-Learning Lab, Center for User Driven Innovation, Learning and Design. His research interests are related to how new media and technologies transform our ways of thinking about and designing for learning. More generally his research interests are within the field of ICT and learning for development, youth and ICT, technology and new media, and socio-cultural learning theories.

**Maggi Savin-Baden** is Professor of Higher Education Research at Coventry University, and Director of the Learning Innovation Research Group. As someone who has always been interested in innovation and change, Maggi's interest in learning has been the focus of her research for many years. Her current research is focusing on the impact of virtual worlds on learning and teaching, funded by the JISC and The Leverhulme Trust. To date she has published six books on problem-based learning and one in 2007 entitled *Learning Spaces,* McGraw Hill. Her next two books tackle new approaches to qualitative research and are to be published with Routledge in 2010. In her spare time she is doing an MSc in e-learning and learning to snowboard.

**Jane Seale** is a Senior Lecturer at the University of Southampton, School of Education. Her teaching and research interests lie at the intersections between disability, technology and education. For twenty years Jane has been researching the role of computers and assistive technologies in promoting independence, identity and quality of life for adults with disabilities. Her 2006 book *E-learning and Disability in Higher Education: Accessibility Research and Practice* is in over 400 libraries worldwide and she has led national and international workshops, seminars and panel discussions focusing on issues of accessibility and digital inclusion. She is also a co-investigator of a JISC funded project called LEXDIS, which aims to explore the e-learning experiences of students with disabilities.

**Neil Selwyn** is a sociologist working at the London Knowledge Lab – part of the Institute of Education, University of London. His research and teaching focuses on the place of digital media in everyday life, and the sociology of technology (non-) use in educational settings. He has written extensively on a number of issues, including digital exclusion, education technology policy-making and the student experience of technology-based learning. Recent books include *Primary Schools and ICT: Learning from Pupil Perspectives* (2009) and *Adult Learning in the Digital Age* (Routledge 2005).

**Rhona Sharpe** is a Principal Lecturer in the Oxford Centre for Staff and Learning Development at Oxford Brookes University where she is responsible for the research and consultancy activities of the unit. She was the project director of the support and synthesis project for the JISC's 'Learner experiences of e-learning' programme and has conducted reviews of e-learning literature and practice for the JISC and Higher Education Academy. She is an editor for the Association for Learning Technology's Journal, *ALT-J, Research in Learning Technology*, and a founder member of Experiences of E-Learning Special Interest Group (ELESIG), a special interest group for those investigating and evaluating learners' experiences of e-learning.

**Cathy Tombs** is a Research Assistant in the Learning Innovation Research Group at Coventry University, and is involved in learning in innovative and new technologies, particularly in virtual worlds. Her work includes the research and development of virtual learning scenarios in various disciplines, and she has had involvement in several projects including the JISC funded Problem-based Learning in Virtual Immersive Educational Worlds (PREVIEW) and Open-Content Employability (OCEP) projects.

**Kathryn Trinder** is a Research Fellow and Educational Development Advisor in the Caledonian Academy at Glasgow Caledonian University. She is a learning technologist involved in a range of activities spanning learning activity design, teaching and staff development in e-learning, and the exploration of emerging technologies. Recent research includes Learner experience of e-learning (LEX) and Learning from Digital Natives (LDN), which investigated e-learning from the student perspective. Her present work and research interests revolve around the use of Web 2.0 and Web 3D technologies. She is currently co-managing several pilot projects within GCU that develop and research Second Life and other 3D virtual worlds as teaching environments.

**Simon Walker** is Head of Educational Development at the University of Greenwich, where he is responsible for a wide range of strategic enhancement-driven projects. These currently include transition, feedback and assessment, and graduate attributes. He is programme co-leader of the Certificate of Professional Development in Transforming Learning with Digital Technologies and Pathway Leader for the MA in Education (e-Learning). He has led a number of national e-learning projects and was awarded a Higher Education Academy National Teaching Fellowship in 2006. He is also responsible for the annual e-learning, and learning and teaching conferences at the University of Greenwich as well as the university's Bicycle Users Group.

# Foreword

The question of how learners experience learning in a technology-rich age is relevant and important. It is thus timely that the book *Rethinking Learning for a Digital Age* now appears. To set the stage for this fine book, we would like to introduce the metaphor of learning footprints for twenty-first century learners. By learning footprints we mean some evidence of where a learner has been or is going and what she is using and possibly leaving behind while she is making the footprints.

Within this metaphor we would like to focus on two questions. The first is of a descriptive nature: what are patterns in these learning footprints? Or, to operationalize this, when, where and how do twenty-first century learners go about their learning activities? The second question brings in issues of causality or at least correlation: how do the affordances of different learning spaces influence learning footprints?

Part of the first question appears to be more or less straightforward. Where and when do learners go to carry out their learning activities? Can we follow their footprints?

But it turns out to be not so easy to address this question. A visit to the JISC Info site of photos showing a large range of learning environments in UK higher education institutions (JISC 2009) immediately makes it clear that the idea of capturing where and when learners go for their learning activities requires multidimensional elaborations. There are dimensions relating to flexibility, to social interaction, to physical aspects such as types of seating and working environments, and to the instructor/learner balance in decision making about when and how to make use of a learning setting. And to further complicate the issue it is clear that learners move seamlessly in and out of, and occupy at the same time, various blends of learning spaces and environments. Milne (2006) notes the interplay between physical spaces and virtual spaces, each further segmented in terms of the extent to which the instructor designates or is present in the spaces. He identifies formal physical spaces (such as classrooms or seminar rooms), physical social spaces (such as coffee lounges), physical transition spaces (such as hallways), physical small group work spaces (such as a meeting room in a library), physical private spaces (such as the learner's own residence), virtual social spaces (such as Facebook or any other social community environment), virtual public communication spaces both formal (course environments in virtual learning environments (VLEs)) and informal (blogs), and virtual private environments (email and instant messaging). For any learning activity, learners may combine or recombine various combinations of these different types of spaces. Clearly the message is that there is a blurring of boundaries when we consider where and when learners carry out learning activities. There are innumerable combinations of physical, virtual, social, private, institutional and non-institutional settings that may at any given time, for any given learner, differ as she goes about a learning activity. Thus the descriptive question of where and when learners go for learning activities does not have a simple answer.

To analyse the complexity even further, let us focus on learners' virtual footprints. We can look at these in terms of verbs: what the learners are doing. At one level, their activities are assimilative. They use digital resources and pathways to listen, to watch, to read. Learners have always done these activities; what differs now are the scope, range and the lack of gatekeeping compared to traditional (i.e. pre-twenty-first century ) settings. The next level of virtual learning activities relates to the transition from assimilating to re-expressing ideas and resources. Again learners have always annotated and adapted and expanded ideas. What is different now is the way that learners can affect resource materials themselves and the magnitude of the scale of influence that their adaptations can have on other learners. Instead of only noting their ideas in their own paper notepads, they can now add their ideas to the original sources or even challenge or adapt the original sources. Their thoughts can be noticed by other learners, from their own context but also outside of their frame of reference.

A further layer of digital learning activity relates to the personal organization of learning. Learners need to capture, store and label what they find or annotate or create. Again these have always been learning activities but what makes the twenty-first century processes different relates to access, linkages and sharing. No longer do learners have to have their notes with them physically; anywhere they have network access they can have access to their learning materials and can combine, link and manage them in ways not feasible with traditional (pre-twenty-first century) tools. The level that particularly escalates learning activities in virtual spaces is that of sharing. Learners can now share not only their ideas but their resources, their bookmark collections, their work in progress, their completed work with whomever they wish, with no limitations based on physical proximity. The learning footprints associated with virtual sharing are of a level of complexity we have never encountered before.

Moving from description to causation (or at least correlation), our second question is: how do the affordances of different learning spaces influence learning footprints? Universities make large investments in both physical and virtual learning environments on the assumption that these will lead to different, and presumably better, learning footprints than in pre-twenty-first century times. But it remains frustratingly difficult to isolate the impact of a particular learning space or intervention on learner development. Again the multidimensionality of learning footprints makes unidimensional conclusions unwise if not impossible. Simplistically we can say that learning footprints are a function of (at least) the personal characteristics of the learner, cohort cultures, time available to the learner for learning, extrinsic and intrinsic motivations for learning, institutional affordances (spaces, tools and support available), technologies used and their affordances, social and personal priorities, and, last but not least, the pedagogies set forward by their instructors for learning. It is not contradictory with a focus on learners to consider the pedagogical practices of instructors as important components of the learner experiences. While learners have always made many decisions for themselves as to how, when and with what tools they will learn, the types of learning activities expected of them in their formal study provide a strong frame around the path of their learning footprints. Learners for whom successful completion of a course means being at lectures, listening, remembering, reading and then remembering for an assessment moment will leave different footprints than learners from whom successful completion of a course means working collaboratively with other students to find, critically decompose and recombine, and create new learning artifacts whose value includes the extent the new contributions will be useful to others. We cannot expect busy learners in higher education to, on their own, develop complex collaborative learning tasks. These are pedagogically steered. We have studied the role of the instructor in a 'contributing student' learning approach (see Collis and Moonen 2007). Left on their own, learners will participate in 'underworlds' of social learning networks – what Benfield and De Laat (Chapter 13 of this volume) call collaboration around the task, invisible to their instructor – and make use of sophisticated digital tools and resources to support their learning but will be constrained or at least steered by what matters for assessment and accreditation in their units and programmes and professions. We cannot expect the learners to have other than a conservative view of their expectations of formal learning in higher education if higher education in return does not appear to value or accredit non-conservative learning activities.

Thus, *Rethinking Learning for a Digital Age* is indeed a timely and important contribution. We applaud and appreciate its examination of learner footprints in the higher education context.

Betty Collis and Jef Moonen
Emeritus Professors,
University of Twente, The Netherlands

## References

Collis, B. & Moonen, J. (2007) The contributing student: Philosophy, technology, and strategy. In: J. M. Spector (Ed.), *Finding your online voice: Stories told by experienced online educators* (pp. 19–31). Mahwah, NJ: Lawrence Erlbaum Associates.

JISC (2009) Planning and designing technology rich learning spaces. Retrieved 2 November, 2009, from http://www.jiscinfonet.ac.uk/infokits/learning-space-design/more/flickr.

Milne, A. J. (2006) Designing blended learning space to the student experience. In D. G. Oblinger (Ed.) *Learning spaces* (Chapter 11). An Educause e-book. Boulder, CO: Educause. Retrieved 2 November, 2009, from http://www.educause.edu/learningspacesch11.

# Acknowledgements

The editors and authors would like to acknowledge the support of the UK Joint Information Systems Committee (JISC) in the writing of this book. The JISC-funded Understanding my Learning and Learner Experiences of E-learning programmes were the starting point for much of the work in this field of research. These programmes supported the original work on which some of the chapters are based and prompted a great deal of further research. In particular, the following chapters were developed from research originally funded by the JISC: Chapter 3 (Creanor and Trinder), Chapter 6 (Sharpe and Beetham), Chapter 9 (Seale and Bishop) and Chapter 11 (Beetham and Oliver). The JISC also supported the early synthesis and dissemination of these findings at conferences and network meetings, such as the Learning and Teaching Practice Experts Group meetings of the JISC e-Learning and Pedagogy programme. We are deeply indebted to colleagues who have attended these meetings and who have helped to refine our materials and ideas. We are also grateful to the reviewers who commented on early drafts of the chapters in constructive and helpful ways, and ultimately have led to this being a better book.

## Acknowledgement of Copyright Permissions

Table 15.1 was originally published in *Confronting the Challenges of Participatory culture: Media education for the 21st Century* edited by Henry Jenkins, with Ravi Purushotma, Margaret Weigel, Katie Clinton and Alice J. Robinson, and is reproduced with the kind permission of the MacAuthor Foundation and MIT Press.

# An Introduction to *Rethinking Learning for a Digital Age*

RHONA SHARPE, HELEN BEETHAM,
SARA DE FREITAS AND GRÁINNE CONOLE

## Learning in a Digital Age

This book is concerned with how learners experience learning in a technology rich age. There is no doubt that for those of us living in the developed world, it is a world full of technology. Technology surrounds us and in the last decade advances in its availability and functionality have changed the way we communicate, find information and even do our shopping. Educational institutions have invested heavily in technology, fitting out computer laboratories, installing electronic whiteboards in classrooms and managed learning environments behind the scenes. Some of the technology that we find in educational institutions is the same, or at least similar to, that found in society more generally but others are distinct to our academic practices. Where we recognize it as being different, we make attempts to induct new students to its use (such as electronic libraries), but other technology is used without so much as a comment (think about electronic presentations and websites on reading lists). In addition, students arrive with their own personal technology to add to the mix – and, just when we think we understand all the tools and resources we have available to us, it changes again. What the experience of the past few years has shown us is how indelibly linked technologies are with social and cultural interactions and interchanges. This should make us even more wary of the dangers of technological determinism, and opening up new potential for more enriched and immersive learning experiences. With this in mind we are watching with interest developments in gaming and ambient technologies for their possible relevance and application within educational contexts. Practitioners and policy makers need to acknowledge how radically learners' relationships with technology are changing, and how this impacts upon their expectations and experience of education.

This collection brings together research that focuses on the experiences of learners in post-compulsory education. While we do draw on findings from studies of children where appropriate – knowing that these will be our learners in a few short years' time – our interest is in adult learners. We focus on the skills that adults are asked to perform in tertiary education, such as analysis, synthesis, collaboration and evaluating resources, and look at how their access to technology is changing how they undertake these tasks. We have attempted to draw links between the established literature on student learning research and the emerging research on digital literacy, such as observing how young people undertake group tasks (Ryberg and Dirckinck-Holmfeld, Chapter 12) and exploring how learners' approaches to study underpin their uses of technology (Goodyear and Ellis, Chapter 7).

Alongside this interest in learning process and practices, we are keen to promote a wider view of the student experience that encompasses other aspects of learners' lives. One of the notable features of learner experience research is the extent to which it has intentionally set out to take such a holistic view. It is about the worlds that learners inhabit themselves as well as the ones we present them with. It is about how they manage their identities as learners at the heart of increasingly complex personal, educational and social networks. So, as well as examining technology use and its influence on expectations and approaches to study, we look at the use of technology more broadly. We examine the role that technology plays in managing the increasing complexity of learners' lives (Creanor and Trinder, Chapter 3) and the interaction between technology used for social, leisure and study purposes that blurs the boundaries between formal and informal contexts for learning and opens up new spaces for interchange and learning (Facer and Selwyn, Chapter 2).

What becomes clear is the extent to which learners are becoming active participants in their learning experiences and are shaping their own educational environments. We reveal digital-age learners as creative actors and networkers in their own right, who make strategic choices about their use of digital applications and learning approaches. Learners are creating their own blends of physical and virtual environments and of informal and formal learning contexts. We are interested in following what Collis refers to as the patterns in the 'footprints' of how twenty-first-century learners make use of the technologies available to them (Collis 2009).

This book sits alongside our previous book: *Rethinking Pedagogy for a Digital Age*. We argued there that technological applications of information and communication technology (ICT) only has the potential to transform education in ways that are beneficial and that it was the role of teachers to exploit that potential through their designs for learning. The skill of teachers to design activities and environments to promote learning is not in dispute. We argue here, in this companion volume, that these actions of teachers are not enough. The reorganization of learning is being driven by learners now, in a way that places a great deal more emphasis upon designing learning from their perspective.

Ultimately it is the learner who learns, and the new applications certainly place more power in their hands, albeit that they are still in need of support with how to use these in educational contexts. For instance, as social technologies have become an integrative and pervasive part of learners' lives, we need to uncover how they experience this and how it interacts with and blends with our designs for learning. The first chapter (de Freitas and Conole, Chapter 1) makes this link between the two volumes explicit, outlining how pedagogic models and new metaphors for learning provide a response to an environment in which tools and their availability changes so rapidly. They detail a range of new tools and applications that can be used to support greater learner empowerment, emphasizing how a deeper consideration of pedagogy can be utilized to support these rapid changes.

## An Overview of Learner Experience Research

There has been a growing body of research looking explicitly at the learner's experience of using technology in an educational context. Part 1 summarizes some of this work. Although we present only a snapshot, the chapters in themselves provide case studies of current research in this field.

Around the mid-1990s represents the time when the use of ICT and the Web were beginning to have a greater impact within institutions: email had become prevalent, the Web was becoming recognized as both a valuable source of information and a useful marketing tool, and there were numerous educational technology-supported interventions, in particular around the role of computer-mediated conferencing (e.g. Mason and Kaye 1989). By the early 2000s more comprehensive virtual learning environments were being rolled out across institutions and integrated with student records systems (see Browne and Jenkins 2003). There were of course evaluations being conducted of these implementations. In the main these focused on recommendations for local improvements, examining the role of the tutor or moderator in online discussions and surveys of the uptake of technology.

In the United Kingdom, the Joint Information Systems Committee (JISC) began a programme of work, which we began with a review of papers that purported to focus on the learner experience (Sharpe et al. 2005). We found that many of the studies focused primarily at the level of course evaluations, rather than on how learners actually use and experience ICT. We argued that there had been a lack of acknowledgement of the learner perspective in the development of tools, pedagogy and teaching practices. We suggested that more in-depth studies were needed to capture the diversity of how learners are using technologies in their studies, as well as to elicit their perceptions of e-learning. As a result, the JISC commissioned two studies of adult learners that established that technology use is pervasive and integrative, with learners making frequent use of technology both at home and within their learning institution (Creanor et al. 2006; Conole et al. 2007). These concluded that there were two main uses of ICT by learners: for information, and to access an underworld of technology-mediated informal learning. Of interest was the dominance of tools from everyday life being reflected in the choices learners made. So learners used everyday tools such as Google and Wikipedia to find information and used social networking sites and instant messaging systems such as MySpace and MSN to communicate with their peers.

About the same time in Australia, Gregor Kennedy and colleagues were using a survey to gather quantitative and qualitative data about students' use of technologies. Published three years later, Kennedy et al. (2008) provided evidence that increased levels of access and new uses of the tools were emerging. The study also found that learners were 'overwhelmingly positive' about the use of ICT, indicating that they used these tools for many aspects of their studies including finding information, communicating with teachers and peers, course administration as well as for general study purposes. Although published before the current wave of Web 2.0 technologies really took effect, this study shows evidence that learners were starting to use social networking sites such as MySpace, and Web 2.0 tools such as wikis and blogs. However, the study found that patterns of use were not homogeneous:

> [Learners were] very tech-savvy. Many students are using a wide range of traditional and emerging technologies regularly in their daily lives. However, there are clearly areas where the use of and familiarity with technology-based tools is far from universal among first year students.
> (Kennedy et al. 2008: 8)

In the United States, Oblinger and Oblinger's (2005) book, *Educating the Net Generation*, provides a kind of watershed in respect of the characterization of how learners were interacting with new tools and how this might be changing the ways in which they were learning. Terms, such as 'Net Generation', 'Nintendo kids'; 'Millennials' (among others) typify this movement (see for example, Tapscott 1998; Prensky 2001; Oblinger and Oblinger 2005; Kennedy et al. 2008). In their introduction, Oblinger and Oblinger note, '... [w]e hope this book will help educators make sense of the many patterns and behaviours that we see in the Net Generation but don't quite understand' (2005: 7). The general arguments the book puts forward are that: technologies are 'interwoven' through all aspects of the lives of the Net Generation, that today's Net Generation have grown up with technology, use and ownership of technologies is becoming near ubiquitous and consequently learners use the Web extensively for homework. In brief, learners view technologies as being 'part of our world', 'embedded in society', 'make things faster' and the new tools enable them to learn more effectively (in their view) and help them to more readily connect with family, peers and teachers.

Although it now seems unlikely that the terms above can be used to accurately describe the characteristics of a whole generation of learners, the technological context in which they find themselves has undoubtedly changed dramatically in recent years, and indeed are still changing. Recent learner experience research has tracked such changes. For example, surveys of usage have monitored the explosion in the use of Web 2.0 technologies. In the UK, the JISC/Ipsos Mori surveys found that 65 per cent of school leavers regularly used social networking sites in 2007 and this had risen to 93 per cent of the same cohort a year later in their first year of university (JISC 2007a; JISC 2008). Similar usage figures have been reported from annual surveys of undergraduates in the US undertaken by Educause (see for example Caruso and Salaway 2008), although not in South Africa where uptake of social software is low (Czerniewicz and Brown, Chapter 10). Learner experience research can be a powerful tool in uncovering the voices behind such usage figures, such as Facer and Selwyn's findings in Chapter 2 around learners' use of social networking. Here we see that we should not assume from the high levels of usage that education should be attempting to 'catch up' with societal trends.

In these changing times, the value of learner experience research has been to provide detailed, rich accounts of actual use alongside an aggregate body of empirical data from which it is possible to extrapolate future trends and patterns of use. The results are useful in terms of providing up-to-date empirical evidence of learners' current learning environments. The findings give a hint of the learners' environment of tomorrow and raise a host of important implications for policy and practice. At an institutional level, we have uncovered learners' lived experience of the intended flexible delivery of content provided by virtual learning environments that has implications for the systems we provide (Creanor and Trinder, Chapter 3). Surely the success or otherwise of such institutional investment should be measured in how it is experienced by its users. It is important that the sector has such research available on which to base decisions – especially as we move into a period of constrained finances.

Learner experience research also has value in surfacing the experiences of individuals whose views might be under-represented. Seale and Bishop (Chapter 9) present the findings of a study into disabled students' experiences of technology in higher education. Their methodology adopts a participatory approach to engage learners in all stages of the research. This approach has been successful both in revealing aspects of the learners' experience that might otherwise be hidden and in presenting it vividly in the learners' own words. Such rich descriptions that illuminate the learner's world are becoming characteristic of this field of research, which draws widely on narratives (Savin-Baden and Tombs, Chapter 5), diaries and logs (Hardy and Jefferies,

Chapter 8) and interviews (Benfield and De Laat, Chapter 13). The words of learners feature strongly in many of the chapters as researchers explore the use of a range of methodologies to see which can provide a suitable combination of rigour and rich description. The multiple methods for social interactions and social expression foreground inadequacies of existing methodologies and approaches to capture and analyse the complexities at work in these new contexts and spaces of learning.

## Contexts for Learning

Part 1 focuses on contexts for learning, making links with available tools, wider changes in society, learning in life and teaching as design. de Freitas and Conole (Chapter 1) take as their starting point that research has failed to adequately acknowledge the learner perspective in the development of tools and pedagogy, arguing that these have been driven by the availability of ICT tools rather than learner needs. Their review of learner experience research shows that learners use a wide range of ICT tools, often interchangeably, and in both formal and informal contexts. A major challenge for institutions is to capture this richness of potential and harness it into quality educational approaches. The use of pedagogy to apply more diverse strategies of learning is posited here, however, the real challenges of adopting these new pedagogies and accessing and leveraging the new metaphors of learning remain significant challenges. As tutors shift from tutor-centred approaches towards more activity-led methods, questions remain as to how effective these approaches will be for supporting the new skill sets that are currently hard to outline and define. The studies collectively indicate a reversal of fortune away from information retrieval and regurgitation and towards user generated content and exploratory learning models, away from single learner study towards participatory and collaborative practices.

One of the challenges of technology-mediated learning is the rate at which contexts change so rapidly. In 2006 we were uncovering 'an underworld' of social networking, which until that point had been operating largely unnoticed by teachers (Creanor et al. 2006). Now we know that 73 per cent of first year undergraduates in the UK use social networking sites to discuss their coursework (JISC 2008). In Chapter 2, Facer and Selwyn specifically review the role of social networks in managing social relationships and managing the logistics of study. In Chapter 3, Creanor and Trinder illustrate the complexity of the contexts in which learners operate. They highlight the interplays between self and institution, study and home, friends and tutors and show how this is acted out and crucially, felt, by learners. With a focus on the use of technology to manage the practical complexity of being a student, they juxtapose the learner perspective of managing their time and learning spaces alongside commonly held institutional views of flexibility.

Dziuban and colleagues in **Chapter 4 explore ways** of measuring the satisfaction of learners in the so-called Net Generation and start to consider some of the social implications of the technologies. In particular, they continue some of the critical questioning begun in the Facer and Selwyn chapter and explore the margins of student identity and social networks as potential learning accelerators. The notion of ethnographic methods of exploring student experiences is similarly taken up by Savin-Baden and Tombs in their study of learners' experiences of virtual **worlds in Chapter 5. Here** the emphasis is on identity and virtual spaces as boundary objects allowing learners to traverse between different kinds of learning experiences, constructing complex relationships between in-world and real-world behaviour.

Together this first part demonstrates the extent to which learning is being rethought and reconstructed by learners. It is their identity, representations and constructions, rather than those of the tutors, which are the tools at the heart of the sets of shifts that allow us to reconstruct how we consider and approach teaching and learning.

**Frameworks for Understanding the Learner Experience**

The preceding brief review of learner experience research and the changing contexts for learning hints at the complexity of the relationships between learners and their technology use. Clearly it is not going to be possible to explain learners' use of technology in terms of generational effects, so other explanations must be sought. In addition, the focus on holistic research has helped us to see the role of technology within the wider context of learners' lives and there have been great strides in developing research methodologies that will elicit from their learners their behaviours, thoughts and attitudes towards technology use. The accounts that are being produced give a fascinating insight into learners' lives (see for example JISC 2007b). They also demonstrate – vividly – the differences between learners in their experiences. As the field of learner experience research matures, the challenge is to make meaning from the many descriptions we now have available (Sharpe 2009a). In Part 2 we present a range of ways in which researchers are developing conceptual accounts to explain such variation. Such conceptual accounts should underpin future research so that we do more than simply collect stories. Indeed, in a field that changes so fast, individual stories rapidly appear dated.

Developing frameworks will also enable us to have confidence in making recommendations on the basis of the research. There is currently a great deal of interest in the 'student learning experience' (House of Commons 2009), and there is pressure to turn research findings quickly into changes in practice (see for example Sharpe 2009b). In this volume alone, we have made recommendations for the design of tools (de Freitas and **Conole, Chapter 1**), the design of learning activities (Goodyear and **Ellis, Chapter 7**), the provision of online materials (Seale and Bishop, Chapter 9), supporting students through transition (Hardy and Jefferies, Chapter 8) and strategies for developing digital literacies (Walker et al. Chapter 15). For a field of research that has the potential to have such impact, and that is being followed so closely by decision makers, it is important that our work is methodologically sound and underpinned by theoretical concepts. Czerniewicz and Brown (Chapter 10) provide a good example of using a combination of empirical research and a theoretical lens to explore complex issues including: boundaries between in and out of the curriculum, social and academic uses of technology and physical and virtual learning environments.

So what frameworks might be useful? There is already a rich literature focusing more broadly on the learner experience beyond the scope of technology mediated learning. Thorpe et al. (2008) encouraged those working in e-learning to make use of this, citing in particular the work of Richardson (e.g. 2005, 2006) and Entwistle (e.g. Entwistle and Ramsden 1983; Entwistle 2009) who have contributed so much to student learning research. In Chapter 7, Goodyear and Ellis take a phenomenographic approach, much used in student learning research, to explain learners' conceptions of learning, and learning with technology. Importantly they demonstrate the importance of context, finding that students can change their learning approach in response to the pedagogic context and the educational intentions of the teacher.

It is noticeable that in both student learning research and learner experience research, there has been a shift from seeing differences between learners as largely stable individual differences and finding that context and time are important variables (Sharpe et al. 2009). Hardy and Jefferies (Chapter 8) take this expectation of change as their starting point, reporting on the findings from two research studies that set out to record experiences of learning during a period of change and transition upon entry to university.

Sharpe and Beetham (Chapter 6) adopt a grounded theory approach to understanding learner development, drawing on the findings of ten research studies conducted over four years and involving nearly 200 learners in extended periods of qualitative data collection. From this, they propose a model of learning development, mapping the data from these studies onto learners' progression towards creative appropriation of technology for learning. This model draws on many of the concepts that others have used to extend our descriptions of learners' uses of technology, including confidence and familiarity (Hardy and Jefferies, Chapter 8; Seale and Bishop, Chapter 9), decision making (Seale and Bishop, Chapter 9; Benfield and De Laat, Chapter 13) and skills and strategies (Sharpe and Beetham, Chapter 6; Walker et al. Chapter 15). Most notable is the finding across many studies that learners who are making good uses of technology to support their learning are those who are willing to explore beyond the confines of the course, what Seale and Bishop (Chapter 9) term 'digital agility'. Czerniewicz and Brown (Chapter 10) provide the link towards Part 3, starting to show how these concepts manifest in new learning practices.

## Developing Learning Practices

As educators, we are ultimately interested in how learners experience learning and technology because we want to find ways of supporting their development more effectively. We are particularly interested in how learners' informal practices with technology and digital media can support their studies, and whether practices in further and higher education need to change to recognize the new contexts for learning. This does not mean always meeting 'learners' expectations' as a client group for educational provision. It does mean enquiring deeply into learners' aspirations, and knowing how best to support them.

The chapters in Part 3 critically examine the evidence that the internet generation exhibits a wholly new set of learning practices. The discourse of today's learners as 'different' owes much to Oblinger and Oblinger's extended characterization of the 'Net Generation' (2005) as discussed previously. They argue that children born post-1980 have had a qualitatively different experience of socialization and learning due to the prevalence of networked information. Unlike children raised on print and broadcast media, they deal with information differently: 'they develop hypertext minds, they leap around', they piece information together from multiple sources rather than following lines of thought (p. 15). They are also said to be naturally more problem-focused and experiential in their approach, rather than being happy to follow a content-led curriculum.

The chapters of Part 3 find that the reality is more complex and differentiated than the headlines suggest. There is no doubt that many, if not most, young people in the developed world have acquired digital capabilities through informal and peer-supported learning, and that these are potentially valuable in supporting their studies. They question, however, whether even very technically capable learners are acquiring the digital practices they need for lifelong learning – including creative production, critical reading and collaborative knowledge building – without active intervention by educators.

Beetham and Oliver (Chapter 11) begin Part 3 by considering the changing contexts of knowledge practice and the new demands being made on learners as a result. Building on the development of effective learning begun in Chapter 6, they develop an account of digital literacy as effective learning for a digital age, and suggest that learners need support to manage the complex and interconnected cultures of academic knowledge and the Web. Ryberg and Dirckinck-Holmfeld (Chapter 12) extend this analysis with a detailed case study of digital literacy in action. Their 'power' users of technology – 13–16-year-old Danish school students – demonstrate the creative potential of young people working in a multimedia environment with tasks of real-world importance to inspire them. Benfield and De Laat (Chapter 13) focus specifically on practices of knowledge-building, and report on two studies of undergraduate learners working in digitally networked situations. They distinguish collaboration 'on the task', which is usually in the context of mandated group work, from collaboration 'around the task', which is undertaken by learners in their own digital spaces, usually invisible from educators. The presence or absence of academic 'surveillance' is, they argue, at least as significant as the technologies used in defining learners' experiences and the meaning they attach to the collaborative practice.

Julie Hughes (Chapter 14) explores the potential of e-portfolio practices to develop learners' personal and professional identities. Again her focus is less on the specific technologies used than on how learners interpret the context in which they are working. Online identities, often described in terms of risk and uncertainty for young people, emerge from Hughes' work as powerful resources for self-determination and development.

Finally, in Chapter 15, Walker et al. report from the front line of learners' emerging literacies. The authors have extensive experience of helping non-traditional university students make the transition to higher education, with a particular focus on bridging the gap between their existing participatory skills and the expectations of university study. Like other authors in this part, they describe a blend of online learning and intensive face-to-face support – individualized where possible – as critical for the development of digitally literate learners.

**Conclusions**

Taken together, the work collected here argues against some commonly espoused myths, warns against the dangers of over-generalizing and presents alternative ways of studying this field. We find that not all learners fit the 'digital native' mould. Even those who are most at home with digital technology may not know how to use it to support learning in the ways required by further and higher education. Rather we find that they arrive at our doors rather conservative in their expectations (Goodyear and Ellis, Chapter 7; Hardy and Jefferies, Chapter 8) and in need of our support. We find that learners differ hugely in their aspirations, expectations, preferences, needs and access to technology. While technology helps to overcome some of the differences that can debar learners from opportunity, it also introduces many new kinds of difference to each student cohort. Educators need to see learners as individuals (Seale and Bishop, Chapter 9) and design for difference. Researchers and learning developers also need to understand these differences if they are to describe the experience of learners – whether digital newcomers or digital natives – in ways that are helpful. While we can usefully define traits (e.g.

Goodyear and Ellis, Chapter 7) and accurately record learners' voices (Creanor and Trinder, Chapter 3), we should be cautious of categorizing learners and should debunk altogether the myth of a common generational learning experience.

One reason for being cautious about categorization is that context has at least as much influence on learners' behaviours and experience as personal traits such as their age or technical competence (see Goodyear and Ellis, Chapter 7; Hughes, Chapter 14; Ryberg and Dirckinck-Holmfeld, Chapter 12). As educators we find this something of a relief. It means that we can make a difference to learners' development, however well resourced they are with devices and digital networks.

Indeed tutoring, learning support and skilled design of learning opportunities emerge as essential, despite our focus on learners this time around. Pedagogy is a theme we find ourselves returning to. Social technologies will continue to engage learners deeply, both for the emotional and informal 'around the task' support that is essential to successful learning, and for collaborative knowledge building practices as we learn more about integrating Web 2.0 capabilities into the design of learning tasks. As we move towards more immersive environments, with more integrated social software capabilities, we see play and discovery becoming the means by which learners approach key concepts. While technology will offer learners the potential to create and share knowledge in ways we can only imagine, it is up to us now to make their learning creative, challenging and open-ended.

Most importantly, these chapters demonstrate that it is endlessly fascinating and inspiring to listen to learners, and critical to build learners' perspectives into all aspects of educational provision, including how their personal and social technologies are supported. Although this is a book largely about research, we hope practitioners will respond to the methods described here and find ways of adapting them to professional reflection, and to engaging learners in the conversation.

## References

Browne, T. & Jenkins, M. (2003) VLE surveys: A longitudinal perspective between March 2001 and March 2003 for higher education in the United Kingdom. Retrieved 27 May, 2005, from http://www.ucisa.ac.uk/groups/tlig/vle/index_html.

Caruso, G. & Salaway, J. (2008) *The ECAR study of undergraduate students and information technology 2008*. Boulder, CO: Educause. Retrieved 21 October, 2009, from http://www.educause.edu/ECAR/TheECARStudyofUndergraduateStu /163283.

Collis, B. (2009) *Learning footprints*. Keynote presented at the Improving Student Learning Conference 2009: Improving Student Learning for the 21st Century Learner. Imperial College London, UK, 7–9 September 2009.

Conole, G., de Laat, M., Dillon, T. & Darby, J. (2007) 'Disruptive technologies', 'pedagogical innovation': What's new? Findings from an in-depth study of students' use and perception of technology, *Computers & Education*, 50(2), 511–524.

Creanor, L., Trinder, K., Gowan, D., & Howells, C. (2006) *LEX: The learner experience of e-learning. Final report* (Report under the JISC e-pedagogy 'Understanding my learner' programme).

Glasgow: Glasgow Caledonian University. Retrieved 20 August, 2009, from http://www.jisc. ac.uk/whatwedo/programmes/elearning_pedagogy/elp_learneroutcomes.aspx.

Entwistle, N.J. (2009) *Teaching for understanding at university: Deep approaches and distinctive ways of thinking (Universities into the 21St Century).* Basingstoke: Palgrave Macmillan.

Entwistle, N.J. & Ramsden, P. (1983) *Understanding student learning.* London: Croom Helm.

House of Commons (2009) *Students and universities.* Report of the innovation Universities Science and Skills Committee. London: House of Commons.

JISC (2007a) *Student expectations study.* Retrieved 19 May, 2009, from http://www.jisc.ac.uk/ media/documents/publications/studentexpectations.pdf.

JISC (2007b) *In their own words.* Bristol: JISC.

JISC (2008) *Great expectations of ICT. How higher education institutions are measuring up.* Retrieved 19 May, 2009, from http://www.jisc.ac.uk/media/documents/publications/ jiscgreatexpectationsfinalreportjune08.pdf.

Kennedy, G., Judd, T.S., Churchward, A., Gray, K. & Krause, K. (2008) First year students' experiences with technology: Are they really digital natives? *Australasian Journal of Educational Technology,* 24(1), 108–122.

Mason, R. & Kaye, A. (1989) *Mindweave: Communication, computers and distance education.* Oxford: Pergamon Press.

Oblinger, D.G. & Oblinger, J. L. (Eds.) (2005) *Educating the Net Generation.* Boulder, CO: Educause. Retrieved 10 June, 2009, from http://www.educause.edu/educatingthenetgen.

Prensky, M. (2001) Digital natives, digital immigrants, *On the Horizon,* 9(5), NCB University Press. Retrieved 27 February, 2009, from http://www.twitchspeed.com/site/Prensky%20 -%20Digital%20Natives,%20Digital%20Immigrants%20-%20Part1.htm.

Richardson, J.T.E. (2005) Students' approaches to learning and teachers' approaches to teaching in higher education. *Educational Psychology,* 25(6), 673–680.

Richardson, J.T.E. (2006) Investigating the relationship between variations in students' perceptions of their academic environment and variations in study behaviour in distance education. *British Journal of Educational Psychology,* 76(4), 867–893.

Sharpe, R. (2009a) Learning from the learners' experiences. In S.Walker, M. Ryan and R. Teed (Eds.) *Learning from the learners' experience. Post-conference reflections* (pp. 11–19). London: University of Greenwich.

Sharpe, R. (2009b) The impact of learner experience research on transforming institutional practices. In T. Mayes, D. Morrison, H. Mellar, P. Bullen and M. Oliver (Eds.) *Transforming higher education through technology-enhanced learning* (pp. 178–190). York: Higher Education Academy.

Sharpe R., Benfield G., Lessner E. & DeCicco, E. (2005) *Final report: Scoping study for the pedagogy strand of the JISC e-Learning Programme.* Oxford: OCSLD. Retrieved 27 February, 2009, from http://www.jisc.ac.uk/whatwedo/programmes/elearning_pedagogy/elp_learneroutcomes. aspx.

Sharpe, R., Beetham, H., Benfield. G., DeCicco, E. & Lessner, E. (2009) *Learner experiences of e-learning synthesis report: Explaining learner differences.* Oxford: OCSLD. Retrieved 21 October, 2009, from https://mw.brookes.ac.uk/display/JISCle2f/Findings.

Tapscott, D. (1998) *Growing up digital: The rise of the Net Generation.* New York: McGraw-Hill.

Thorpe, M., Conole, G. & Edmunds, R. (2008) *Learners' experiences of blended learning environments in a practice context.* Paper presented at Sixth International Networked Learning Conference, Halkidiki, Greece, 5–6 May, 2008. Retrieved 13 February, 2009, from http://kn.open.ac.uk/ document.cfm?docid=12129.

# Part I
## New Contexts for Learning

# 1

# The Influence of Pervasive and Integrative Tools on Learners' Experiences and Expectations of Study

SARA DE FREITAS AND GRÁINNE CONOLE

## Editors' Introduction

This chapter focuses its discussion on the learner's experience through a discussion around differing positions of how the use of social software and other innovative technologies are influencing the learner directly. Drawing on a range of studies and case studies, the authors note a move towards multimodal learning and that this move is well supported through the new tools. Notably the capabilities of these are leading to new and diverse models and metaphors for learning that are set to influence learning in future years. The chapter brings together an overview of this trend and introduces some case studies from practice to illustrate the significant shifts in learning that are outlined in the move towards greater uptake of social software and immersive learning tools.

## Introduction: The Future for Learners' Experiences

The opening paragraphs of any recent policy documents are a testimony to the recognized importance of e-learning in education. As the case studies in this book also attest, e-learning models and theories, simulations, computer modelling and social software are now an integral part of most learners' experience and environment. Similarly, institutions now recognize the strategic importance of ICT and have central policies in place to ensure that there is a technical infrastructure available to support all aspects of the learner's lifecycle, from recruitment through to assessment.

Research in recent years, focusing specifically on learner use of ICT, has given us a rich picture of how learners of all ages are appropriating new tools within their own context, mixing different applications for finding and managing information and for communicating with others. With respect to this trend, a recent report on the impact of ICT in the US, commissioned by the National Science Foundation, begins with a scenario of a learner of the near future:

> Imagine a high school student in the year 2015. She has grown up in a world where learning is as accessible through technologies at home as it is in the classroom, and digital content is as real to her as paper, lab equipment, or textbooks. At school, she and her classmates engage in creative problem-solving activities by manipulating simulations in a virtual laboratory or by downloading and analyzing visualizations of real-time data from remote sensors. Away from the classroom, she has seamless access to school materials and homework assignments using inexpensive mobile technologies. She continues to collaborate with her classmates in virtual environments that allow not only social interaction with each other but also rich connections with a wealth of supplementary content ...
>
> (Borgman et al. 2008: 7)

Other policy documents echo this vision of the future that promotes a seamless interchange with ubiquitous and ambient technologies (e.g. Becta 2008; European Commission 2008). The overall picture is of a rich personalized learning environment mediated through a plethora of tools and integrated applications. The suggestion is that this provides unique opportunities for authentic, rich learning experiences and that learners are developing new digital literacy skills that will enable them to work effectively in a constantly, changing social context. Skills such as curiosity, play, inventiveness and imagination appear to be becoming more important than traditional competences such as knowledge recall, organization and domain expertise. Skills mediated by enriched experiences seem to be the order of the day, and a shift away from more text-based approaches to more rich representationally-based social interchanges rings the changes. This chapter surveys the main trends with respect to social software and other innovative tools such as virtual worlds and games and considers new models and metaphors for bridging between pedagogies and tools, considering virtual worlds and digital spaces as new metaphors for exploration of learning concepts and user generated content.

To illustrate this transition, it is worth considering in a little more detail the ways in which ICT and Internet technologies have had an increasing impact in education. Pea and Wallis (cited in Borgman et al. 2008: 13) for example, suggest there are five main phases of general technological advancement. Each phase can also be considered in terms of the mediational context for learning. The first wave is simple face-to-face communication, harking back to the origins of human communication and learning such as Socratic dialogue. The second wave is the introduction of symbolic representation (written language, mathematic representations and graphics), which act as mediating artefacts between people, each providing different lenses on the intended meaning and what is and isn't foregrounded in the interaction (see for example Daniels et al. 2007 for a recent edited collection on this). The third wave is the introduction of communicative tools such as the telephone, radio and television. Again these tools offer different lenses on intended mediation and have different associated affordances (sound, visualization, asynchronicity vs. synchronicity). The fourth wave is associated with networked computers and the Internet and the fifth is what they refer to as cyberinfrastructure including participatory technologies (which in essence equate to what others refer to as Web 2.0 technologies). Waves three to five see a progressive and dramatic increase in the types of tools available, the different ways in which users can interact and communicate and the ways in which information can be displayed, visualized, manipulated and distributed. Pea and Wallis conclude: 'We can now interact at a distance, accessing complex and useful resources in ways unimaginable in early eras' (Pea and Wallis, in Borgman et al. 2008: 13).

It is important to note that each phase builds on, rather than replaces, the previous phase, but also that the introduction of each new approach to technological usage requires a reorientation and adaption of practice to incorporate it. For example, recent alternatives to email for communication, such as Short Message Service (SMS), chat and microblogging services such as Twitter, have not replaced email but have altered the ways in which individuals communicate.

We argue that there has been a shift in the use of tools, which emphasizes the more participatory and communicative capabilities of new technological applications, such as social software tools. For example, compare typical tool functionality pre-2005 with tools today. Each shows a shift from individual to more collective use. For example, Google Documents (Google Docs) for manipulating text compared to Word, and Slideshare for sharing and presenting as opposed to PowerPoint. Whereas pre-2005 the majority of communication occurred in email, chat and forums, learners now have a much richer and more complex set of communicative tools, including social networking tools such as Facebook and Ning, SMS and microblogging services such as Twitter, and audio/video conferencing. What is powerful about these new technologies is the way in which they can be integrated across platforms and between services, so that a message can be sent once, but distributed in a variety of different ways. The nature of content, both in terms of production and distribution, then has shifted with greater control for the individual as producer and as user.

Seely Brown and Adler (2008) argue that this trend supports people with common interests, for example allowing them to meet, share ideas and collaborate in innovative ways. They argue that the so-called 'Web 2.0' tools such as social networking sites, blogs, wikis and virtual communities have produced a new form of participatory medium that is ideally suited for multimodal learning.

So far we have argued that there has been a co-evolution of tools and their use and a commensurate increasing impact of these tools on practice. The rhetoric around so called 'Web 2.0' hints at the suggestion that the ways in which these tools are being appropriated is more than just a gradual shift to new tools and progressively enhanced technological mediation, and that in fact there are fundamental changes in practice occurring as a result of tool-user co-evolution. So whereas initial use of the Web (Web 1.0) was essentially fairly static, with hyperlinked information pages displaying information (often created by 'subject experts' and maintained by 'webmasters', and email acting as the primarily communication tool), Web 2.0 shifts towards a more active and distributed network with user generated content and a much richer interconnected network of communicative channels. Along with O'Reilly's original definition (O'Reilly 2005), phrases such as 'user participation' (O'Reilly 2004), architecture of participation (O'Reilly 2004), wisdom of the crowds (Surowiecki 2004) and everything is miscellaneous (Weinberger 2007) became synonymous with this practice.

In addition to Web 2.0 tools, other technologies are beginning to change practice, for example gaming technologies, virtual worlds, haptic technologies, large-scale distributed data networks and cloud computing. The annual Horizon reports (Johnson et al. 2009) paint a picture of an ever increasingly complex, rich technologically mediated environment. At the time of writing, mobiles, cloud computing, geo-everything, the personal Web, semantic-aware objects and smart objects are the top six technologies to watch (Johnson et al. 2009). Taken together, these technologically mediated contexts for learning can be characterized as:

- ubiquitous and networked;
- context and location aware;
- representational and simulatory;
- mobile and adaptive;
- distributed and interoperable.

A retrospective look at user–tool interactions in recent years indicates that there have been a number of changes in practice. The first is a shift from information being a 'scarce, expensive commodity' produced by those in authority to an 'abundance of information'. Information is no longer the provost of authoritative texts and encyclopaedia but can be produced and distributed by anyone and is available at the click of a button via Google. The notion of the nature and value of content has fundamentally changed; there is an increasing expectation that content should be free. Secondly traditional notions of authority are being challenged; many argue that the wisdom of the

**Table 1.1** New Tools Mapped onto Pedagogic Usage

| Trends in the uses of applications and tools | Pedagogical drive |
|---|---|
| New Web 2.0 practices | From individual to social |
| Location-aware technologies | Contextualized and situated |
| Adaptation and customization | Personalized learning |
| Virtual and immersive 3D worlds | Experiential learning |
| Google it! | Enquiry learning |
| User-generated content | Open educational resources |
| Badges, World of Warcraft | Peer learning |
| Blogging, peer critique | Reflection |
| Cloud computing | Distributed cognition |

crowds prevails. Thirdly, content can be distributed and rendered in multiple ways: text posted in one service can be automatically made available in a range of other services; non-text-based modes (such as podcasts, videos, animations and avatars) offer rich alternative methods for getting across meaning.

The description above paints a picture of a rich and exciting technological environment to support learning, with a multitude of mechanisms for rendering content, distributing information and communicating. There seems to be a tantalizing alignment between many of the social capabilities of the tools and practices evident with new technologies and what has emerged as 'good' pedagogy in recent years. Table 1.1 lists some of the key characteristics and trends associated with technologies, illustrating how these can be mapped pedagogically. What is striking about the table is that it shows the potential these technologies have to support what is currently perceived to be 'good pedagogy' (Conole 2009a).

However, despite this, there is a fundamental gap between the potential and actual uptake in the use of technologies in practice (Conole 2009b; Conole and Culver 2009).

- A lot of content seems to be the same; there is little evidence of innovative use of the new technologies.
- There is a spectrum of learners: good learners are able to harness and appropriate technologies effectively, whereas weak learners – confronted with so much choice – are even more lost.
- Despite the rhetoric around the notion of the 'Net Generation' immersed in technology (Oblinger and Oblinger 2005), in reality many learners don't have a good grasp of technologies – particularly not in terms of how technologies can be used for academic purposes.

Oblinger and Oblinger (2005) have made some bold statements suggesting that children born post-1980 are qualitatively different because of these changes in social behaviour. They argue that individuals raised with the computer deal with information differently compared to previous cohorts: 'they develop hypertext minds, they leap around'. A linear thought process is much less common than bricolage, or the ability to piece information together from multiple sources (p. 15).

A key argument is that the Net Generation is digitally literate – they are intuitively able to use and navigate around the Internet. It is suggested that they are more visually literate than previous generations and their approach to understanding is more surface level and multifaceted. Another claim about the characteristics of the Net Generation is that they are virtually connected and more socially orientated, as well as extrinsically motivated. The capabilities that the use of these technologies offer the learner includes immediacy, and hence learners expect quick responses to queries posted and operate very much on a 'just in time' basis.

Kennedy et al. (2008's) Australian survey of students' use of technologies provided evidence that the trend identified by Oblinger and Oblinger (2005) was still observable; indeed with increased levels of access new uses of the tools were emerging. In terms of use of particular technologies, two patterns of response were evident. The first pattern showed those technologies the majority of students wanted or were using, such as a computer to create documents, access to the Web, a learning portal, chat facility and access to university administration. The second pattern was more divergent – these technologies included social networking tools, personal digital assistants (PDAs), web conferencing, Really Simple Syndication (RSS) feeds and blogs. This reinforces the observation from Seale and Bishop (Chapter 9) that there is a core set of technologies that all learners are using and that additional technologies are taken up (or not) depending on personal preferences, individual ways of working and subject-discipline differences.

### An Overview of Key Themes Emerging From Learner Experience Practice: Case Studies

We have conducted a review of some of the projects that are engaging learners centrally. Table 1.2 summarizes the key themes arising from the review and illustrates these with case study examples identified in the wider literature survey. This section provides a pointer to some concrete cases studies of how new technologies are being used by learners, focusing upon examples of use of Web 2.0 tools, virtual worlds, games and e-science as well as highlighting a potential impact on education.

The case studies were identified from a number of recent reviews and research reports including the NSF-commissioned study on Cyberlearning (Borgman et al. 2008), the IPTS reviews of 'Learning 2.0' in formal and informal contexts (Ala-Mutka 2009), along with individual case studies that

**Table 1.2** Case Studies Mapped by Thematic Area

| Theme area | Case study | Brief description of case study | Potential impact upon education |
|---|---|---|---|
| Scaffolded | VEOU (Willis et al. 2004) | Virtual continuing professional development (CPD) and scaffolded support for publication | Potential to change the ways in which professional CPD is delivered, offering more tailored, personalized and just-in-time training |
| Open | E-Bank – towards truly 'Open research' (Cole et al. 2006) | Access to open learning materials designed to support tutors and learners alike | Democratization of education in terms of content production and delivery. Wider access to materials for casual learners and to support informal learning as a 'taster' for formal learning qualifications |
| Cumulative | CCK09 (Siemens 2009) – education for free! | An experimental course in which both the content and expertise was free | What is the role of traditional educational institutions in a world in which content and expertise is increasingly free? |
| Social | Cloudworks (Conole and Culver 2009) | Social networking for an educational context | Social networking applied to education has the potential to change the ways in which teachers exchange information, with the potential to lead to proactive sharing and reuse of educational resources |
| Authentic environments | WISE project (SecondReiff Aachen School of Architecture); Stanford Medical School simulations using Olive platform (cited in Ala-Mutka et al. 2009) | Authentic real-time modelling environment in Second Life for architecture and medical students | Scope for training in new and realistic environments. Pedagogic models include exploratory learning (ELM), inquiry learning and problem-based learning approaches |
| Fostering inquiry learning | Personal Inquiry Project (Scanlon et al. 2010) | Development of inquiry-based learning skills for students to enhance their understanding of science | Through independent learning approaches, peer learning is encouraged and analytical skills may be fostered |

Continued …

## Table 1.2 continued

| Theme area | Case study | Brief description of case study | Potential impact upon education |
|---|---|---|---|
| Enhancing life experiences | Mundo des estrellas (cited in Ala-Mutka et al. 2009); JISC MyPlan project (de Freitas et al. 2009) | Young people in hospitals, interactive gaming, life swapping and sharing of experience. MyPlan project providing tools for lifelong career decisions and educational choices using visualization of learners' timelines (http://www.lkl.ac.uk/research/myplan) | The potential for these tools to support lifelong learning opportunities and enhance life experiences |
| Broadening access | Notschool and Schome projects (cited in Ala-Mutka et al. 2009) | Notschool for virtual home schooling for disaffected children and Schome project for gifted and talented kids | The impact of this includes outreach to children and excluded, talented learners. Using familiar media-based metaphors rather than traditional school-based metaphors-new learners may be reached |
| New forms of collaboration | CSCL pedagogical patterns (Hernández et al. forthcoming) | Structured pedagogical patterns to support different forms of collaborative activities | Broader application of pedagogical patterns and other scaffolded forms of pedagogical have the potential to transfer good practice from research into practice in an effective way. Automation of such patterns can be embedded in pedagogy tools |
| Co-construction of understanding | Welker's Wikinomics (cited in Ala-Mutka et al. 2009), The Decameron Web (http://www.brown.edu/Departments/Italian_Studies/dweb/dweb.shtml) | Collaborative co-construction of understanding of economics | Blurring research and teaching: examples of how the Web can provide access to scholarly materials and give students the opportunity to observe and emulate scholars at work |
| Aggregating and sharing content | Wikipedia | Co-construction of knowledge through collaboration and iterative development | New tools provided for learners at all stages, and interaction between learners and publication of shared knowledge |

exemplify different facets of technology appropriation. The examples selected have been summarized in Table 1.2 to indicate the breadth and variety of uses of Web 2.0 tools. In each case a brief description is provided, along with an indication of potential impact.

## New Models and Metaphors for Analysing and Enriching Learner Experiences

This review of learner experience literature and practices indicates that we need to devise new models and metaphors for understanding learner and teacher interactions with technologies, along with new pedagogical models that can help guide the design of effective and innovative learning interventions. In this section we describe a number of models and metaphors that have been developed. This is very new research work, the examples provided are put forward mainly as examples of thinking and visualizing technology-enhanced learning differently. We suggest that further work is needed to fully explore how these can be used to guide both the design and enactment of learning experiences occurring in technology-enhanced learning environments.

We argue that traditional time–space based metaphors used to describe technologies and users' interactions with these technologies are no longer adequate to describe the rich, multifaceted ways in which practices are now being shaped by technologies and the complex, distributed nature of the associated temporal-spatiality:

> There is a need for new approaches to help navigate through the digital environment and also to help make sense of it and the impact it is having on our lives. Simplistic descriptions of the digital environment replicating physical spaces are no longer appropriate, it is necessary to take a more holistic view and describe technologies and users together emphasising the connections between them.
>
> (Conole 2008)

We argue that spatial descriptions of digital spaces quickly evolved in the early stages of the Internet – the concept of 'virtual universities' was born with associated virtual cafes, libraries and lecture halls trying to mimic real-life educational spaces. However, it is also evident that as we have co-evolved with these tools, use has become more complex, and more temporally/spatially fragmented. Conole has suggested that there are four foci to describing digital spaces (Table 1.3). A consideration of these in combination can provide a richer, more accurate description of use of tools.

**Table 1.3** Descriptions of Digital Space

| Focus | Aspects of the digital space this emphasizes |
| --- | --- |
| Spatial | Made up of objects that are connected in a typology of hyperlinks |
| Temporal | Evolving over time, with events happening over different time frames |
| Functional | Represented as the different functions of the tools; tools acting on 'data' in the system leading to transformation in some way |
| Connected | A connected network of different types of objects (tools, resources, people) interacting |

## Pedagogies of the Future

New models and metaphors are emerging to provide a conceptual basis for the kinds of changes going on that relate to education and training practices, as highlighted above. While these changes are clearly more socio-cultural than technologically based, nonetheless they have presented tutors and the wider policy development community with real challenges. The speed of uptake of the new social software and game-based tools has been sufficiently rapid to merit conceptualizations and conceptual models that are prepared on the fly, rather than developed incrementally over long periods of time. This has led to a whole set of challenges that we are only now beginning to meet. The main issues of speed of uptake and the general model of user-led innovations and validations of software tools, coupled with the pervasiveness of the Web and broadband connectivity, alongside service-orientated architectures that allow us to integrate technological applications more easily together, have collectively led to significant changes in education. The lag between research and tool use and the relative lack of critical and conceptual models have jointly been problematic. However, generic sets of approaches are emerging and here we outline examples of such conceptual models that may be deployed to help evaluate and validate new tools and applications.

We have previously used a four-dimensional framework (de Freitas and Oliver 2006) as a specific toolset for tutors using games and simulations in their learning and teaching practices. The framework originally envisaged as a tool for selection of games has since been tested to support the design, use and evaluation of serious games (games for educational purposes) (e.g. de Freitas and Jarvis 2008). The framework has, however, a wider applicability for approaches that combine learning design and participatory approaches involving the active participation of learners. The 'dimensions' include the learner, the pedagogies used, the representation selected and the context within which learning is grounded. Notably here, representation is an increasing area of interest as the social software and simulation tools become more prevalent, cheaper and easier to access, and as the processes of learning and knowledge exchange, social interactivity and networking become more complex.

The learner dimension in turn becomes a more active mode of engagement with role play and game-based approaches, and the interaction between social actors in the process of learning. In particular the interchange between learners in the cycle of peer learning underpins this social dimension. The pedagogies used in terms of learning theories and models and approaches taken similarly play a central role in the process of learning as a whole. The context of learning is central to the selection of learning tools used and processes adopted. *Where* learning takes place as much as *how* learning takes place can have an impact upon the learner cohort and place constraints or freedoms upon the social interactions taking place. Whether the context is considered in terms of access to materials, location and place of learning or disciplinal framework used, it is undeniably a central aspect of the learning interchange both individually and in group work.

These four dimensions serve to highlight the main processes of learning design, and foreground a dynamic and changing nature of learning as well as highlighting the social interactive dimension of learning that the teachers and tutors are serving to support. The model can also be used in non-tutorial contexts to evaluate and measure the effectiveness of learning content, the learning design process and innovative approaches to learning (e.g. game-based, social software).

In other work, we have used pedagogical schema to guide learning and teaching (Conole 2008) and we have argued that these can be used as guidance to help both effective design of learning interventions, and in particular how technologies can be appropriated, as well as guidance during the learning process. One of these provides a conceptual map of the learning process, enabling the learner to focus not so much on the tools but *how* they are being used. Any learning intervention consists of four interrelated facets:

- thinking and reflection;
- conversation and interaction;
- experience and activity;
- evidence and demonstration.

A second tool, the pedagogy profile, focuses more on providing support for mapping a set of learning activities in terms of the types of tasks the learner is undertaking. The work derives from a learning activity taxonomy (Conole 2007) that characterizes the types of tasks learners undertake into six types: assimilative (attending and understanding content), information handling (e.g. gathering and classifying resources or manipulating data), adaptive (use of modelling or simulation software), communicative (dialogic activities, e.g. pair dialogues or group-based discussions), productive (construction of an artefact such as a written essay, new chemical compound or a sculpture) and experiential (practising skills in a particular context or undertaking an investigation).

In addition to these conceptual models, wider metaphors are also emerging worthy of consideration. One such approach being investigated in the UK (at the Serious Games Institute, UK) and in the 'Spaces for Knowledge Generation' project in Australia (http://www.skgproject.com/) is the concept around 'smart spaces' and 'hybrid spaces'. These projects are extending the spatial metaphors beyond current usage and into new areas of application. For example, in the smart spaces project at the Serious Games Institute the more seamless use of real and virtual spaces, is being engineered with industrial partners using bridging technology that allows changes in real spaces to be reflected in virtual spaces, and vice versa. The applications are being used primarily for environmental controls and monitoring purposes; however, the potential of the integrative approach to open up new concepts and metaphors of space and our social interactions within different spaces is clear. The work in Australia is exploring how new technologies might be better appropriated to enhance learning both on campus and virtually. Themes include 'designing more effective collaborative learning spaces', 'sunburnt wifi: what makes a really great outdoor learning space?' and 'the corners of our minds – how should we be using eddy spaces' (i.e. reconceptualizing current 'dead' spaces).

### Virtual Worlds as Metaphors for Learning

The new virtual worlds themselves open up scope for new and multiple uses of metaphors for learning. They can take literal representations of current training situations such as in the Olive training example where Forterra's OLIVE (Online Interactive Virtual Environment – 1.0) platform allows developers to build and maintain persistent virtual worlds, supporting users for training, rehearsal and analysis. Or indeed whether the virtual world is being used as a classroom for learning interactions such as in the Seely Brown and Adler 'Terra Incognita' project of the University of Southern Queensland (Australia), which has built a classroom in Second Life, the online virtual world that has attracted millions of users. In addition to supporting lecture-style teaching, Terra Incognita includes the capability for small groups of students who want to work together to easily 'break off' from the central classroom before rejoining the entire class. Instructors can 'visit' or send messages to any of the breakout groups and can summon them to rejoin the larger group.

The scope for using virtual worlds to 'play' with our conceptions of learning and to interrogate these conceptions in different contexts is only now being explored in education.

In addition to new metaphors of learning space, new and specific pedagogical angles on technology use are emerging to help tutors and institutions deal with the kind of rapid changes that are predicted for future learning provision, and with a particular focus upon letting the learner's voices become part of the design of learning. The ways in which technologies can be harnessed to personalize learning is a strong part of current rhetoric. O'Donoghue (forthcoming) provides a summary of cases on this. The vision is that technologies can enable a more personalized delivery of learning according to learner requirement and profile. Similarly there is now considerable interest in exploring how technologies can facilitate more inquiry-based approaches to learning. (See for example the Centre for Inquiry-based Learning in the Arts and Social Sciences, http://www.shef.ac.uk/cilass/home.html, and the personal inquiry project, http://www.pi-project.ac.uk/.) These indicate the necessity of learner-led approaches, and imply a greater emphasis upon social interactions as part of the process of learning and assessment.

Inevitably, this leads us to consider not only the roles of tutors and learners but also the learning models that will be used to support onward development. As Walker and colleagues point out, in this volume (Chapter 15), the concept of skills can be unhelpful as it can lead to a separation of learning approaches, which can be problematic, as in real lived practice often skills need to be integrated together, for example for decision making. The roles of tutors and learners do seem to be altering with the adoption of e-learning approaches, in particular the relationships between learners seems to be strengthening, leaving the tutor in a more mediatory role.

The new pedagogic models that reflect social learning are beginning to emerge, such as the exploratory learning model (ELM) (de Freitas and Jarvis 2008; de Freitas and Neumann 2009), and reflect a greater emphasis upon the social dimensions of learning between peers. However, as pointed out in the earlier volume of this series, models that support social interactive learning are still relatively sparse leading to a need for more conceptual modelling and better critical categories for complex social interchanges (Mayes and de Freitas 2007). Methodologies such as 'social network analysis' (e.g. Wasserman and Faust 1994) may perhaps provide new approaches for developing new learning theories and approaches, whilst other directions of study focus upon neurological processing and demonstrate some potential for further opening up this difficult and complex area of how we learn (e.g. Rebolledo-Mendez et al. 2009).

## Conclusions

This chapter has opened up some of the key questions and themes associated with learners' experience and voice, while outlining some of the key challenges facing education as a whole (see Table 1.4 for a summary of these). The vision of the future learner as proposed at the outset of this chapter has been broadly supported by the review undertaken by the authors. Indeed the sets

**Table 1.4** Mapping the Changes Between Traditional and Non-traditional Modes of Learning

| Traditional modes | New modes | Impact of the changes |
|---|---|---|
| Closed private systems | Shift to broader notions of openness, e.g. Open Educational resource movement | Greater engagement of non-participating learners |
| | Flat but spikier worlds (e.g. Friedman 2005) | |
| Hierarchically organized systems of education | Multi-distributed systems of education (e.g. Weinberger 2007) | Potential for international models of education and greater distribution of learner cohorts |
| From individual modes | To more social modes | Adoption of more socially-based pedagogies (e.g. communities of practice) |
| Static/passive models of the learner | More user participation and engagement | Greater reach of education into non-traditional learner cohorts. Greater scope for lifelong learning practices. |
| Predominantly linear and textual | More multi-modal and non-linear forms adopted | Move towards multimodality and multi-skill development |
| Expertise | Wisdom of crowds | Blurring between teacher and learner roles |
| Changing nature of the notion of content production by tutors for learners | Content production by tutors and learners | Blurred line between producers and consumers of content |

of changes impact upon the individual learner as much as the fabric of the educational institutions.

Indeed these changes that are affecting the role of learners as more active participants in their lifelong learning journeys reflect a wider socio-cultural trend of democratisation of the education system. However, the resulting greater complexity that we experience in our everyday lives driven by greater opportunities to learn in different places and different ways has the real potential to dilute the quality of learning experiences. This 'double bind' of more opportunities and less quality needs to be considered critically if we are to adapt our education systems to maximize our learners' skills and qualities, future opportunities and enthusiasm for learning. Indeed, the notion of 'what are the necessary skills' is a subject that is considered in Walker et al. (Chapter 15 in this volume) and is being hotly debated across the sector, e.g. are skills required specific or generic? Do we need to involve industry in the process of development of skills and education? Many of these considerations centre upon the notion of the learner, e.g. who is the learner, how can they be modelled and how can learning be customized for them? How can we best support their future needs when there is so much debate about what skills will be needed to support our future societies; digital literacy is clearly only a small part of the skill set needed for the future by tutors and learners alike.

Additional issues raised here include: a need for consideration of the digital divide – are individuals opting in and out freely or are there still real issues to deal with in terms of access and accessibility? In this way do tools need to be personalized or made more generic, and will the market forces ultimately decide what we use and do not use in practice?

Finally, the chapter has raised the central question: how do we support new approaches to design and delivery of courses to make more effective use of technologies that lead to an enhanced learning experience? While the literature is positing change in this way, ultimately the main challenge lies in the real transition to a less tutor-led approach to learning. In the future the contexts for learning will diverge and so models of learning will necessarily be more diverse, and this will be challenging for how we evolve and use pedagogical models. Content will not be delivered to learners but co-constructed with them. This paradigm shift is only beginning to be addressed and this volume provides a starting point for this substantial revision.

## References

Ala-Mutka, K., Bacigalupo, M., Kluzer, S., Pascu, C., Punie, Y. & Redecker, C. (2009) *Review of learning 2.0 practices,* IPTS technical report prepared for publication, IPTS: Seville. Retrieved 18 April, 2009, from, http://ipts.jrc.ec.europa.eu/publications/pub.cfm?id=2139.

Alvino, S., Dimitriadis, Y., Asensio-Pérez, Juan, I. & Hernández-Leo, D. (2009) Supporting the reuse of effective CSCL learning designs through social structure representations. *The American Journal of Distance Education* 30(2): 239–258.

Becta (2008) *Harnessing technology: Next generation learning 2008–14,* Becta, Coventry. Retrieved 8 February, 2009, from http://publications.becta.org.uk/display.cfm?resID=37348&page=1835.

Borgman, C. et al. (2008). *Fostering learning in the networked world: The cyberlearning opportunity and challenge,* National Science Foundation. Retrieved 12 October, 2009, from http://www.nsf.gov/pubs/2008/nsf08204/nsf08204.pdf.

Coles, S.J., Frey, J.G., Hursthouse, M.B., Light, M.E., Milsted, A.J., Carr, L.A., DeRoure, D., Gutteridge, C.J., Mills, H.R., Meacham, K.E., Surridge, M., Lyon, E., Heery, R., Duke, M. & Day, M. (2006) An e-Science environment for service crystallography – from submission to dissemination. *Journal of Chemical Information and Modeling,* Special Issue on eScience 46(3) 1006–1016.

Conole, G. (2007) Describing learning activities: Tools and resources to guide practice. In H. Beetham and R. Sharpe (Eds.) *Rethinking pedagogy for a digital age: Designing and delivering e-learning* (pp. 81–91), London: Routledge.

Conole, G. (2008) New schema for mapping pedagogies and technologies, *ARIADNE* magazine. Retrieved 10 August, 2009, from http://www.ariadne.ac.uk/issue56/conole/.

Conole, G. (2009a, June) *Personalisation through technology-enhanced learning.* Keynote at the E-Portfolio 2009 conference: Innovation, creativity and Accountability, City University, London.

Conole, G. (2009b) Research methodological issues with researching the learner voice. In L.T.W. Hin & R. Subramaniam (Eds.) *Handbook of research on new media literacy at the K-12 level: Issues and challenges* (pp. 669–82), Hershey, PA: IGI Global.

Conole, G. & Culver, J. (2009) The design of Cloudworks: Applying social networking practice to foster the exchange of learning and teaching ideas and designs. Paper accepted for *Computers and Education,* CAL special issue.

Daniels, H., Wertsch, J. & Cole, M. (2007) *The Cambridge companion to Vygotsky*, Cambridge: Cambridge University Press.

de Freitas, S. & Jarvis, S. (2008) Towards a development approach for serious games. In T.M. Connolly, M. Stansfield & E. Boyle (Eds.),*Games-based learning advancements for multi-sensory human-computer interfaces: Techniques and effective practices* (pp. 215–231), Hershey, PA: IGI Global.

de Freitas, S. & Neumann, T. (2009) The use of 'exploratory learning' for supporting immersive learning in virtual environments, *Computers and Education*, 52(2), 343–352.

de Freitas, S. & Oliver, M. (2006) How can exploratory learning with games and simulations within the curriculum be most effectively evaluated? *Computers and Education*, 46(3), 249–264.

de Freitas, S., Rebolledo-Mendez, G., Liarokapis, F., Magoulas, G. Poulovassilis, A. (2009) Developing an evaluation methodology for immersive learning experiences in a virtual world. In G. Rebolledo-Mendez, F. Liarokapis, & S. de Freitas (Eds) Proceedings of 2009 Conference in Games and Virtual Worlds for Serious Applications, IEEE, pp. 43–50.

European Commission (2008) An updated strategic framework for European cooperation in education and training, Communication from the Commission to the European Parliament, the Council, the European Economic and Social Committee and the Committee of the Regions (December). Retrieved 8 February, 2009, from http://ec.europa.eu/education/lifelong-learning-policy/doc28_en.htm.

Friedman, T.L. (2005) *The world is flat: A brief history of the twenty-first century*, New York: Picador.

Johnson, L.F., Levine, A. & Smith, R.S. (2009) *Horizon Report*, Austin, TX: The New Media Consortium.

Kennedy, G., Judd, T.S., Churchward, A., Gray, K. & Krause, K. (2008) First year students' experiences with technology: Are they really digital natives, *Australasian Journal of Educational Technology*, 24(1), 108–122.

Mayes, T. & de Freitas, S. (2007) Learning and e-learning: The role of theory. In H. Beetham and R. Sharpe (Eds.) *Rethinking pedagogy for a digital age: Designing and delivering e-learning* (pp. 13–25), London: Routledge.

Oblinger, D.G. & Oblinger, J.L. (Eds.) (2005) *Educating the Net Generation*, Boulder, CO: Educause. Retrieved 16 January, 2009, from http://www.educause.edu/educatingthenetgen.

O'Donoghue, J. (Ed.) (Forthcoming).*Technology supported environment for personalised learning: Methods and case studies*, New York: IGI Publications.

O'Reilly, T. (2004) *The architecture of participation*. Retrieved 11 December, 2008, from http://www.oreillynet.com/pub/a/oreilly/tim/articles/architecture_of_participation.html.

O'Reilly, T. (2005) *What is Web 2.0: Design patterns and business models for the next generation of software*. Retrieved 11 December, 2008, from http://oreilly.com/web2/archive/what-is-web-20.html.

Rebolledo-Mendez et al. (2009, July) *Assessing the usability of a Brain-Computer Interface (BCI) that detects attention levels in an assessment exercise*. Paper presented at 13th International Conference on Human-Computer Interaction, San Diego, California.

Scanlon, E., Kerawalla, L., Twiner, A., Mulholland, P., Collins, T., Jones, A., Gaved, M., Littleton, K., Blake, C. & Conole, G. (2010) Personal inquiry: Scripting support for inquiry learning by participatory design, 9th International Conference on Computer Based Learning in Science, 4–7th July, Warsaw, Poland.

Seely Brown, J. & Adler. R. (2008) Minds on fire: Open education, the long tail, and Learning 2.0, *EDUCAUSE Review*, 43(1), 16–32.

Siemens, G. (2009), Connectivism and Connective Knowledge 2009, blog post, 5th July, http://ltc.umanitoba.ca/connectivism/?p=189.

Surowiecki, J. (2004) The wisdom of crowds: Why the many are smarter than the few and how collective wisdom shapes business, economies, societies and nations, London: Little, Brown Book Group.

Wasserman, S. & Faust, K. (1994) *Social network analysis: Methods and analysis*, Cambridge: Cambridge University Press.

Weinberger, D. (2007) *Everything is miscellaneous – the power of the new digital disorder*, New York: Times Books.

Wills, G., Miles-Board, T., Bailey, C., Carr, L., Gee, Q., Hall, W. & Grange, S. (2005) T*he Dynamic Review Journal: A scholarly archive*. New Review of Hypermedia and Multimedia, 11(1): 69–89. ISSN 13614568.

# 2

# Social Networking
## *Key Messages From the Research*

### KERI FACER AND NEIL SELWYN

## Editors' Introduction

This chapter centrally provides a valuable overview of developments in social networking within education. It explores how learners' use social networking sites to represent their identities to others in a way that reinforces their sense of belonging within particular groups. While the authors see the potential of appropriating these sites for informal education, they problematize the use of these for formal educational contexts, although arguing for benefits where learners maintain control over interactions.

## Introduction

The emergence and exponential growth in popularity of social networking sites such as MySpace and Facebook present new opportunities to young people, learners and students. Alongside the basic functions of finding and maintaining contacts, such networks offer increasingly sophisticated tools for sharing and building knowledge, such as social bookmarking, shared favourites, networked applications and many more. It has never been easier to identify like-minded other people to share ideas with, and these self-organized groups offer opportunities as well as challenges to traditional learning. This chapter explores recent findings on learner-created networks, and asks whether they have a legitimate role to play in extending learning beyond the boundaries of the institution. Do learners welcome the incursion of universities and colleges into 'TheirSpace'? What impact is this having on their experiences and expectations?

The first years of the twenty-first century are proving exciting times in which to be studying education and technology. In particular, many writers and researchers are associating the rapid development of Internet technologies with the emergence of new forms of teaching and learning. There has been much discussion, for instance, of a general recasting of education provision along more fluid and democratic lines, and built around the empowerment of engaged and enthusiastic learners (see Davies and Merchant 2009). Yet such predictions are tempered both by those who argue that emergent technologies are leading to an imminent decline in 'basic skills' by a generation of digitally dependent learners, and by a concern that such a fundamental recasting of educational power relations and provision may be dependent upon more than the appropriation of the technologies of popular digital cultures. Educationalists therefore face new variations on long-standing questions, not least whether the change associated with this new wave of education innovation can be said to be truly novel or simply the latest development in the relationship between formal and informal learning.

Whilst often imprecisely defined and used, 'Web 2.0' can be seen as an umbrella term for a host of Internet applications such as blogging, wikis, folksonomies, virtual societies, multiplayer online gaming and 'mash-ups'. Perhaps the most prominent and most prevalent of these applications over the past five years has been social networking services (SNS) – especially popular commercial applications such as MySpace, Facebook, hi5, Friendster and Piczo.

In this chapter we explore the main debates surrounding the educational significance of social networking and, in particular, review the key messages emerging from the research literature with regards to the use of social networking in formal education and informal learning. From this basis we are able to highlight a number of key issues that merit sustained attention by those seeking to ensure an informed and intelligent response by formal education to the emergence of social networking sites and their associated cultural practices.

**What is Social Networking?**

One of the defining features of social networking applications is that they mark a progression from what Tufekci (2008) terms the 'instrumental Internet' to the 'expressive Internet'. Whilst social networking applications can be used for the instrumental purpose of 'information seeking and knowledge gathering', their distinctive strength lies in the use of the Internet to 'perform and realize social interactions, self-presentation, public performance, social capital management, social monitoring, and the production, maintenance and furthering of social ties' (pp. 547–548). In this sense social networking applications mark a distinct progression from the Internet applications of the 1990s' 'cyberspace' era in that they are predicated on the appropriation and sharing of content amongst communities of users, resulting in various forms of user-driven communication, collaboration and content (re)creation. Thus unlike earlier applications, social networking is built upon 'interactive' rather than 'broadcast' forms of exchange, with information shared between 'many-to-many' rather than transmitted from 'one-to-many' (Shirky 2003; O'Reilly 2005).

The popularity of social networking is unparalleled, even in comparison to other Web 2.0 technologies (by 2007 there were over 250 million profiles in such sites, Redecker 2009). Such popularity is also being mobilized to build new relationships between producers and consumers, between fans and cultural icons in a range of areas of cultural, political and economic life (Reich 2009). The Obama election campaign, for example, effectively mobilized social networks to create a self-sustaining army of volunteers; in contrast, film buffs created blogs about the film *Snakes on a Plane*, and produced viral video clips so popular that the lines written for them ended up in the film; in contrast again, companies as diverse as Dell and Proctor & Gamble are using social networking sites to discuss products and gain ideas and feedback from consumers.

Yet whilst social networking services certainly continue to be of increasingly personal and social significance to individuals and groups of all ages and across diverse areas of their lives, we should take time to detach ourselves from the considerable hyperbole, and consider carefully the extent to which SNSs can be said to have an educational significance.

## The Education Potential of Social Networking

Social networking's rapid rise to prominence in the lives of individuals and learners of all ages has prompted great enthusiasm amongst educators. SNSs are being talked of in some quarters as leading a Web 2.0 inspired transformation of educational provision and student learning: first, by offering new ways of achieving long-standing educational goals; and second, by offering new democratic and collaborative models of educational practice to enable students to 'rehearse for 21st century situations' (Reich 2009: 15).

It has been argued, for example, that social networking applications share many of the qualities of a good 'official' education technology in terms of their mechanisms for peer feedback and their fit with the social contexts of learning such as the school, university or local community (Mason and Rennie 2007). One of the main educational uses of social networking is seen to lie in the support of interactions and exchanges between learners facing the common dilemma of negotiating their studies (Smith and Peterson 2007).

Other potential benefits of social networking services are argued to include the connection of learners with others into new networks of collaborative learning, often based around interests and affinities not catered for in their immediate educational environments (Maloney 2007: 26). This has prompted some educationalists to explore the potential of social networking to augment 'conventional' interactions and dialogue between students and academic staff. Indeed, some educators have welcomed the capacity of social networking services such as Facebook to offer teachers a forum for 'easy networking and positive networking with students' (Lemeul 2006).

As these latter examples imply, strong links have been made between the nature of social networking activity and socio-cultural perspectives on learning that see knowledge as constructed actively by the learner within communal social settings comprising people and objects where knowledge can be created and supported.

Such approaches are seen to be particularly appropriate for the perceived demands of 'the 21st century' (Redecker 2009) at the heart of which is a vision of a new role for the learner as active participant in, rather than passive recipient of, learning experiences. In this sense social networking services have been heralded by some commentators as offering 'the capacity to radically change the educational system ... to better motivate students as engaged learners rather than learners who are primarily passive observers of the educational process' (Ziegler 2007: 69).

## The Education Problems of Social Networking

Whilst persuasive, these enthusiastic hopes for social networking are not shared unanimously across the education community. Indeed, other commentators argue that social networking services may cause harm to formal educational attainment. For example, negative discourses have developed around a range of issues in which social networking is seen as contributing to the heightened disengagement, alienation, distraction and disconnection of learners from education (Bugeja 2006; Cassidy 2006). Fears abound that, when used in certain ways, social networking could be a key contributing factor to what Ziegler (2007) has termed 'the mis-education of Generation M', and the intellectual and scholarly de-powering of a 'Google generation' of students incapable of independent critical thought (Brabazon 2007). Other commentators have pointed towards the contribution of SNS use to 'the development of a culture of disrespect' between learners and formal education providers (Ziegler 2007: 70). To date, much of the professional debate around education institutions and learner social networking use has centred on issues of regulation and permissiveness. And much of the public debate has centred on students' use of SNSs to criticize or undermine teacher authority – what a past UK education minister termed 'the sinister downside of modern technology' (Johnson 2007).

## Social Networking: Key Messages From the Research

Social networking feeds into a set of wider contemporary educational debates, from the realignment of power within the student/teacher relationship that is at the heart of learner voice and children's rights agendas, to the types of knowledge that are valued in educational settings.

What is far from clear, however, is how far this debate is informed by the lived experiences and practices of learners; in other words, by demands from learners themselves for changed educational practice in the light of their uses of social networking services, and how far SNSs are simply the latest battleground for conducting the long-standing educational debates between progressives and conservatives.

Indeed, much of the public debate in this field has failed to consider what learners are *actually* doing with social networking (as opposed to how educationalists would prefer learners to be using social networking), and certainly fails to listen to learners' perceptions and understandings of social networking. As Bill Dutton concluded recently, 'there is a clear need within the educational debate over web 2.0 technologies for more empirical data and theoretically driven empirical research ... we have a wealth of alternative theoretical perspectives, but very few facts' (Dutton 2008: 29).

With this thought in mind, this chapter will now go on to consider the emerging research evidence on the current relationships between social networking, informal learning and formal education – thus providing an empirical perspective on the debates and controversies outlined above.

## Prevalence of Use of Social Networking Services

Whilst it is estimated that 17 per cent of UK adult Internet users maintain an online social networking profile (Dutton and Helsper 2007), it is clear that SNS use is heavily age-dependent. A recent survey of UK primary school pupils aged between seven and eleven years reported 21 per cent make regular use of a social networking service (Selwyn et al. 2009), while a similar UK survey of eleven to sixteen year olds report that 74 per cent have social networking accounts (Crook and Harrison 2008). In the US, data from the Pew Internet survey suggest that over half of 12–17-year-old Internet users use social networking services (Lenhart and Madden 2007), with this figure rising to over 90 per cent of undergraduate students (Ipsos MORI 2008).

Yet when discussing these general levels of usage we should remain mindful that a significant number of learners remain peripheral to these trends. For example, Boyd's (2008) ethnography of SNS usage amongst US teenagers identified two types of non-participants – what she labels as 'disenfranchised teens' and 'conscientious objectors':

The former consists of those without Internet access, those whose parents succeed in banning them from participation, and online teens who primarily access the Internet through school and other public venues where social network sites are banned. Conscientious objectors include politically minded teens who wish to protest against Murdoch's

News Corp. (the corporate owner of MySpace), obedient teens who have respected or agree with their parents' moral or safety concerns, marginalized teens who feel that social network sites are for the cool kids, and other teens who feel as though they are too cool for these sites.

### The Use of Social Networking Services for Collaborative Knowledge Production

The sorts of learning practices manifest in social networking activities are explored in Luckin et al. (2009). Whilst most learners express a generally positive orientation towards using the Internet to support their learning, their actual interests were mainly focused on supporting familiar school activities (such as formal presentations) or for communication:

> learners seem cautious about other values associated with the Web 2.0 initiative, such as the shared construction of knowledge in a public format. There was little evidence of groundbreaking activities and only a few embryonic signs of criticality, self-management or meta-cognitive reflection.

These findings lend support to the general conclusion that learners' uses of Web 2.0 applications at home and at school tend to involve what Crook (2008) terms a 'low bandwidth exchange' of information and knowledge, more accurately described in terms of co-operation or co-ordination between individuals than true collaboration and knowledge building. This conclusion was recently reinforced in the findings from a six-country survey that found that the use of social networking sites by libraries did not increase the likelihood of young people saying that they would self-publish creative work, share ideas with others, share photographs and videos, participate in online discussion groups or meet others with similar interests (De Rosa et al. 2007).

Rather than necessitating a shift towards radically new models of knowledge production and collaboration, therefore, social networking services are, in the main, appropriated by learners within familiar and bounded models of learning and interaction.

### Learner Attitudes Towards Use of Social Networking in Teaching

The research literature presents a mixed picture of learner enthusiasm for using social networking in teaching courses. Whilst the recent Ipsos MORI (2008) survey of UK undergraduates found that over half of undergraduate students reported seeing social networking sites as potentially useful in 'enhancing their learning', only a third thought that their lecturers or tutors should use social networking sites for teaching purposes, and indeed over a quarter expressed the opinion that university staff should definitely not use social networking in their teaching.

Similarly, in response to libraries constructing profiles in MySpace and Facebook, recent researchers argue that 'there are clearly dangers in trying to appear "cool" to a younger audience. In fact, there is a considerable danger that younger users will resent the library invading what they regard as their space'. Instead, as the Ipsos Mori researchers argued, 'evidence shows that using these sites in education are more effective when the students set them up themselves; lecturer-led ones can feel overly formal' (Ipsos MORI 2008).

### Learners Managing the Logistics of Education

In terms of logistical co-ordination, ethnographic studies have shown how SNSs are used by learners alongside technologies such as Microsoft's MSN and texting to gain procedural and logistical information about the conduct of their studies, for instance the requirements of assessment and examination tasks, the timing and location of lessons and so on (Selwyn 2009).

Learners also use SNSs as forums for discussion of education experiences – not least the rating and occasional ridicule of teachers and courses (see Beer and Burrows 2007). Indeed, learners' growing use of SNS-based information is beginning to prompt educational institutions to consider officially sanctioned information sharing. Oradini and Saunders (2008) suggest that there can be 'added value' in this bounded sociality in supporting communities of learners in their social and leisure pursuits.

### Learners Managing Their Social Ties

There has been considerable evidence of learners using SNSs for a range of social and emotional activities relating to their learning. Recent research by Madge et al. (2009) details, for instance, how incoming undergraduate students make use of Facebook before joining the university as a means of making new friends, as well as then keeping in touch with existing friends and family at home. Social networking services are therefore reported to be important social tools used by a majority of students to aid the 'settling-in' process and develop an understanding of university life.

These uses notwithstanding, Madge found little evidence of formal educational benefits to accrue from this use, concluding that for many students Facebook 'is more for socialising and talking to friends about work than for actually doing work' (p. 141). In a similar study of US undergraduate students, Ellison et al. (2007) also reported a strong association between Facebook use and the development of 'bridging' ties between students in loose groups that otherwise did not overlap socially on campus. Similarly, Facebook was also found to be used for maintaining strong 'bonding' links between learners in tight-knit, emotionally close offline relationships.

### Learners' Identity Production

Finally, learners' SNS use has also been found in many studies to relate to issues of (re)presentation of self and maintenance of learner identities. In particular it is acknowledged that social networking sites are complex and often awkward sites of identity performance where users attempt to construct and maintain a (quasi) public image (Boyd and Heer 2006). For instance, Greenhow and Robelia's (2009) study shows how MySpace was being used by US high school students to formulate and display 'all sides of themselves' and for exploring physical, sexual, occupational and ethnic dimensions of their identities within a bounded network of friends. Similarly, Selwyn's (2009) research noted how Facebook is now established as a prominent arena where university students become versed in the 'identity politics' of being a student. Rather than necessarily enhancing or eroding what Goffman (1959) would term students' 'front-stage' engagement with their formal studies, Selwyn's data suggest that Facebook provides a site where the 'role conflict' that students often experience in their relationships with coursework, teaching staff, academic conventions and scholarly expectations can be worked through in a relatively closed 'backstage' area.

In this sense, the research literature shows social networking services to be important arenas within which the 'behind the scenes work' of being a learner is being performed.

### Social Networking: Emerging Issues Requiring Further Attention

These studies confirm that social networking is an important element of many young people's lives and a prominent part of their engagement with new technology. Yet this empirical evidence also suggests that the claims for social networking services generating radical transformations in informal knowledge production and exchange, and in necessitating significant shifts in the organization and structure of formal education, are harder to sustain. Similarly, the demand to appropriate social networking services within formal teaching practices does not seem to originate from students themselves. Instead, students seem to be mobilizing existing educational assumptions – that learning is organized around the individual and that it is oriented around content rather than process and that there should be clear divides between social interaction and 'educational interaction' – when assessing the potential of SNS to assist their learning. At the same time, much of the research reviewed above would suggest that educators might need to pay attention to social networking sites as important for the social construction of identity, including personal, social and learner identity.

With these thoughts in mind, the chapter concludes by considering briefly the issues arising from this review of research evidence that merit sustained attention from the education community.

## Developing New Pedagogies to Support Knowledge Building

On the basis of current evidence, there is little to suggest that learners are 'naturally' and 'intuitively' developing radically new models of collaborative knowledge production outside formal educational settings that can easily be appropriated to the ends of formal education. Despite the rhetoric of Web 2.0 technologies opening up individuals and institutions on a persistent, replicable basis to mediated invisible audiences (Boyd 2007), we have seen how learners' uses of social networking are often closed, private and party to a restricted networked 'public'.

Should educators wish to promote new models of collaborative learning and knowledge production, therefore, such models, and the cultural and cognitive practices that enable them, will need to be consciously and carefully built in educational institutions. SNS technologies, and students' use of them outside formal educational settings, will not in and of themselves offer a 'silver bullet' in transforming educational power relationships, pedagogies and structures.

## Respecting Informal and Resistant Cultures

If social networking sites such as Facebook are acting as 'backstage' spaces for resistance – contesting the asymmetrical power relationship built into the institutional offline positions of student and lecturer (Bourdieu and Passeron 1977) – then a strong case can be made for school and university authorities to avoid appropriating them in order to respect their distinctive role as sites of challenge.

A strong case can be made for school and university authorities to remain purposively unaware of how learners are using social networking in their course of 'doing university' – as Richard Sennett observed in 'The Fall of Public Man', 'civilised relations between selves can only proceed to the extent that nasty little secrets of desire, greed or envy are kept locked up' (Sennett 1974: p. 4).

As Kitto and Higgins (2003) argue, as soon as school or university authorities get involved then there is a danger that SNSs such as Facebook become technologies that 'enable the governing of bodies and actions "at a distance"' (p. 25) – indeed, the increasingly commercial use of SNSs to elicit consumers' opinions and ideas points to one direction in which educational engagement in this area might head. In this sense, social networking services should be recognized as learners' spaces, rather than spaces for learning. As Boyd reasons:

> ... teens often argue that MySpace should be recognized as *my* space, a space for teenagers to be teenagers. Adults typically view this attitude as preposterous because, as they see it, since the technology is public and teens are participating in a public way, they should have every right to view this content. This attitude often frustrates teenagers who argue that just because anyone *can* access the site doesn't mean that everyone *should*.
>
> (Boyd 2008: 25)

### Empowering Learners to Critically Examine SNS

This does not, however, suggest that social networking practices are not of interest to educators. Instead, it suggests that the interest might be oriented towards different questions. If SNSs are important sites for students' identity production and social participation, educators may need to ask whether they might move beyond questions of regulation and management of such practices to productively work with learners to critically reflect upon the nature of these sites.

For instance, Beer and Burrows (2007) identify a number of important issues that could act as a focus for critical reflection: the changing relations between the production and consumption of content; the mainstreaming of private information posted to the public domain; and, our main focus here, the emergence of a new rhetoric of 'democratisation'. There is clearly an important role for schools and universities to work with learners on developing critical understanding of the role of social networking in commodifying the individual (and more importantly the individual's user profile), and embedding the individual within the 'cultural circuits of capital' (Thrift 2005) that underpin Web 2.0 technologies. Similarly, learners can be supported in developing critical understanding of the shifting nature of 'privacy' and notions of public/audience entailed in social networking's mainstreaming of private information posted to the public domain.

### Conclusion

We have attempted to argue that the debate on education and SNS needs to move beyond a simple question of whether education needs to 'catch up' with the changing world of social networking, or whether such changes should be resisted.

Instead, we suggest that as educators, we need to critically examine the extent to which our own aspirations for education are inscribed in our 'reading' of the significance of social networking; we need to explore what it is that really constitutes effective attainment of competence in such practices; we need to challenge our assumption that educational institutions have the automatic right to attempt to colonize such tools for formal educational purposes; and we need to ask what critical literacies will enable us to respond to and interrogate the changes that are happening outside the institutional walls (see also Walker et al., Chapter 15). As our latter discussions have implied, these issues involve uncomfortable but essential questions of power, culture, inequality and identity; the politics and policies of education and technology; issues of space and place; philosophical perspectives on technology and education; and issues underlying the production and consumption of education technologies.

Such questions may not lead to the wholesale adoption of particular technologically mediated practices, they may not lead to the radical redesign of education, but they should lead to the development of a better understanding of how, precisely, we can equip young people to flourish in the context of networked social interactions.

## References

Beer, D. & Burrows, R. (2007) Sociology and, of and in web 2.0: Some initial considerations, *Sociological Research Online*, 12(5). Retrieved 15 October, 2009, from http://www.socresonline.org.uk/12/5/17.html.

Bourdieu, P. & Passeron, C. (1977) *Reproduction in education, society and culture*, London: Sage.

Boyd, D. (2007) The significance of social software. In T. Burg & J. Schmidt (Eds.) *BlogTalks reloaded: Social software research and cases* (pp. 15–30), Norderstedt: Books on Demand.

Boyd, D. (2008) Why youth (heart) social network sites: The role of networked publics in teenage social life. In D. Buckingham (Ed.) *MacArthur foundation series on digital learning – youth, identity, and digital media volume* (pp. 119–142), Cambridge, MA: MIT Press.

Boyd, D. & Heer, J. (2006) Profiles as conversation: Networked identity performance on Friendster. In Proceedings of the Hawai'i International Conference on System Sciences, Persistent Conversation Track. Kauai, HI: IEEE Computer Society. 4–7 January.

Brabazon, T. (2007) *The university of Google: Education in the (post) information age*, Aldershot: Ashgate.

Bugeja, M. (2006) Facing the Facebook, *The Chronicle of Higher Education*, 52(21), p.C1.

Cassidy, J. (2006, 15 May) Me Media. *The New Yorker*, 50–59.

Crook, C. (2008) Theories of formal and informal learning in the world of Web 2.0. In S. Livingstone (Ed.) *Theorising the benefits of new technology for youth: Controversies of learning and development*, University of Oxford/ London School of Economics. Retrieved 15 October, 2009, from http://www.education.ox.ac.uk/esrcseries/uploaded/08_0314%20ESRC%20report_web.pdf.

Crook, C. & Harrison, C. (2008) *Web 2.0 technologies for teaching and learning at key stages 3 and 4*, Coventry: Becta. Retrieved 15 October, 2009, from http://partners.becta.org.uk/upload-dir/downloads/page_documents/research/web2_ks34_summary.pdf.

Davies, J. & Merchant, G. (2009) *Web 2.0 for schools: Learning and social participation*, New York: Peter Lang.

De Rosa, C., Cantrell, J., Havens, A., Hawk, J. & Jenkins, L. (2007) *Sharing, privacy and trust in our networked world*, Dublin, OH: OCLC Online Computer Library Center.

Dutton, B. (2008) Discussant comments on 'Developing the technological imagination'. In S. Livingstone (Ed.) *Theorising the benefits of new technology for youth: Controversies of learning and development*, London: University of Oxford/ London School of Economics. Retrieved 15 October, 2009, from www.education.ox.ac.uk/esrcseries/uploaded/08_0314%20ESRC%20report_web.pdf.

Dutton, W. & Helsper, E. (2007) *The Internet in Britain: 2007*, University of Oxford: Oxford Internet Institute.

Ellison, N., Steinfield, C. & Lampe, C. (2007) The benefits of facebook 'friends:' Social capital and college students' use of online social network sites, *Journal of Computer-Mediated Communication*, 12(4), 1143–1168.

Goffman, E. (1959) *The presentation of self in everyday life,*. Harmondsworth, Penguin.

Greenhow, C. & Robelia, B. (2009) Informal learning and identity formation in online social network, *Learning, Media and Technology*, 34(2), 119–140.

Ipsos MORI (2008) *Great expectations of ICT: How higher education institutions are measuring up*, Bristol: JISC.

Johnson, A. (2007) Speech to the NASUWT Annual Conference, Belfast, 10 April.

Kitto, S. & Higgins, V. (2003) Online university education: Liberating the student? *Science as Culture*, 12(1), 23–58.

Lemeul, J. (2006) Why I registered on Facebook, *The Chronicle of Higher Education*, 53(2), p. C1.

Lenhart, A. & Madden, M. (2007) *Social networking websites and teens: An overview*, Washington DC: Pew Internet and American Life Project Data Memo.

Luckin, R., Clark, W., Logan, K., Graber, R., Oliver, M. & Mee, A. (2009) Do Web 2.0 tools really open the door to learning: Practices, perceptions and profiles of 11–16 year old learners, *Learning, Media and Technology*, 34(2), 87–104.

Madge, C., Wellens, J. & Meek, J. (2009) Facebook, social integration and informal learning at University: 'It is more for socialising and talking to friends about work than for actually doing work', *Learning, Media and Technology*, 34(2), 141–155.

Maloney, E. (2007) What Web 2.0 can teach us about learning, *The Chronicle of Higher Education*, 53(18), 5 January, p. B26.

Mason, R. & Rennie, F. (2007) Using Web 2.0 for learning in the community, *Internet and Higher Education*, 10, 196–203.

Oradini, F. & Saunders, G. (2008) *The use of social networking by students and staff in higher education*. Paper presented at iLearning Forum, European Institute of E-Learning, Paris, France.

O'Reilly, T. (2005) *What is Web 2.0: Design patterns and business models for the next generation of software*. Retrieved 11 December, 2008, from http://oreilly.com/web2/archive/what-is-web-20.html.

Redecker, C. (2009) *Review of learning 2.0 practices: Study on the impact of Web 2.0 innovations on education and training in Europe*, Brussels: JRC European Commission, Scientific and Technical Reports.

Reich, J. (2009) *Reworking the Web, reworking the world: How Web 2.0 is changing our society, review prepared for the Beyond Current Horizons Project*, Bristol: Futurelab. Retrieved October, 2009, from http://www.beyondcurrenthorizons.org.uk.

Selwyn, N. (2009) Faceworking: Exploring students' education-related use of Facebook, *Learning, Media and Technology*, 34(2), 157–174.

Selwyn, N., Potter, J. & Cranmer, S. (2009) Primary pupils' use of information and communication technologies at school and home, *British Journal of Educational Technology*, 40(5), 919–932.

Sennett, R. (1974) *The fall of public man*, New York: Norton.

Shirky, C. (2003) *Social software and the politics of groups*. Retrieved 15 October, 2009, from http://www.shirky.com/writings/group_politics.html.

Smith, R. & Peterson, B. (2007) Psst ... what do you think? The relationship between advice prestige, type of advice, and academic performance, *Communication Education*, 56(3), 278–291.

Thrift, N. (2005) *Knowing capitalism*, London: Sage.

Tufekci, Z. (2008) Grooming, gossip, Facebook and Myspace: What can we learn about social networking sites from non-users, *Information, Communication and Society*, 11(4), 544–564.

Ziegler, S. (2007) The (mis)education of Generation M, *Learning, Media and Technology*, 32(1), 69–81.

# 3
# Managing Study and Life With Technology

LINDA CREANOR AND KATHRYN TRINDER

## Editors' Introduction

This chapter surveys issues around learners' uses and attitudes to technology-enhanced learning. The findings of the JISC LEX study, which adopted a phenomenological method, found that use of technology is complex and often centres around informal as well as formal interventions. The authors conclude that institutional provision of technology needs to adopt a broadly flexible approach helping learners to mesh together different content delivery mechanisms around their own lives.

## Introduction

Fitting study around life is essential for today's learners as they attempt to balance competing responsibilities in an increasingly fast-paced living and learning environment. Advances in technology over the last two decades, most recently manifested in the proliferation of Web 2.0 tools for collaboration and sharing, have extended opportunities for more varied and flexible approaches to learning. Nevertheless, formal learning remains for the most part premised on a traditional model of timetabled, classroom-based instruction that does not easily accommodate learner demands for more flexible approaches.

Flexible learning has been defined variously as widening access to learning through part-time or distance learning; addressing managerial concerns with regard to the effectiveness and efficiency of learning; restructuring educational practices to meet the needs of employers and professional bodies; redesigning the curriculum to incorporate a more student-centred pedagogy; and of course exploiting new technology to achieve these aims (e.g. Nunan 1996). It can also incorporate flexible admissions, recognition of prior informal and experiential learning, student support, advice and guidance, and continuing professional development (QAA Briefing Paper 2006). From the institutional perspective, flexibility is viewed as an aspect of learning that can be controlled and managed: 'Flexible delivery is regarded by institutions as a means of making learning opportunities more accessible to larger and more diverse groups of learners in a resource-constrained environment, whilst still maintaining a quality-driven approach' (QAA Report 2005).

In this context, technology-enhanced learning is often perceived as a means of increasing flexibility through providing easier access for learners to course content and learning activities, usually within a 'safe' virtual learning environment (VLE). Until recently, however, there has been little attempt to discover how this relates in a holistic way to other aspects of learners' lives including the wider digital environment that increasingly pervades their day-to-day activities.

Speculation on changing learner expectations in direct response to this digital environment has been widespread (e.g. Seely Brown 2000; Prensky 2006). For those learners born mainly between 1980 and 1995 and described variously as Millennials (Howe and Strauss 2000), Net Generation (Tapscott 1998) and Generation Y (following on from the 'Generation X' coined by Hamblett and Deverson in the 1965 novel of that name), it is suggested that technology has been a central feature of their everyday life since birth. Whether portrayed as Prensky's 'digital natives' (2001) or White's 'Residents' (2007), such categorisations have captured the popular imagination and in an educational context have prompted an academic 'moral panic' (Bennett et al. 2008) around the need for a redesign of learning to engage these confident, digitally literate learners (Oblinger and Oblinger 2005). Nevertheless, the lack of empirical evidence for these pronouncements and the acknowledgement that learner cohorts cannot be conceived of as homogeneous groups highlight the need for further investigation (Kennedy et al. 2006).

This chapter will focus on one study, the Learner Experience of E-Learning (LEX), which aimed to address this major gap in our understanding by focusing solely on the learner perspective. It will begin by outlining the background to the study and describing the innovative methodology adopted by the research team. It will present a sample of the rich data collected, which, through the learners' own voices, encapsulates the challenging complexity of their lives and the impact of the digital environment on their ability to create the flexibility they need. In conclusion, it will critically relate the findings of this study to more recent developments in the field and identify key issues for future research and development.

## Background

The foundation for LEX was a Scoping Study commissioned by the Joint Information Systems Committee (JISC) in the UK to conduct a literature review of the learner experience of technology-enhanced learning (Sharpe et al.

2005). The review discovered that, whilst there was no shortage of studies from a teacher, course or technology perspective, the learner viewpoint appeared in only seven of the eighty-eight publications cited. The report concluded that:

> There is in general a scarcity of studies of the learner experience. In particular there is a scarcity of studies which can be characterised as expressing a 'learner voice' i.e. in which the learners' own expressions of their experiences are central to the study.
>
> (Sharpe et al. 2005: 3)

The scoping study was undertaken before Web 2.0, social networking and 3D virtual worlds had become as pervasive as they are today, therefore its findings relate mainly to the learning technologies that were prevalent at that time. A significant proportion of the literature (around 50 per cent) focused on asynchronous online discussions that make visible certain aspects of student behaviour through a rich and easily observable data resource (Cox et al. 2000; Shephard et al. 2003; Bird 2004; Cramphorn 2004).

Participation in online forums and the reification of that interaction in threaded discussions offer a legitimated communication structure and a valid focus for research (Wenger 1998). Inevitably, however, they capture only one aspect of learner communication and disregard the unseen behaviour that may take place elsewhere, including in the less formal but highly important networks of peers, family and friends with whom learners interact.

A recent study (Trinder et al. 2008) explored the potential of informal technologies to support formal learning. It focused on two disciplines across two institutions (engineering and social work undergraduates), with a mix of learner ages. The learners in the study talked about how they harnessed technology tools to support their learning through the use of both informal personal tools such as social networking sites or mobile phones, and formal institutionally provided tools such as a VLE. These learners used digital and Web 2.0 tools in informal ways to help them tap into these personal and peer networks. Sometimes this communication was explicit and encouraged by the teachers, at other times it was hidden and unsupported, or even discouraged, by the institution.

Other studies have examined the impact of blended learning (e.g. Sweeney et al. 2004), distance learning (e.g. Alstete and Beutell 2004) and mobile learning (e.g. Kukulska-Hulme and Traxler 2005). However, the findings were mainly contextualised, predominately in higher education, and were often specific to a particular course or technology. There clearly remain significant gaps in our knowledge of the learner experience, especially with regard to personal use of technology to enhance the effectiveness and flexibility of learning.

LEX was one of two groundbreaking studies that aimed to broaden and deepen our understanding of these less discernible aspects of the learner experience. It was the first UK-wide and fully cross-sectoral study to explore in-depth the varied, and hitherto invisible, behaviours and attitudes of learners towards technology in all aspects of their lives (Creanor et al. 2006).

### Researching the Learner Experience

It was necessary to choose an appropriate methodology that would allow an exclusive focus on the learner voice, and after much deliberation an interpretive phenomenological analysis (IPA) methodology was adopted. The grounded theoretical approach that underpins IPA ensures that the participants' lived experiences remain central to the study. Previously, it had been administered predominantly in the health psychology domain (e.g. Smith 2004) therefore its application to a technology-enhanced learning context was new and untested. A detailed critique of the methodology and its merit in this field is presented in a separate report (Mayes 2006).

Individual interviews augmented by a small number of focus group sessions formed the main data gathering interventions. Of the fifty-five learners interviewed, 44 per cent were male and 55 per cent female. In addition to their studies, the majority (71 per cent) were employed either full- or part-time. Although a few (less than 6 per cent) were studying completely online, most were undertaking traditional face-to-face courses that incorporated technology to varying degrees. The aim was not to conduct a comparative study with respect to this diversity, but rather to draw out common themes from the experiences of individual learners to inform our understanding of their use of, and feelings about, technology for learning.

### Influencing Factors

IPA requires a rigorous data analysis that, through an increasingly high level of scrutiny, brings to the fore connections, interrelationships and patterns, thus gradually reducing the levels of complexity (Reid, Flowers and Larkin 2005; Smith and Osborn 2003). To minimise the influence of the researchers' subjective perspectives on the outcome of the analysis, a sequence of individual and team-based encoding techniques was employed alongside a review of a random selection of encoded transcripts by an experienced and objective critical friend. In this way, a robust triangulation across the various categories of analysis was ensured (Denzin 1978). Two overarching, learner-focused questions informed the development of the resulting conceptual framework:

- What factors influence what I do with my learning?
- What factors influence how I feel about my learning?

A detailed conceptual map was developed that captured the structural relationships between these emerging factors. The analysis identified five main categories defined as life, formal learning, technology, people and time, with each category possessing five underlying dimensions of control, identity, feelings, relationships and abilities.

The remainder of this paper will focus on the interplay between these emerging factors and their influence on learners' lives. It will also highlight some of the strategies adopted by learners in their use of technology to minimise the disruption of competing responsibilities and enhance opportunities for flexibility in their learning.

## Convenience or Necessity?

From an institutional perspective, flexibility in learning can often be conceived of as an additional option rather than an essential feature of the learning experience. For many learners, however, it can be fundamental to their ability to undertake a course of study.

> When I was at university [the first time] I was single, stayed myself, found it quite easy to find time to get the work done. Now three years down the line I'm married with a boy of four years old and I find it quite hard to find the time to sit and do course work.
>
> (Male college student)

> I find we're under pressure all day when we come up here. We have to be here for nine in the morning, we're leaving home after seven, and then at lunchtime we run to the library … you don't get enough time really to access the things that you want to and I do try and leave quite sharp-ish in the evening to be home for the children.
>
> (Female college student)

Technology was perceived as a key factor in enabling learners to manage these competing commitments.

> Yes, I had to leave early last week because my childminder was off and I had to pick up my son from the nursery so I missed the afternoon lecture so I went onto the message board and asked for information about what I'd missed. People were kind enough to log on … and they let me know what groups I was in and what the presentation was about and things like that, so it was good for catching up in that respect.
>
> (Male college student)

The flexibility inherent in well-designed technology-enhanced learning that affords access to resources, tutors and fellow students at the learner's convenience, often through a virtual learning environment, was seen by learners as a major benefit. However, LEX also uncovered the alternative routes adopted by learners through employing their own preferred tools and techniques, often bypassing the institutionally controlled systems. Indeed, participants expressed great pride in the fact that they had taken control of the learning process in this way. This behaviour clearly had a positive impact on learners' confidence and self-esteem but it was generally invisible to tutors, resulting in what we described as an 'underworld' of activity in support of learning (Creanor et al. 2006: 27).

> I use [the discussion board] like once or twice a week but ... we contact each other in the evenings over MSN Messenger if we're doing work quite a lot, or just text ...
>
> (Female postgraduate student)

> So my [group] we always text each other and say, 'oh are you coming in at this time' or 'we'll meet at this time' and so it looks on the face of it from the university website that we haven't been communicating all year but we have, it's just outside of that [discussion] board.
>
> (Female postgraduate student)

We were left in no doubt that technology played an important role in the lives of all the learners interviewed, with many displaying the multitasking and 'always connected' behaviours that often underpinned their approach to study and their ability to link different aspects of their lives.

> I think in the future people can't cope without their laptops. My main use of it is I guess social networking. It would be MySpace and Messenger and e-mail things like that and then secondary would be information gathering ... my home page is the technology website and current affairs, news. I have alerts coming in to me so I get information and then I use search engines for academic purposes ... [laughs].
>
> (Female undergraduate student)

Alongside this sense of necessity, the flexibility to control and personalise learning environments, both physical and virtual, emerged as another important theme.

### Personal Technology and Personalising Learning Environments

Learners have variable preferences in their choices of technology, both for personal use and for learning. Some learners naturally mix their learning activity, communication and their everyday life, supported by their personal technology and institutionally provided tools, whereas others compartmentalise their activities and prefer to keep a clear distinction between learning, life and the tools that they use for each.

I find it very, very distracting being in the library as ... I need to set everything out and all. I feel that I'm in too close proximity to other people to be able to use the computer ... I prefer to do my studying at home.

(Female college student)

I have two [mobile phones], my personal phone for my own personal use and I have a works phone where work can keep in touch with me and find out where I am ... My own phone is just for personal use, to keep in touch with my own family.

(Focus group participant)

The methods they chose for study, and their preferred modes of communication with their personal support networks also allowed learners to express their individual sense of identity.

I'd sooner talk to someone or phone so I'm not that big on MSN really ... my girlfriend uses it all time you know ... but I suppose it's just how everybody is, it just depends what you enjoy.

(Male undergraduate student)

However, although technology was integral to their daily activities, several participants expressed reservations towards embracing a new technology for learning without a strong justification.

I don't really like to just go headlong into using something new because I always like to see what it is that the new technology's going to do for me ...

(Female postgraduate student)

Where they were convinced of its benefits, they recognised that technology enabled them to blur the boundaries between life and learning in positive and helpful ways.

I guess [the Internet] expands all your horizons in completely different ways and helps you to apply academic stuff to everyday life and see where current affairs and things fit into the academic. I guess it provides that interface ... that wouldn't have been there before.

(Female undergraduate student)

Technology makes it a lot easier for me to learn, if I didn't have access to the internet I think I wouldn't be at the point where I've been able to pass some subjects.

(Female undergraduate student)

This combination of highly valued tools and networks to choose from, and the ability to adapt them to their personal needs, allowed learners the scope to pull together the appropriate environments for them as individuals, giving them the flexibility they required to support fitting their learning into their lives in a more seamless way.

### Confidence and Motivation

The aim of LEX was to elicit common themes from the learner experiences rather than compare differences, however, unsolicited comments from participants pointed to a general perception that younger learners had an advantage over their more mature counterparts because of their greater familiarity and confidence with digital tools.

> The kids know everything there is to know about new technology, so if you've got a young person around then they would be able to show you everything there is to know about it.
>
> (Focus group participant)

> Our generation has grown up with [technology] ... so we just take it all for granted ... and we'll just use it.
>
> (Female undergraduate student)

Despite this, our findings indicate that the impact of this perceived advantage on learning effectiveness was minimal. This may be in part because of the discontinuity between the technologies and tools used for formal learning, such as institutional VLEs, online discussion boards, specialised databases and e-portfolios, and those that constituted the personal digital environments of many of the participants, e.g. mobile devices, Google, Wikipedia and social networking sites.

Another influencing factor was the motivation and self-determination identified by those who believed they had some ground to make up with regard to digital competences:

> I think a lot of the stuff that younger people would find a lot easier I find harder, but then again I think to compensate for that I try harder ...
>
> (Male undergraduate student)

> ... when I first went on and started to look at it I thought, 'oh my God! I don't know whether this is for me' but then I thought, 'calm down a bit and sit down and go through it step by step'.
>
> (Female Adult and Community Learner)

Several participants reported that whereas they may have begun as digital novices, they had quickly developed the necessary skills and confidence to allow them to minimise any perceived gap between themselves and their peers. When asked how this had been achieved, most reported relying on a combination of self-direction, including trial and error, and a strong support network of family, friends, colleagues and fellow students. Interestingly, there was little mention of formal institutional training in this regard. The sense of achievement gained as confidence and skill levels increased appeared to have had a positive motivational impact on their experience as learners.

> You get a wee boost the first time you do something, you get a, 'oh right, I've done that myself' and then … you'll go to the next step, you know. The first time you hit a brick wall … you go 'aargh!', but when you do it [successfully] the first time you think 'I did that' and then move on to the next thing. It's definitely worth it.
>
> (Focus group participant)

There was also an acknowledgement that, even amongst the most confident participants, an expanded set of digital literacies was required. Indeed several participants noted that, although they considered themselves reasonably expert, their self-confidence was challenged by the realisation that formal learning encompassed unfamiliar technologies and approaches:

> I thought it would be OK because I'm so used to doing word processing … I didn't realise that I would need to go on to the internet [to use the VLE] and so I was feeling quite confident, but I don't feel as confident about that now.
>
> (Focus group participant)

> … the internet is the main thing that we end up using and just trawling through all these websites, you never know if the knowledge is actually good or not, so I'm always worried that I'm handing something in which is completely just one guy's opinion.
>
> (Female undergraduate student)

Although the participants reported a wide range of views on, and experiences with, technology, it was clear that they shared the common attributes of self-motivation and a strong determination to make the most of their learning experience. This included using technology in a way that maximised opportunities for flexibility to fit learning successfully into their everyday lives.

## Discussion

More recent surveys have shed further light on the role of technology in learners' lives as they attempt to balance study with part- or full-time employment, personal and family commitments, and leisure activities. One large-scale study of over a thousand first year undergraduate students (Ipsos Mori 2008) found that a large majority of respondents (87 per cent) reported that the technology provided by their universities either met or surpassed their expectations, but at the same time highlighted the fact that their most common use of technology '... is simply to support daily life' (p. 40). This suggests that learners have lower expectations of technology to support learning than we might have assumed, and that formal learning is still not sufficiently attuned to the reality of technology use in the daily lives of learners.

The LEX findings have also been validated by subsequent learner experience research studies, some of which have investigated a more focused, sectoral or subject specific context (Sharpe et al. 2009). The Learning from Digital Natives (LDN) final report found that whilst there was some tool use difference between disciplines, perception and misperception of the value of tools and their actual uses varied widely (Trinder et al. 2008). Like LEX, this report also concluded that learners are adaptable and active, and will pull in tools to support activity as and where required, and often in spite of any institutional provision. So far though, there appears to be no clear evidence emerging that points to a significant difference in the way students of different disciplines use technology to support their studies.

Flexibility is clearly a key factor for today's learners, and technology is increasingly central to the personal networks and constantly evolving 'ecologies' that learners construct to support the various elements of their lives. The subversive behaviour reported with such delight by many of the LEX participants emphasises the complex interplay between human agency and institutional structure that continues to cause much angst amongst educators and senior managers (Czerniewicz et al. 2009).

Institutional control, standardisation of learning systems and the policing of technology to safeguard security sit increasingly uneasily with the shifting sands of Web 2.0, virtual worlds, mobile devices and, more importantly, the concept of the independent, self-regulated learner (e.g. Fazey and Fazey 2001). It has been suggested that the aforementioned 'moral panic' is setting in (Keen 2007); however, more recent reports (Bradwell 2009) show the beginnings of a culture shift that recognises that flexibility of provision is vital in sustaining twenty-first century learning.

**Conclusions**

LEX did not deliberately set out to capture the experiences of those learners who approached technology with reluctance or apprehension. Nevertheless, many of our participants referred to a time when they were less confident technology users, and described the journey they had taken to achieve the levels of confidence that had allowed them to gain the digital competences that impacted positively on their learning. Indeed, these personal journeys of discovery can perhaps provide deeper insights into the design of technology-enhanced learning than a focus on generational differences or the affordances of the latest Web 2.0 tools.

Perhaps we now need to focus our attention on the intersections of the diverse communities that learners inhabit and investigate the discontinuities between them. By so doing, we would be better placed to identify opportunities for learning through the development of appropriate learning activities that encourage creativity and higher levels of autonomy by allowing for a greater degree of learner choice. Professional development for tutors should focus on identifying and explicitly addressing the barriers and opportunities offered by these intertwined socio-technical factors. 'Now we need to give teachers the time, the tools, and the trust to develop their use of digital technologies according to the needs of their learners' (Laurillard, 2008: 34).

The role of human agency is also vital: by nurturing a collaborative approach through increased student involvement in designing the process (for example, which technologies and tools might be most appropriate for a particular activity) as well as the outcomes of learning activities, we can scaffold their development as independent learners whilst at the same time enhance the experience and understanding of their tutors.

Many LEX participants stated how valuable they found their institutional VLE for interacting and communicating with peers and tutors; gaining and offering support via their learning communities; accessing course materials; receiving formative feedback through online tests; and reflecting on their learning in e-portfolios. The learners' main concern was the lack of consistency in its use by their tutors and by institutions. The core system of the institutional VLE, as a well supported technology supporting well understood pedagogies, can provide a stable and invaluable backbone of activity when effectively utilised. This backbone can be enhanced by new tools and technologies as they emerge, and by the personal choices of the learners themselves. 'Through their institutional capital, universities can use technology to offer more flexible provision and open more equal routes to higher education and learning (Bradwell 2009).

By ensuring that these core systems provide a consistently high quality 'safety net' of activities and resources for all students, it is evident that institutions can make real difference to the learner experience and their demands for flexibility.

To ensure our learners are equipped to face the real world of choices in the broader knowledge economy, however, we also need to embrace the fact that they will be creative, even subversive, in their use of new technology and find a way of acknowledging, even rewarding, this behaviour. While we cannot predict learner strategy in the use of technology, we can incorporate more flexibility within our learning systems and processes and, most importantly, allow the learner voice to inform our future thinking.

**54** • Linda Creanor and Kathryn Trinder

## References

Alstete, J.W. & Beutell, N.J. (2004). Performance indicators in online distance learning courses: A study of management education, *Quality Assurance in Education*, 12(1), 6–14.

Bennett, S., Maton, K. & Kervin, L. (2008) The 'digital natives' debate: A critical review of the evidence, *British Journal of Educational Technology*, 39(5), 775–786.

Bird, C. (2004) Sinking in a C-M sea: A graduate student's experience of learning through asynchronous computer-mediated communication, *Reflective Practice*, 5(2), 253–263.

Bradwell, P. (2009) Edgeless University: Why higher education must embrace technology, Demos Report. ISBN 978-1-906693-16-9. Retrieved 26 June, 2009, from http://www.jisc.ac.uk/media/documents/publications/edgelessuniversity.pdf.

Cox, E.S., Clark, W.P., Heath, H. & Plumpton, B. (2000) The impact of gender on effective online discussion groups. Proceedings of *Distance Education: An Open Question?* Conference, 11–13 September 2000. Retrieved 27 February, 2009, from http://www.unisanet.unisa.edu.au/cccc/papers/refereed/paper12/Paper12-1.htm.

Cramphorn, C. (2004) An evaluation of the formal and underlying factors influencing student participation with e-learning web discussion forums. In S. Banks et al. (Eds.) *Proceedings of Networked Learning* (pp. 417–442).

Creanor, L., Trinder, K., Gowan, D. & Howells, C. (2006) *LEX: The learner experience of e-learning. Final report* (report under the JISC e-pedagogy Understanding my learner programme). Glasgow: Glasgow Caledonian University. Retrieved 20 August, 2009, from, http://www.jisc.ac.uk/whatwedo/programmes/elearning_pedagogy/elp_learneroutcomes.aspx.

Czerniewicz, L., Williams, K. & Brown, C. (2009) Students make a plan: Understanding student agency in constraining conditions, *ALT-J, Research in Learning Technology*, 17(2), 75–88.

Denzin, N.K. (1978) *The research act: A theoretical introduction to sociological methods*. New York: McGraw-Hill.

Fazey, D. & Fazey, J. (2001) The potential for autonomy in learning: Perceptions of competence, motivation and locus of control in first year undergraduate students, *Studies in Higher Education*, 26(3), 345–361.

Hamblett, C. & Deverson, J. (1965) *Generation X*, London, Universal-Tandem Publishing Co Ltd.

Howe, N. & Strauss, W. (2000) *Millennials rising: The next great generation*, New York: Vintage Books.

Ipsos Mori (2008) *Great expectations of ICT: How higher education institutions are measuring up*, research study conducted for the Joint Information Systems Committee (JISC). Retrieved 27 February, 2009, from http://www.jisc.ac.uk/publications/publications/studentexpectations.

Keen, A. (2007) *The cult of the amateur: How today's internet is killing our culture*, New York: Doubleday/Currency.

Kennedy, G., Krause, K.L., Gray, K., Judd, T., Bennett, S., Maton, K., Dalgarno, B. & Bishop, A. (2006) Questioning the Net Generation: A collaborative project in Australian higher education. In L. Markauskaite, P. Goodyear and P. Reimann (Eds.) *Who's learning? Whose technology?* Proceedings of the 23rd annual Ascilite conference, 3–6 December, Sydney, Australia.

Kukulska-Hulme, A. & Traxler, J. (Eds.) (2005) *Mobile learning: A handbook for educators and trainers*, London: Routledge.

Laurillard, D. (2008) *Digital technologies and their role in achieving our ambitions for education*, Inaugural Professorial Lecture, Institute of Education, University of London, 26 February. Association for Learning Technology (Occasional Publication).

Mayes, J.T. (2006) LEX methodology report. Retrieved 27 February, 2009, from http://www.jisc.ac.uk/media/documents/programmes/elearningpedagogy/lex_method_final.pdf.

Nunan, T. (1996) *Flexible delivery: What is it and why is it a part of current educational debate?* Paper presented at the Higher Education Research and Development Society of Australasia Annual Conference, *Different Approaches: Theory and Practice in Higher Education*, Perth, Western Australia, 8–12 July.

Oblinger D. and Oblinger J. (2005) Is it age or IT? First steps towards understanding the Net Generation. In D. Oblinger and J. Oblinger (Eds.) *Educating the Net Generation*, Educause. Retrieved 27 February, 2009, from http://www.educause.edu/educatingthenetgen/.

Prensky, M. (2001) Digital natives, digital immigrants, *On the Horizon*, 9(5), NCB University Press. Retrieved 27 February, 2009, from http://www.twitchspeed.com/site/Prensky%20-%20Digital%20Natives,%20Digital%20Immigrants%20-%20Part1.htm.

Prensky M. (2006) Listen to the natives. *Educational Leadership*, 63(4), 8–13.

QAA Report, (2005), *Flexible Delivery Consultation: The Institutional Perspective, Steering Committee for Quality Enhancement Theme: Flexible Delivery,* The Quality Assurance Agency for Higher Education. Retrieved 5 February, 2010, from http://www.enhancementthemes. ac.uk/documents/flexibleDelivery/Institutional_Consultation_Final_Report.DOC.

QAA Report (2006) *Flexible delivery: An evaluation of the use of the virtual learning environment in higher education across Scotland,* The Quality Assurance Agency for Higher Education. Retrieved 27 February, 2009, from http://www.enhancementthemes.ac.uk/documents/ flexibleDelivery/Flexible_delivery_QAA_128.pdf.

Reid, K., Flowers, P. & Larkin, M. (2005) Exploring lived experience, *The Psychologist,* 18(1), 20–23.

Seely Brown, J. (2000) Growing up digital: How the Web changes work, education, and the ways people learn, *US Distance Learning Association Journal,* 16(2) Retrieved 27 February, 2009, from http://www.usdla.org/html/journal/FEB02_Issue/article01.html.

Sharpe R., Benfield G., Lessner E. & DeCicco E. (2005) *Final report: Scoping study for the pedagogy strand of the JISC e-Learning Programme,* Oxford: OCSLD. Retrieved 27 February, 2009, from http://www.jisc.ac.uk/whatwedo/programmes/elearning_pedagogy/elp_learneroutcomes. aspx.

Sharpe, R., Beetham, H., Benfield, G., DeCicco, E. & Lessner, E. (2009) *Learners' experiences of e-learning synthesis report: Explaining learner differences.* Retrieved 28 June, 2009, from https://mw.brookes.ac.uk/display/JISCle2f/Findings.

Shephard, K., Riddy, P., Warren, A. & Mathias, H. (2003) Exploring the role of on-line discussion in academic staff development for new lecturers, *Innovations in Education and Teaching International,* 40(3), 245–253.

Smith, J.A. (2004) Reflecting on the development of interpretative phenomenological analysis and its contribution to qualitative research in psychology, *Qualitative Research in Psychology,* 1, 39–54.

Smith, J.A. & Osborn, M. (2003) Interpretative phenomenological analysis. In J.A. Smith (Ed.) *Qualitative Psychology,* London: Sage.

Sweeney, J., O'Donoghue, T. & Whitehead, C. (2004) Traditional face-to-face and web-based tutorials: A study of university students' perspectives on the roles of tutorial participants, *Teaching in Higher Education,* 9(3), 311–323.

Tapscott, D. (1998) *Growing up digital: The rise of the Net Generation,* New York: McGraw-Hill.

Trinder, K., Guiller, J., Margaryan, A., Littlejohn, A. & Nicol, D. (2008) Learning from digital natives: Integrating formal and informal learning. *Final project report,* Higher Education Academy, UK. Retrieved 14 April, 2009, from http://www.academy.gcal.ac.uk/ldn/ LDNFinalReport.pdf.

Wenger, E. (1998) *Communities of practice: Learning, meaning, and identity,* Cambridge: Cambridge University Press.

White, D. (2007) Not 'natives' & 'immigrants' but 'visitors' & 'residents', Blog post. Retrieved 20 May, 2009, from http://tallblog.conted.ox.ac.uk/index.php/2008/07/23/not-natives-immigrants-but-visitors-residents/.

# 4
# Constructs That Impact the Net Generation's Satisfaction With Online Learning

CHARLES D. DZIUBAN, PATSY D. MOSKAL,
GEORGE R. BRADFORD, JAY BROPHY-ELLISON AND
AMANDA T. GROFF

**Editors' Introduction**

This chapter assesses differences in how the so-called 'Net Generation' are interacting with technology such as social software tools. The chapter surveys ethnographic concepts such as 'boundary objects' and prototype theory through a lens of ambivalence and uncertain mediation. In this way the learner's experience is a refracted and reorganized set of mediations whereby learner satisfaction becomes a moving target.

**Introduction**

In this chapter we focus on Net Generation, or digital native students, as they interact with emerging technologies and express satisfaction with online and technology-enhanced educational environments. Although we consider these elements separately, each forms complex interactions with multiple factors in the educational environment leading us to three conclusions. First, it is virtually impossible to anticipate how an intervention will evolve in a complex system such as a university or a classroom. Second, many of the outcomes we achieve will be counterintuitive, and finally there will be unanticipated side effects, both positive and negative that must be accommodated (Forrester 1993).

Before presenting the results of our current research we discuss some characteristics of students and higher education systems that force us to function in what Setenyi calls an environment of 'uncertain mediation' (1995).

Very often we must make decisions, reach conclusions and take action in the face of incomplete or ambiguous information.

## The Net Generation

Understanding the Net Generation's relationship to technology and the resulting interaction that impacts current educational practices remains one of the most active research agendas in online learning. Questions persist about whether we should respond to these students' personal characteristics, learning preferences and lifestyles by designing new teaching paradigms, or hold the line on important traditional standards such as proper sources, copyright and intellectual honesty. In the frenzy to build a workable prototype for this learner cohort we describe them at various times as collaborative, open, independent and inclusive (Tapscott 1998); special, sheltered, achieving and conventional (Howe and Strauss 2000); multitasking, graphically oriented, connected and active (Prensky 2001); or narcissistic, cynical and self-absorbed (Twenge 2006). Interestingly, these prototypes represent only a portion of the models proposed by investigators who attend to this student group (Wendover 2002; Coomes and DeBard 2002; Prensky 2009). In marked contradiction, these young people have been characterized as the greatest generation (Howe and Strauss 2000) and the dumbest generation (Bauerlein 2008).

As fascinating as this research and theorizing are, they heighten our ambivalence by raising a number of important ambiguities. Is this digital generation driven by personal and mobile technologies in the acquisition of knowledge or is it simply transfixed with the social networking capabilities of platforms that do little to enhance learning? Are they living in the Eduardo of ambient findability where anyone can find anything, anywhere, at any time (Morville 2005) or are they experiencing Taleb's (2008) toxicity of the information age? Do their emerging learning styles demand attention in the educational enterprise or is the study of learning style a vacuous pursuit? Is the Net Generation genuinely dissatisfied with the current educational system that they see as non-responsive or are they simply ambivalent toward learning under the transmission of information model? Should students have a participatory voice in their education or are they imposing a consumer mentality on learning that undermines rigour and high standards?

## Net Generation (Digital Native) Ambivalence

There is little doubt that uncertainties predominate our modern pluralistic society (Taleb 2005). Those uncertainties become a fertile ground for Net Generation students to express ambivalent feelings about their curriculum, their classes and their instructors. Ambivalence is a situation where students experience at least two contradictory feelings that push them in one direction and pull them in another. For instance, they appreciate the convenience and flexibility of online classes but lament the lack of face-to-face contact with their instructors. Students can dislike formal writing for their class assignments, but produce several hundred Facebook posts in a single month. They may gravitate toward knowing exactly where they stand on multiple choice tests, yet express a desire for more real world, authentic assessment. Historically, more traditional societies provided role expectation models for their members (Weigert 1991). Everyone belonged to a metaphorical tribe (Godin 2008) and they knew where they were supposed to be and what they were supposed to do. There was a beginning and an end. In today's information societies individuals have a diminished sense of those beginnings and endings.

## Boundary Object

Each of these ideas convinces us that the Net Generation has become what Star and Griesemer (1989) define as a boundary object:

> Boundary objects are objects which are both plastic enough to adapt to local needs and constraints of the several parties employing them, yet robust enough to maintain a common identity across sites. They are weakly structured in common use, and become strongly structured in individual-site use. They may be abstract or concrete. They have different meanings in different social worlds but their structure is common enough to more than one world to make them recognizable means of translation. The creation and management of boundary objects is key in developing and maintaining coherence across intersecting social worlds.
> ( Star and Griesemer 1989: 387–420)

Therefore, Net Generation is a notion in which many communities find themselves invested, but an idea that allows them to vector their own frames of reference. For instance, it seems reasonable to assume that faculty members, instructional designers, students, administrators and learning theorists might have varying perspectives but still come together under the generational framework. Those constituents tend to operate at the periphery of the generation notion while remaining connected to each other. The concept serves as a means of coordination and alignment, as well as a vehicle for translation across communities and a strong basis for knowledge production. Ultimately, boundary objects such as the Net Generation, or digital native, become repositories for large and valuable bodies of knowledge that complement each other and foster emerging theory and practice in technology-enhanced learning. The Net Generation as a boundary object frees us from the gruelling task of a precise definition with the associated negative side effects (e.g. protracted and unproductive definitional arguments). After all, most definitions are neither correct nor incorrect, they are either useful or not.

*Prototype Theory*

In considering online learning we use the terms Net Generation and digital native interchangeably. Although there are those who would argue that they are not synonymous, we contend that they are metaphorically joined at the hip (Lakoff and Johnson 1980). For the sake of argument let's consider the category digital native and the characteristics and behaviours that qualify a student for that designation. These attempts strive to construct what Rosch (1973) defines as a prototype basic level effect. That is, we seek to find a category at the most responsive level that resonates with our conception of students interacting with technology in the educational environment (Lakoff 1987). In her work, Rosch points out that any single category, such as digital native, features a fundamental asymmetry. Within these singular categories there is wide variation in the characteristics of those bearing the same designation. Some digital natives are more digitally native than others. While this may seem obvious to the reader, virtually everyone who has written on this topic concentrates on the prototype at the expense of the within-group variation, possibly the most important feature of categories.

## Towards a Construct of Satisfaction for the Net Generation

Colleges and universities have learned that the twenty-first century student is different, both demographically and geographically, from students of previous generations. These differences affect everything from admissions policy to library services. Reaching these students, and serving them appropriately, are major challenges to today's institutions.
(Lezberg 2003: 432–433)

Net Generation students are high stakes players in the evolving saga of student satisfaction with the online environment. Traditionally, they respond to end-of-course survey protocols that purport to index varying aspects of courses and instructors (Wang et al. 2009). They publish their own evaluations making them available through a number of channels. They vote organically by registering for or avoiding courses taught by certain instructors. In addition, every campus has an effective gossip network where instructors' reputations are influenced by word-of-mouth and electronically distributed student comments. The emergence of RateMyProfessors.com takes expression of student satisfaction to another level. For better or worse, that site has created a worldwide forum for students to express their views, enabling them to communicate their preference to an audience of astounding size. Web 2.0 further levels the playing field so that social networks have become an archive for student satisfaction. In real time, students can tweet what is happening in class via Twitter or asynchronously post something on YouTube or Facebook.

## Expanding the Student Satisfaction Construct

In a study funded by the Alfred P. Sloan Foundation to identify the components that underlie Net Generation student satisfaction, we leveraged three approaches in a mixed model approach. Consistent with current thinking that this cohort prefers active learning, collaboration and co-creation, we sought to have digital natives become active participants in the research process. Initially, we scrutinized three well known literature reviews on satisfaction and harvested a number of preliminary elements having potential for developing measurement protocols and assessing student satisfaction (Muilenburg and Berge 2005; Sun et al. 2008).

The second phase of the study involved ten Net Generation focus groups of approximately ten students each to review the literature elements, and eliminate those that failed to resonate with these students or in their judgement misrepresented them. We arrived at a final decision on each construct after a negotiation process. Upon completion of this phase the student groups working with the facilitators refined those dimensions. Finally, the students added components they believed represented their generation and should be used for developing a measurement protocol.

The students went on to review existing satisfaction instruments identifying items they believed were valid for measuring some aspect of the underlying constructs. In some cases they were able to identify one-to-one component correspondence while in other instances they were more generalized in their selection criteria. Finally, the students constructed items that they believed were valid for assessing satisfaction levels for their peers in online classes. The item clusters underwent a final review by students with priority recommendations. The research associates and staff of the Research Initiative for Teaching Effectiveness at the University of Central Florida, working with online faculty, selected, revised and validated a final set of 24 five-point Likert scale items and assembled them into a data collection protocol. Those items are contained in Table 4.1. The survey was distributed online to 2,230 Net Generation students who were involved in online courses at the time of the study; 1,350 complied for a response rate of approximately 59 per cent.

## Data Analysis

The responses to the Likert items were intercorrelated and subjected to principal component analysis. Prior to that procedure, however, we determined whether the data in hand were appropriate for factoring procedures by assessing their domain sampling properties. This is a recommended procedure developed by Dziuban and Shirkey (1974) that answers the question of whether or not the items under consideration comprise a valid sample from a domain under study. This is the psychometric sampling issue that investigators address much less often than statistical sampling in the literature, but one of fundamental importance. Although one can never be completely sure about an item sample, there is evidence to show that if one has an adequate psychometric sample of items the inverse of the correlation matrix will approach an identity. Using this property, Kaiser (1974) developed his measure of sampling adequacy (MSA), a unitary index that varies from 0 to 1. As the measure approaches 1 the items have increasingly improving sampling properties. We computed the MSA for our data and obtained a value of 0.95 providing evidence that the correlation matrix under consideration does possess excellent psychometric properties and is appropriate for component analysis.

Components were extracted according to the eigenvalues of the correlation matrix greater than one and rotated according to the promax procedure developed by Hendrickson and White (1964). This procedure produces component correlation giving a more interpretable pattern matrix. Coefficients greater than 0.4 were used for interpretation purposes. The derived component pattern matrix is presented in Table 4.1

Six components were retained suggesting a multiple dimension construct of Net Generation student satisfaction with online learning. The components are quite direct in their interpretation

## 1. More Effective Institutional Responsiveness

A major contributing dimension to satisfaction derives from students believing that their institutions make some effort to accommodate their lifestyle needs. Their ability to pursue educational goals in a flexible environment where they are relieved from rigid schedules and large lecture sections creates for them the perception of an extended and responsive university. They experience a sense of localness whether they are at a great distance from, near or on campus.

## 2. Increased Educational Engagement

A second major consideration for students relates to engaging with their educational environments. They do this by interacting with their peers and instructors, having an enhanced ability to ask questions and clarify their concerns. In addition, this component identifies their ability to learn collaboratively as an element that leads to satisfaction.

## 3. More Explicit Role Expectations

This component suggests that students are more satisfied with courses in which they have a clear vision of the rules of engagement. Their satisfaction is inextricably related to valid assessment of their academic progress in a manner that they believe is responsive and equitable. Interestingly, the student focus groups' conversations indicated that they prefer assessment of their academic progress to change from procedures that are objective, non-authentic and non-contextual to those that are reflective, authentic and contextual.

**Table 4.1** Promax Transformed Pattern Matrix for the Principal Components Analysis of the Student Questionnaire Responses (n = 1,325)*

|  | 1 | 2 | 3 | 4 | 5 | 6 |
|---|---|---|---|---|---|---|
| Online classes allow me to work where I want | 90 | | | | | |
| Online classes are easier to schedule | 93 | | | | | |
| Online courses help me control my life | 53 | | | | | |
| Online classes free me from large classes | 52 | | | | | |
| Overall, I am satisfied with online courses | 59 | | | | | |
| Online classes allow me to work when I want | 91 | | | | | |
| Online classes make my life more flexible | 88 | | | | | |
| Online classes make life more convenient | 87 | | | | | |
| Learn more in online classes than small class | | 76 | | | | |
| More likely to ask questions online | | 83 | | | | |
| More opportunities to collaborate online | | 68 | | | | |
| Learn more online than in large classes | | 62 | | | | |
| Amount of interaction better with faculty online | | 70 | | | | |
| Amount of interaction better with students online | | 69 | | | | |
| Expectations for courses clearer online | | | 54 | | | |
| Assessment of my performance better online | | | 54 | | | |
| I feel I am treated more fairly online | | | 63 | | | |
| Working to get my degree is increasing stress in my life | | | | 85 | | |
| More likely to get degree because of online classes | | | | 62 | | |
| Online experience increased ability to use information | | | | | 57 | |
| Overall, I am satisfied with my courses | | | | | 83 | |
| Online experience increased ability to evaluate information | | | | | 56 | |
| Working hard for degree | | | | | | 84 |
| I am very committed to getting a degree | | | | | | 80 |

* Decimals omitted. Measure of sample adequacy = 0.95
1 = More effective institutional responsiveness
2 = Increased educational engagement
3 = More explicit role expectations
4 = Reduced ambivalence
5 = Increased information fluency
6 = Increased commitment to obtaining an education

## 4. REDUCED AMBIVALENCE

Earlier in this paper we argued that Net Generation or digital native ambivalence with the current higher education learning infrastructure is a major force in designing new learning environments. However, often these ambivalent feelings become confused with genuine dissatisfaction. This fourth component in our solution confirms that satisfied students have in some way lessened their ambivalent feelings toward their educational requirements. Quite likely this is because they perceive institutional responsiveness, experience a heightened sense of engagement and have a clearer understanding of the expectations that will be placed upon them. This component appears to be a function of the first three elements of the component model.

## 5. INCREASED INFORMATION FLUENCY

This element suggests that students express concerns about the overwhelming amount of information to which they are exposed to, given the absence of any effective filtering mechanisms. They are uncomfortable with their ability to locate, evaluate and use information properly in an ethical manner. Increased satisfaction reflects itself in classes that assist them with information literacy, technology literacy and critical thinking. Students express greater satisfaction with online classes that help them ground information browsing into a more systemic algorithm that frees them from random foraging through information sources.

## 6. INCREASED COMMITMENT TO EDUCATION

This final component bears an interesting relationship to the first five components that seem to identify satisfaction as a function of a responsive, facilitative and structured environment that empowers students with a sense of agency. In this solution, commitment derives its meaning from a strong sense of goal commitment and progress toward those educational goals. Interpreted at face value this component would suggest that more committed students tend to be the most satisfied with their technology-enhanced learning. Intuitively, this seems to make sense. However, the next data elements of this study cause us to examine this assumption.

### The Relationship Among the Components

The reader will recall that one of the by-products of the promax rotation procedure is the correlation matrix among the satisfaction dimensions. That correlation matrix may be examined in Table 4.2.

The correlations among the components portray an interesting set of relationships. Responsiveness, engagement, role expectations, ambivalence and information fluency exhibit a positive manifold relationship: they are all positively related to each other. This suggests that what leads to student

**Table 4.2** Correlations Among the Satisfaction Components*

|  | Responsive-ness | Engagement | Role expectations | Information fluency | Commit-ment |
|---|---|---|---|---|---|
| Engagement | 58 |  |  |  |  |
| Role expecta-tions | 42 | 50 |  |  |  |
| Ambivalence | 59 | 52 | 38 |  |  |
| Information fluency | 53 | 52 | 32 | 52 |  |
| Commitment | −11 | −23 | −17 | −29 | −12 |

*Decimals omitted

satisfaction with online learning is a generalized environment that requires the presence of each element in order for the educational experience to be perceived as effective. Another way to interpret this finding is that if the students' believe online classes represent institutional responsiveness, then there is the likelihood that these classes will be engaging, have clearly defined expectations, help students negotiate information sources and thereby reduce their ambivalence toward obtaining an education.

The correlations of those elements with commitment present quite a different set of relationships. All of those coefficients are negative with those for responsiveness, role expectations and information fluency close to zero. Those for engagement and ambivalence are small and negative but slightly higher. At best this suggests that a student's commitment to obtaining an education as a component of satisfaction is independent of a positive educational environment. In some cases it appears to be slightly negatively related. To us this suggests that the educational environment provided by the institution may or may not impact a student's commitment to the educational process. Uncommitted students may not express satisfaction no matter how excellent the educational climate becomes.

## A Narrative for the Satisfied, Net Generation Student

Satisfied digital natives in technology-enhanced courses wish to lessen their ambiguity toward formal education by gaining some sense of a well-defined path to success and relevancy of their studies to their present and future lives. They need a sense of self-worth supported by recognition, respect, responsiveness and reward from their instructors and peers. Students who are conflicted with ambivalence about taking courses (they want to participate and don't want to participate at the same time) require resolution of those conflicting feelings through believing in the added value of higher education. They want an active rather than a passive learning environment, and because they participate in a highly interactive world, they expect the same from their classes, responding poorly to situations that don't fit this design. Students in higher education want more outlets for their creativity and their collaborative nature. Ultimately, satisfied Net Generation students respond to the increased freedom and latitude that the anytime model provides.

## The Net Generation and Satisfaction Issues

The transformational impact of technology on education is undeniable, having been characterized as the great unbundling (Carr 2008). This phenomenon is playing out in music, in newspapers, in banking, in real estate, in publishing including academic journals, in information search, in copyright and most certainly in education. Shirky (2008) explains this as an increase in our ability to share and cooperate with each other, allowing us collective action outside the framework of traditional organizations and institutions. He suggests that going viral is easy when the cost of publishing globally has become virtually nil by removing the transaction costs of organizations. There is no better example of this than the YouTube video 'A Vision of Students Today' created by Michael Wesch and his students at Kansas State University (2007) with millions of hits at the submission of this paper.

## Dangerous Ideas

Technology-enhanced education is full of dangerous ideas, notions that undermine traditional values about effective education. Seife (2000) documents how dangerous an idea the number zero was and what a difficult time it had gaining traction. Zero simply misbehaved. It refused to get bigger and it refused to make any other numbers bigger. Such dangerous ideas foster ambivalence and ambiguity. Online learning and Web 2.0 are dangerous ideas; they unbundle the traditional classroom, expanding it far beyond lecture halls and Monday, Wednesday and Friday classes.

## Idealized Cognitive Models

We make the point that the Net Generation qualifies as a boundary object, but there is another possibility. Lakoff (1987) describes extensive work on the notion of idealized cognitive models. At its basic level, idealized cognitive models (ICMs) are constructs that don't organically exist in nature but have been fabricated by human beings to facilitate the understanding of theories or behavior. For instance, any particular day of the week (e.g. Friday) is an idealized cognitive model developed within the context of another model termed 'week'. Essentially, they were developed because we needed some metric for the passage of time. Obviously, these models are arbitrary and can take on multiple forms just like boundary objects. Lakoff points out that other cultures around the world, the Balinese for example, have a completely different cognitive model for the passage of time. The Net Generation and digital natives appear to qualify as idealized cognitive models as well as boundary objects. As fascinating as they are, arbitrary designations become useful only to the extent that we can better engage our students in the learning process.

### A Measurement Issue

There is another important consideration. The seeming antithesis of digital native is digital immigrant creating a binary classification scheme (Prensky 2001). Therefore, depending on affiliation with identifying characteristics, one acquires the label of native or immigrant. However, just how one acquires the label digital native is a fascinating measurement problem. Does a student have to ring true on all semantic descriptors, or is four out of six enough and so on (Prensky 2001)? Let's assume another measurement model other than the nominal where digital native and digital immigrant are anchors at the opposite ends of a continuous scale that is capable of responding to the fundamental asymmetry of prototype theory. Depending on the granularity of the scale, one can see that there are almost an unlimited number of points where a student may fit between native and immigrant. Given this tenet of classical test theory what score must I obtain in order to be a digital native? Where is the break point and how do I determine it? Here is the fundamental measurement reality of this situation. There is a score above which there is no question that I am a digital native; there is a score below which there is very little doubt that I am a digital immigrant, and there are a large number of scores between those two cut scores where I am unable to make an assignment to a proper category. This reframes the situation into another more plausible classification scheme of unequally probable outcomes: digital native, digital immigrant and undetermined, the category with the highest marginal probability. Sometimes there is simply not enough information to assign a category label. Digital native and digital immigrant oversimplify the classification scheme. Anyone who has taken a test, however, knows exactly how the situation resolves itself. There is only one score used to define the two categories. If you score above it you get your driver's license. If not, you come back in a week and try again. Now we are back to yet another Net Generation classification problem.

### The Taylor Russell Problem Revisited

The next issue with identifying Net Generation students involves the relative opportunity costs of making classification errors. Invariably when most authors write about digital natives, the Net Generation, Millennial students or Generation Y, they do so in a generalized context rarely proposing assessment protocols for individual students. However, it is at the individual level that classification error takes its toll. To frame the problem in terms of our driver's license example, what does it cost to issue a license to someone when they do not have the requisite knowledge to be a safe driver, versus the costs of failing to issue a license to someone who is qualified? While the second error is unfortunate, the first one is potentially catastrophic and should be protected against at all costs.

The psychologists Taylor and Russell (1939) addressed this problem and developed methods for minimizing selection errors – that is, hiring someone who is unqualified and not hiring someone who is qualified. Their decision model was based on three factors: the correlation of the selection criteria with job performance, the base rate of success on the job and the selection ratio. Let's translate the first two factors into our consideration of the Net Generations in higher education as they seem particularly important. Do we have any kind of protocol that is valid for identifying whether or not a student behaves like the so-called digital native other than his or her birthday and hypothesized characteristics, behaviors and preferences? Secondly, do hypothetical characteristics carry valid information that gives us the ability to make an accurate individual Net Generation classification? The answer to the first question is probably not beyond the nominal levels. The second answer is that because entrance preselection restricts ranges, correlations are attenuated.

This leads us to the potential classification errors we can make about the Net Generation and their possible costs. Classifying a student as a digital native when they are really not net-savvy runs the risk of assigning them into a technological education system for which they are ill-equipped, thereby adversely affecting their satisfaction. Putting a true digital native into a traditional educational system where they are unable to use their personal technologies to learn presents a satisfaction problem as well. Both potential errors are costly in terms of student engagement and increased ambivalence toward education.

## Conclusion

The Net Generation, digital natives and student satisfaction are loosely defined constructs that defy precise definition but generate productive conversations about effective teaching and learning in the online environment. Because of mounting uncertainty in our modern society those constructs are becoming increasingly complex and dynamic, complicating meaningful baseline comparison. Roberts summarizes the phenomenon this way:

> The idea of shifting baselines is familiar to us all and does not relate only to the natural environment. It helps explain why people tolerate the slow crawl of urban sprawl and loss of green space, why they fail to notice increasing noise pollution, and why they put up with longer

and longer commutes to work. Changes creep up on us, unnoticed by younger generations who have never known anything different.

(Roberts 2007: 256)

In addition, concepts such as satisfaction tagged by convenience and flexibility are multidimensional, requiring several components to form a comprehensive explanation. Interestingly, the counterintuitive relationship among those elements suggests that Net Generation student commitment to learning may be independent of the educational environment quality.

Many of our definitional problems arise from increasing ambivalent feelings in the digital native cohort. Their satisfaction with technology-enhanced education cannot be assessed effectively by assuming that the polar opposite of satisfaction is dissatisfaction. A lack of satisfaction with a course is better characterized by simultaneous positives and negatives that confound into a collage of contradictory perceptions. There appear to be multiple reasons for this. We can agree that most of us are overwhelmed by the sheer volume of available information and our inability to process it satisfactorily. As a result most of us resort to Bates's (1989) berry picking model where we forage through the forest often happening on useful information purely by chance. We experience the impact of Nassim Taleb's black swan (2008), in terms of unpredicted monumental events that change the course of history and our lives. The Internet, Google, 9/11 and the recent economic crises are all prototype examples of essentially random events that become epiphanies for us. After the fact, society creates a back-filled narrative that portrays incremental cause and effect relationships intended to convince us that if only we had seen the clues we could have predicted the outcome. Rarely, however, do predictive models forecast such events. Some black swans are instantaneous in their impact (like 9/11) while others develop slowly (like the Internet) but are no less monumental. Technology-enhanced education is a developing black swan and a dangerous idea because of its potential for unbundling centuries of educational practice. Johnson describes those events this way:

> History has its epic thresholds where the world is transformed in a matter of minutes – a leader is assassinated, a volcano erupts, a constitution is ratified. But there are other, smaller, turning points that are no less important. A hundred disparate historical trends converge on a single modest act – some unknown person unscrews the handle of a pump on a side street in a bustling city – and in the years and decades that follow, a thousand changes ripple out from that simple act. It's not that the world is changed instantly; the change itself takes many years to become visible. But the change is no less momentous for its quiet evolution.

(Johnson 2006: 162)

Black swans heighten the ambivalence of our younger generation, possibly explaining the commitment issues we seem to have uncovered. Another plausible explanation for ambivalence in the student population can be found in large numbers of mixed messages about technology our educational system sends to them. We talk about digital natives with their mobile and personal technologies citing their dependency on them, yet we tell our students to check all those devices at the classroom door. We delight in Web 2.0 technologies but our students experience dissonance in the educational setting. For example, Wikipedia is a popularized information source accepted in one class and vilified in another, reinforcing an ambivalent perspective.

Since modern education presents so many opportunities for learning, some of the historical constructs undergo a reframing. Student satisfaction, especially for the Net Generation, is a moving target where constantly changing inputs modify students' perceptions of their educational experiences. Evaluating courses in complete packages may not be as viable as it once was because the traditional boundaries for what comprise courses as we have known them are beginning to blur. However, there are certain constants in the Net Generation satisfaction equations (Wang et al. 2009). Students celebrate instructors that facilitate their learning, are able to communicate effectively, show respect for them, assess their progress effectively and conduct an organized class. This is independent of course mode or discipline. It's true face-to-face and it's true online. It's true in sciences and it's true in humanities.

Ultimately, what is it that we can say about this Net Generation and their satisfaction? We believe that it is this. Digital natives build their own personal geographies of learning depending on their personalities, their sophistication, their intellect, their education, their maturity and their character development (Long 1985). These geographies, individually crafted, have some communality but they are unique to each student and in a state of constant flux. Hopefully, we can have some influence on the development of those personal learning spaces. However, we can be assured that they will continue developing long after we have any direct influence on our students. In the end it may be that the Net Generation will never be satisfied with its education. Perhaps that is precisely what will motivate them to continue their learning, but we can be equally sure that they intend to have a voice in the process.

## Acknowledgements

This study was conducted with funding from the Alfred P. Sloan Foundation, however, the findings and the opinions are those of the authors and do not necessarily reflect the position of the funding agency.

## References

Bates, M. (1989) The design of browsing and berrypicking techniques for the online search interface, Online Review, 13, 407–424.

Bauerlein, M. (2008) The dumbest generation: How the digital age stupefies young Americans and jeopardizes our future, New York: Tarcher.

Carr, N. (2008) Is Google making us stupid? The Atlantic, July/August. Retrieved 28 June, 2009, from http://www.theatlantic.com/doc/200807/google.

Coomes, M. & Debard, R. (2002) Serving the millennial generation, New Directions for Student Services, 106, 5–16.

Dziuban, C. & Shirky, E. (1974) When is a correlation matrix appropriate for factor analysis? Some decision rules, Psychological Bulletin, 81(6): 358–361.

Forrester, J.W. (1993) System dynamics and the lessons of 35 years. In K.B. DeGreene (Ed) System-based approach to policymaking (pp. 199–240). Norwell, MA: Kluwer Academic Publishers.

Godin, S. (2008) Tribes: We need you to lead us, New York: Penguin Books.

Hendrickson, A. & White, P.O. (1964) Promax: A quick method for rotation to oblique and simple structure, British Journal of Statistical Psychology, 17, 65–70.

Howe, N. & Strauss, W. (2000) Millennials rising: The next great generation, New York: Vintage Books.

Johnson, S. (2006) The ghost map, New York: Roverhead Books.

Kaiser, H.F. Rice, J. (1974) Little Jiffy, Mark IV Journal of Educational and Psychological Measurement, 34(1), 111–117.

Lakoff, G. (1987) Women, fire and dangerous things: What categories reveal about the mind, Chicago, IL: University of Chicago Press.

Lakoff, G., & Johnson, M. (1980) Metaphors we live by, Chicago, IL: University of Chicago Press

Lezberg, A.K. (2003) Accreditation: Quality control in higher distance education. In M.G. Moore and W.G. Anderson (Eds.) Handbook of distance education (pp. 425–434). Mahwah, NJ: Lawrence Erlbaum.

Long, W.A. (1985) The practitioner and adolescent medicine, Seminars in Adolescent Medicine, 1(1), 85–90.

Morville, P. (2005) Ambient findability, Sebastopol, CA: O'Reilly Media, Inc.

Muilenburg, L.Y. & Berge, Z.L. (2005) Student barriers to online learning: A factor analytic study, Distance Education, 21(1), 29–48.

Prensky, M. (2001) Digital natives, digital immigrants, part II: Do they really think differently? On the Horizon, 9(6), 1–6.

Prensky, M. (2009) H. sapiens digital: From digital immigrants and digital natives to digital wisdom, Innovate, 5(3). Retrieved 1 July, 2009, from, http://www.innovateonline.info/index.php?view=article&id=705.

Roberts, C. (2007) The unnatural history of the sea, Washington, DC: Shearwater.

Rosch, E. (1973) Natural categories, Cognitive Psychology, 4, 328–350.

Seife, C. (2000) Zero: The biography of a dangerous idea, New York: Penguin Books.

Setenyi, J. (1995) Teaching democracy in an unpopular democracy. Paper presented at What to Teach about Hungarian Democracy conference. 12 May 1995, Kossuth Klub, Hungary.

Shirky, C. (2008) Here comes everybody: The power of organizing without organizations, New York: Penguin Books.

Star, S.L. & Griesemer, J.R. (1989) Institutional ecology, translations as boundary objects: Amateurs and professionals in Berkely's Museum of Vertebrate Zoology, Social Studies of Science, 19(4), 387–420.

Sun, P., Tsai, R., Finger, G., Chen, Y. & Yeh, D. (2008) What drives a successful e-learning? An empirical investigation of the critical factors influencing learner satisfaction, Computers & Education, 50(4), 1183–1202.

Taleb, N. (2005) Fooled by randomness: The hidden role of chance in life and in the markets, New York: Random House Inc.

Taleb, N. (2008) The black swan: The impact of the highly improbable, New York: Random House Inc.

Tapscott, D. (1998) Growing up digital: The rise of the net generation, New York: McGraw-Hill.

Taylor, H.C. & Russell, J.T. (1939) The relationship of validity coefficients to the practical effectiveness of test selection, Journal of Applied Psychology, 23(5), 565–578.

Twenge, J.M. (2006) Generation me: Why today's young Americans are more confident, assertive, entitled – and more miserable than ever before, New York: Free Press.

Wang, M.C., Dziuban, C.D., Cook, I.J. & Moskal, P.D. (2009) Dr. Fox rocks: Using data mining techniques to examine student ratings of instruction. In M.C. Shelley, L.D. Yore and B. Hand (Eds) *Quality research in literacy and science education* (pp. 383–398). New York: Springer.

Weigert, A.J. (1991) *Mixed emotions: Certain steps toward understanding ambivalence*, New York: State University of New York Press.

Wendover, R.W. (2002) *From Ricky & Lucy to Beavis & Butthead: Managing the new workforce* Aurora, CO): The Center for Generational Studies, Inc.

Wesch, M. (2007) *A vision of students today. Digital ethnography*, Kansas: Kansas State University. Retrieved 15 October, 2009, from http://www.youtube.com/watch?v=dGCJ46vyR9o.

# 5
# Provisionality, Play and Pluralism in Liminal Spaces

MAGGI SAVIN-BADEN AND CATHY TOMBS

## Editors' Introduction

This chapter provides a stepping-off point for a consideration of notions of changing identities. The chapter outlines some of the key challenges with using virtual worlds for supporting learning, and opens up a consideration of virtual identities as a new problematic for pedagogic design and adoption as part of formal and informal learning approaches. The chapter also considers the notion of opening new spaces for learning predicated upon liminality, multiple identities and central notions of play.

## Introduction

To date, learning in immersive worlds is under-researched and the extensive possibilities for its use need to be better understood in order to realise its potential. Furthermore, the impact of learning in such worlds in terms of students' conceptions of reality, their relationship between in-world and real-world behaviour and issues of representation along with perceptions of honesty, disclosure and collaboration, bear further research. This chapter will present a study that used the methodological approach of narrative inquiry to examine students' experiences of learning in Second Life.

## Background

Much of the recent research to date has been undertaken into students' experiences of virtual learning environments, discussion forums and perspectives about what and how online learning has been implemented (for example, Sharpe et al. 2005; Creanor et al. 2006; Conole et al. 2006). These studies, although using relatively small data sets, would seem to indicate students' experiences of e-learning are more complex and wide-ranging than many university tutors realise. Current research into learning in immersive worlds centres around cognitive learning theories. Laurillard (2002), in particular, argues for an information-rich environment in which the student has control in discovering knowledge, but the discovery is supported and scaffolded by extra guidance functions. Yet virtual world learning seems to offer new perspectives relating to the study of the socio-political impact of learning in higher education. This is because virtual worlds such as Second Life (SL) are universal, not bound by time or geography, and in particular adopt different learning values from other learning spaces (Savin-Baden 2007). The overall aim of the study presented here was to explore the impact of learning in immersive worlds on end-users and their practice. The focus of this chapter, however, is on the student experience.

## Methodology

Data were collected from diverse disciplines, which enabled the research themes to be explored across disciplinary boundaries. Research sites were chosen to reflect a range of uses of virtual-worlds across a variety of disciplines. Data were acquired through narrative inquiry, since stories are collected as a means of understanding experience as lived and told, through both research and literature. However, narrative inquiry is seen in a variety of ways and tends to transcend a number of different approaches and traditions such as biography, autobiography, life story and more recently life course research. Narrative inquiry is used to study educational experience since it is argued by those in this sphere that humans are storytelling organisms who lead storied lives. Those who use this research method argue that stories are the closest we can come to shared experience. For example, Clandinin and Connelly argued: 'Experience ... is the stories people live. People live stories and in the telling of them reaffirm them, modify them, and create new ones' (Clandinin and Connelly 1994: 415).

Some researchers would argue that narratives are structured with a beginning, middle and an end, held together by some kind of plot and resolution. However, we would argue against this, suggesting instead that narratives do not necessarily have a plot or structured storyline, but are interruptions of reflection in a storied life. What counts as 'story' varies within methodological fields. We suggest that when using narrative inquiry it is important that the researcher is not only able to ask questions that elicit stories but also that they are able to position themselves so that stories can be analysed effectively. Further, we increasingly believe that the distinction between different types of narrative inquiry tends to be in the co-construction and strategies for interpretation rather than between the traditions.

## Data Collection

An initial review was undertaken of existing data available, via databases and ESDS Qualidata. Data was collected through semi-structured interviews face-to-face, by telephone and in-world with ten staff and ten students, and analysed interpretively to examine the subtext of data. The students involved were from a range of disciplines and transpired from both undergraduate and postgraduate courses.

### Ethics

Ethical approval was sought from the relevant university ethics committees. Data collected was confidential. Safeguards to confidentiality included the coding of data and the code was kept separate from the raw data. All names used throughout were fictitious to preserve the identity of participants. However, it should be acknowledged that the individuals concerned might recognize some excerpts within the text used to illuminate the interpretation of data.

### Trustworthiness, Honest and Informed Consent

In the context of a study such as this, a shift was needed away from validity or trustworthiness, and the assumption that it is possible to find shared truths and clear themes and categories. Instead 'honesties' was adopted – a category that allowed for the acknowledgement that trust and truths are fragile and encourages engagement with the messiness and complexity of data interpretation in ways that reflect the lives of participants (Major and Savin-Baden 2010). Honesty allowed for recognition of not only the cyclical nature of 'truths' but also that informed consent is not unproblematic. Participants signed informed consent forms and were supplied with information sheets.

## Findings

Learning in immersive worlds appears to change the nature of social interaction and affects learning practices. For us it introduced questions about immersive virtual worlds and learning in such spaces that may or may not change communication, collaboration and learning practices in higher education. The findings presented here represent the themes and issues that emerged from student narratives, which include:

- playing to learn;
- provisionality;
- dialogic learning;
- runaway pluralism.

## Playing to Learn

Issues were raised by students about learning, play and fun and how we also play in and through our identities in virtual spaces. Rieber et al. (1998) have suggested that the notion of 'serious play', which is characterized as an intense learning experience, involves considerable energy and commitment and suggests that serious play is important for the development of high order thinking, commitment and engagement. Playing to learn seemed to enable an exploration of the ways in which past, current and future identities are present and embodied and multiply interacting with each other in these spaces. Yet the notion of playing to learn seemed to be at odds between staff and students. Students saw play as part of or integral to learning whereas their perception was that staff did not always see it as such. Chris and Meg both saw SL as space for play and experimentation, which they felt was unexpected by staff:

> I was instantly engaged. I like debating and this fitted the bill. I also don't mind a bit of humour and a few jokes and that is inevitably involved in SL ... There is a real dimension there to do all sorts of creative things you might not have thought of ... For a few the whole thing is off-putting, not really serious, you know old boy, that sort of thing. When I speak to friends who are teachers you have to overcome their prejudice that it's all just a joke.
>
> (Chris)

> I think the course tutors, they are supportive but they can be quite directive on the course at points and I think their understanding of what education in an online space was quite different from mine. And also I was being quite experimental and in a way I think they hadn't expected and I think they were quite thrown by that.
>
> (Meg)

The sense of doing things differently, playing with learning, playing around and exploring were all seen as advantages to learning in immersive virtual worlds (IVWs). Yet these advantages were often seen by staff as troublesome in the sense that the learning boundaries were not necessary controlled and managed by them, but by the students. Yet for students it was the opportunity to play, which challenged the immutability of knowledge and the perception that learning was static and tutor centred. Yet such liquidity in the learning also brought with it a sense of unease about the provisionality of learning and identity in such spaces.

## Provisionality

Throughout the study participants spoke of a sense of everything seeming or feeling provisional and this in turn resulted in a sense of liminality. Liminality is a betwixt and between state often spoken of in studies or rituals or rites of passage as a kind of in-between state. For example, Mandela (1994: 33) described his own experience of the Xhosa rite of passage into manhood, which requires payment by animals, whisky and money. In his biography, Mandela speaks of the rituals, where after the circumcision ceremony in which he was declared a man, he returned to the hut. Clearly the position in which Mandela found himself after circumcision was a liminal space; although declared a man, this was the space in which he was located before he would enter manhood properly. This theme captured the idea that the liminal quality of Second Life and the sense of chronic uncertainty challenged students to consider how to live, work and learn with provisionality. For example, the location of one's avatar in spaces such as Second Life poses particular complexities, because of the interaction of five interrelated concerns that play out in the 'social space'. These are:

- the 'real' body, in the sense the interlocutor of the avatar, the 'author';
- the choice of physical representation and the way the avatar is presented to others;
- the relationship between the avatar and the author;
- the author's lived experience and the social representations made through the avatar;
- the intentional meanings represented through the avatar.

Student experience seemed to indicate that language and speech were not only representations that mirrored experience, but also created it, thus the meanings ascribed and inscribed in and through avatars are always on the move. For example, Ken found that SL opened up possibilities for creativity and freedom for students:

> If you let your restraints go and see the funny side of it then it becomes imaginative fun and very creative. I once answered a questionnaire Dave had and it asked how you would feel if your avatar died. I said it would be like losing a sort of artistic creation like a good painting. So I think it can help you to be creative. The format allows you to try out new problem solving skills. I also think it could be good for those who are shy of public debate and discussion. They can just watch and join in, in a disguised way.
>
> (Ken)

For Ken the lack of restraint allowed for experimentation in new learning spaces, and the opportunity to explore and play with learner identity. Further, the notion of avatar as art indicated a sense of it being both a creative expression and an extension of one's self. It might be that liminality could be seen as a trope for understanding avatar identity/pedagogy, or possibly that provisionality and representation might be seen as subcategories of liminality itself. Yet it is probably more likely that provisionality and representation are issues that inform our understanding of liminality. For example, struggles with understanding of what might constitute provisionality and how representation affects avatar identity and avatar pedagogy seemed to influence different forms and formulations of liminality that occur in IVWs. Thus issues of provisionality and representation and their relationship with liminality introduced questions about whether liminality differs in real life (RL) compared with 3D virtual worlds and whether different forms of liminality exist and/or can be delineated.

### Dialogic Learning

Dialogic learning is learning that occurs when insights and understanding emerge through dialogue in a learning environment. It is a form of learning where staff and students draw upon their own experience to explain the concepts and ideas with which they are presented, and then use that experience to make sense for themselves and also to explore further issues. The promotion of such forms of learning can encourage both staff and students to critique and challenge the structures and boundaries within higher education and industry, whether virtual or face-to-face. This is because learning through dialogue brings to the fore, for students and tutors, the value of prior experience to current learning and thus can engage them in explorations of and (re) constructions of learner identity. However, Flecha (2000) has developed the concept of dialogic learning further, suggesting seven principles that include egalitarian dialogue, the valuing of cultural intelligence and transformation.

In this study SL was seen as a more informal learning space by students than discussion forums, and therefore students felt more able to ask questions about assignments and tutor expectations of both the standard of work expected and their participation in seminars. However, it also allowed opportunities for students to question what counted as learning and what learning meant for them. For example, Kay's learning and dialogue was something that was continually changing and on the move:

> I find that throughout this course and other things that I do that people talk about learning in lots of different ways. So it means the same thing every time they're using it and actually when you try and pin it down it disappears, what we're talking about. We're not quite talking about the same thing. And the learning for me that's coming from Second Life, it doesn't quite answer your question I don't think, but it's giving me almost, not quite a mirror but something, a trigger to look at other things, why am I reacting in this way, to what I'm seeing? Some of the things I've been saying to you. And it's forcing me to look anew at things, looking in a different way at things and I think that's quite powerful.
>
> (Kay)

Such a sense of liminality prompted her to question her own pedagogical stance and explore issues of agency and identity in both RL and SL. Yet thinking of the impact of learning in such spaces and the shift in dialogue occurring also raised issues for students in terms of the imposition of pedagogic frameworks and models by staff on students. For example Meg argued:

> I don't know whether it will or whether it won't [virtual worlds will enhance learning in the future] – I think it's here to stay but I think the problem is that it can go the same way as virtual learning environments and be very contained and linear and I know there are projects that are already doing that – they're moving Gilly Salmon's five steps to good e-learning or whatever she calls it, um into Second Life and I'm not sure that's what it's about, so I'm kind of quite unhappy with some of that – I do think it's quite experimental and I do think that people are being prepared to take risks and I think it's starting to interrupt knowledge and what learning means a bit more in higher education, and I'm glad about that because I don't think there's enough of that going on. We're too obedient ...
>
> (Meg)

For Meg the imposition of frameworks from virtual learning environments seemed to restrict dialogic possibilities and impose containment that was seen as unhelpful and unnecessary. For her the linguistic and dialogic shifts were coupled with a sense of pluralism and chaotic-ness, and a sense of things being out of control was something she valued in a way that others perhaps did not.

## Pluralism

Pluralism stresses the difference between potential and actual power and in this instance refers to the potential or the possibility of power, rather than actual power of such a position. Further, although one of the authors has argued elsewhere for the importance of liquid learning (Savin-Baden 2007), pluralism is both a space of possibility and also of unruliness. There was a sense across the data that anything and everything was possible. Although many participants acknowledged this to be a somewhat utopian stance, the idea of the possibility of 'runaway' pedagogy, although not spoken about quite in those terms, appealed to many. The kinds of pluralism seen in SL related not just to the idea of power flowing from multiple sources, but that power was often intersecting, divided and confused by shifting and changing identities, roles and understanding of learning. This is largely because in SL, power and resources changed and moved and were not subject to the political whims and constraints of RL in the same kinds of ways. Further, the lack of entrapment of identities in essentialist ways has also resulted in an interruption of RL identities, thus to some extent prompting a move away from the tendency to move towards particularity, resulting in vulnerability to discrimination as both concept and practice.

However, at the same time there were unusual issues of actual power in terms of the impact of IVWs on ascribing in world behaviours, but this affected both staff and students. The way in which digital spaces are created for staff, by commercial organizations that are politicized and contained by universities, and used by students enables, but perhaps more often occludes, ways of seeing where information is located. One of the students, Chris, reflected:

> I would like to see a flourishing of all sorts of educational groups using the format. I attend a number of evening classes all now threatened by government funding problems so SL could offer an alternative. I would like to see online learning expand into this dimension as the University seems to be trying to explore. I would like to see this format used in schools in dozens of different areas.
>
> (Chris)

The sense of pluralism therefore related to identities being on the move and almost out of control in terms of space/place/agency and in terms of both colliding and interrupting. There was also a sense of confusion occurring about issues of positioning and representation. Gee's work on video gaming offers some sense not only of the multiplicity of identities involved in online learning, but also the possibilities for relationships between some of them. One of the difficulties related to game-based learning would seem to be that of identity. Gee (2004: 112–113) developed a theory of identity, based on experience of videogaming. It is a tripartite identity comprising:

1. The real identity: who we are in the physical world.
2. The virtual identity: who we are in the virtual space. Thus, Gee argues, our virtual self should be able to 'inherit' some of our real attributes.
3. The projected identity: this refers to identity that is developed through engaging with the character, through the interaction of the first two identities.

However, Gee's conception of the virtual self here is located in gaming and the character within the games, and his notion of identity here seems to equate with 'role' rather than identity per se. Further, he has argued that identities are projected identities, but this introduces interesting psychoanalytic difficulties. Projections are usually unwanted feelings that we invariably choose not to own. We therefore believe that someone else is thinking/feeling them instead, such as anger or judgement (see for example, Jung 1977). Avatars in Second Life seem, in general, to capture wanted elements, or the chosen components of our identities that we wish to present to/in the world. Thus in immersive worlds it would seem that the identities presented are more likely to be the functional or ideal sides rather than the projected 'unwanted' sides. The realization that one is playing with one's identities prompts both questions and realizations that our identities are troublesome and uncertain.

## Discussion

What all of this does seem to point to is a form of liminality between our various identities and in-between identities. Such identities would seem to be provisional, constantly changing and thus are always necessarily on the move. When students are exposed to the SL environment they necessarily add a range of SL identities to their established RL identities such as family member, ethnicity, religious affiliation, together with such temporary RL identities as student, part-time job holder and entrant to their chosen profession.

The overarching temporary RL identity of student carries with it many possibilities of entering liminal spaces after a period of 'being stuck'. In the main, students are initially worried rather than excited about being stuck; it starts off as a negative experience, normally painful to wrestle with, and can be worsened by avoidance or retreat, although ultimately can be positive if dealt with successfully. Many liminal identity issues arising in SL can be related to established areas already familiar in RL. The areas of RL liminality already experienced by students may help or hinder their understandings of their new liminal experiences in SL, which in turn can add new insights back to their existing RL liminal spaces.

Students had a significant variety of SL identities ranging over the four findings, from being positively playful and/or mischievously subversive through to being confused or interrupted, and at worst disempowered and demotivated. It is the positively playful and/or mischievously subversive identities that may offer the best way that SL can help RL sufferers, as this liminality starts by being positive: students are initially excited rather than being worried about their new experience.

These varied identities seldom sat easily with one another, therefore collision and uncertainty resulted in disquietude and a sense of fragmentation. Such disquietude served to confirm that identity work was not only an ongoing task but also a form of musical chairs:

> There are 'musical chairs', of various sizes and styles as well as of changing numbers and position, which prompt men and women to be constantly on the move and promise no 'fulfilment', no rest and no satisfaction of 'arriving', of reaching the final destination, where one can disarm, relax and stop worrying.
>
> (Bauman 2000: 33–34)

## Conclusion

What these data appears to indicate is that although liminal states may share certain characteristics, the experience of liminality differs between people, and invariably relates to identity transitions and transformations in IVWs. Thus it would seem that liminal states are not only affected by the spaces in which they occur but also the pace of change. Playing to learn, provisionality, dialogic learning and pluralism are introducing new spatial zones and practices that need to be taken account of in emerging pedagogies and in explorations of student experience in higher education of the future.

## References

Bauman, Z. (2000) *Liquid modernity,* Cambridge: Polity Press.

Clandinin, D.J. & Connelly, F.M. (1994) Personal experience methods. In N.K. Denzin & Y.S. Lincoln (Eds.) *Handbook of qualitative research,* Thousand Oaks, CA: Sage.

Conole, G., de Laat, M., Dillon, T. & Darby, J. (2006) LXP: Student experiences of technologies – final report. Retrieved 19 June, 2009, from http://jisc.ac.uk/media/documents/programmes/elearningpedagogy/lxp_project_final_report_nov_06.pdf.

Creanor, L., Trinder, K., Gowan, D. & Howells, C. (2006) *LEX: The learner experience of e-learning. Final report* (report under the JISC e-pedagogy 'Understanding my learner' programme), Glasgow: Glasgow Caledonian University. Retrieved 20 August, 2009, from http://www.jisc.ac.uk/whatwedo/programmes/elearning_pedagogy/elp_learneroutcomes.aspx.

Flecha, R. (2000) *Sharing words: Theory and practice of dialogic learning,* Lanham, MA: Rowman and Littlefield.

Gee, J.P. (2004) *What video games have to teach us about learning and literacy,* Hampshire: Palgrave Macmillan.

Jung, K. (1977) *The symbolic life: Miscellaneous writings the collected works of C.G. Jung,* Volume 18, Princeton: Princeton University Press.

Laurillard, D. (2002) *Rethinking university teaching. A conversational framework for the effective use of learning technologies,* London: Routledge.

Major, C. & Savin-Baden, M. (2010) *A practical guide to qualitative research synthesis. Managing the information explosion in social science research,* London: Routledge.

Mandela, N. (1994). *The long walk to freedom,* London: Abacus.

Rieber, L.P., Smith, L. & Noah, D. (1998) The value of serious play, *Educational Technology,* 38(6), 29–37.

Savin-Baden, M. (2007) *Learning spaces: Creating opportunities for knowledge creation in academic life,* Maidenhead: McGraw Hill.

Sharpe, R., Benfield, G., Lessner, E. & DeCicco, E. (2005) *Final report: Scoping study for the pedagogy strand of the JISC e-Learning Programme.* Retrieved 19 October, 2009, from http://www.jisc.ac.uk/index.cfm?name=elp_learneroutcomes.

# Part II
## Frameworks for Understanding Learners' Experiences

# 6

# Understanding Students' Uses of Technology for Learning
## *Towards Creative Appropriation*

### RHONA SHARPE AND HELEN BEETHAM

## Editors' Introduction

This chapter opens Part 2, which is concerned with frameworks that can be used to make sense of the data arising from learner experience research. The authors explore how 'effective learners' use the technology at their disposal. Drawing on data from ten research projects and locating their findings with current literature, they use a developmental framework to explain how higher level skills and attributes are founded on functional access to technology. They propose that the pinnacle of effective learning in the digital age is creative appropriation – where learners have developed and practised strategies for making use of technology in creative ways to meet their own personal and/ or situational needs.

## Introduction: Developing Effective E-learners

This chapter attempts to describe and conceptualize learners' effective use of technology for higher learning. There is a large literature and tradition of thinking about effective learning (Kember 1996; Marton and Booth 1997; Cuthbert 2005). This has aimed to show how learners develop understanding and the influence of learners' intentions on the approaches they adopt. In recent years, this research has progressed to explore the influence of different pedagogical and cultural environments (e.g. Case and Marshall 2004; Marton et al. 2005). This research then focuses on the individual and their cognitive processes as demonstrated within the context of a planned educational intervention. As Haggis (2009: 377) expresses it in her review of forty years of student learning research, 'one of the main concerns of this research has been to find out what is wrong with students who do not engage in the ways that their tutors wish them to'.

There have been few investigations of how approaches to and conceptions of learning are influenced by the online environment (Ellis et al. 2007; Goodyear and Ellis, Chapter 7) and even fewer that recognize that e-learning is not a separate way of learning but part of the normal everyday experience for students (Ellis and Goodyear 2009). Drawing on student learning research then, how we understand the processes by which students learn is still informed by a dominant cognitive and pedagogic perspective. However, the recent learner studies of experiences of learning in technology-rich environments, such as those brought together in this book, show that learners are engaged in all sorts of technology mediated activities outside of the context of the course (primarily social networking and searching for online resources). In a review of the role of theory in studies of learning in immersive virtual worlds, Savin-Baden (2008: 154) notes that:

> such studies [of the learner experience] would also seem to indicate that linearity, narrow problem solving and bounded approaches to learning where knowledge is managed and patrolled by staff is likely to be inappropriate for learning at the university in the twenty-first century.

The challenge then is to bring these two fields of work into alignment. When learners develop their skills, habits, practices and conceptions of learning, they do so in an environment that is now inherently digital. Even those learners who are making conscious choices to unplug from digital networks for some aspects of study, or who lack functional access to technology, can no longer be seen as developing in some non-digital bubble. The social world they move through, the work they do, the institution that accredits their learning, and the information they are handling, will all at some point be touched by the ubiquity of digital networks. To what extent do models of effective learning need to reflect the experience of learning in a digital age?

It is easy to see how traditions of understanding effective learning can be moulded to be relevant in the digital age. As an example, Higgins et al. (2005), who were looking mainly at research in schools, concluded that effective learning has five attributes: readiness, resourcefulness, resilience, remembering and reflecting. These can all be reinterpreted when new technologies are available to support them (for example e-portfolios, time management software on PDAs, memory sticks and so on). Perhaps it is more intriguing to ask, what would a model of effective learning look like if it was designed from now, based on what today's learners tell us about how they are learning?

In our earlier research we were particularly interested to hear from learners who were considered by their tutors to be effective in technology-rich courses. We defined effective e-learners as those who were choosing and using technology in positive ways to support their learning. We recognize that such learners are not representative of most learners, concurring with others who have found few, if any, examples of learners making creative, effective uses of technology (Margaryan and Littlejohn 2008). We reasoned that these learners, despite being in the minority, would be able to demonstrate practices that would be become mainstream in the future. The LEX study (Creanor et al. 2006) purposively sampled learners who had been identified by their tutors as succeeding in technology-rich courses. Interviews with these learners demonstrated that they: were active participants in multiple communities, managed their online identities, built and shared knowledge using multiple sources, used a mixture of personal and institutionally provided technologies, understood the affordances of different technologies to help them make appropriate choices to meet the demands of novel situations, and had developed learning and organizational skills to study and manage the distractions of online study.

Other researchers have talked about this digitally astute minority in other terms. Green and Hannon (2007: 46), working with school age children, referred to a group of 'digital pioneers' and expressed their interest to 'learn from [these] children who interact creatively with digital culture'. Seale et al. (2008: 133) talked about the 'digital agility' of some of the disabled learners they interviewed who were:

- customizing computers to suit preferences;
- swapping and changing from a range of technologies; well-informed about the strengths and weaknesses of particular technologies in relation to design, usability, accessibility and impact on learning;
- developing a range of sophisticated and tailored strategies for using technology to support their learning;
- using technology with confidence;
- feeling comfortable with technology so that it holds no fears;
- being extremely familiar with technology;
- being aware of what help and support is available.

Whether children or adults, this group is characterized by operating beyond the bounds of the course or institutional provision, and are engaged in creative activities that others (their parents, teachers, other peers) are not aware of. They demonstrate a belief in their own efficacy with technology, a willingness to take risks and an expectation that technology will support their efforts.

It has been noted throughout this book that it is not possible to talk about 'the learner experience' but rather that studies of 'learners' experiences' show many and varied voices. Similarly, even within a subset of 'effective e-learners', they are not a homogenous group. Sometimes, like the international students and students with disabilities, they had developed personal strategies with technology to overcome barriers to access, and used the agility this gave them to good advantage in their studies (Seale and Bishop, Chapter 9; Thema 2009).

Sometimes a personal preference or interest led them to adopt technologies in ways that were ahead of their peers. We are not talking here about learners who get high grades in an online course, but learners for whom technologies have acquired a particular personal resonance, or for whom technology lends a particular learning advantage.

Many learners have extensive skills in the use of social software, in networking and in sharing information online. Some even host their own websites and create their own content, including podcasts. Their skills, their willingness to experiment, their use of multiple personal technologies and their lack of respect for organizational boundaries all pose a challenge. Such adept users have an expectation of being able to access their favourite technologies within their place of learning and alongside the more formal technologies they are offered. However, their effectiveness is not just about access and skills. Just as student learning research has shown the links between students' beliefs and study strategies, increasingly we understand that effective e-learning involves complex strategies and sophisticated approaches, in which personal beliefs, values and motivations are also a factor.

## Exploring the Model

The model presented in this section is one way of understanding how effective e-learners can be developed. The emphasis here is on learner development. The model sets out what is known about the strategies, beliefs, behaviours and attitudes of learners and illustrates them with the words of learners themselves. It has been developed from the data arising from the JISC 'Learner experiences of e-learning' programme (https://mw.brookes.ac.uk/display/jiscle2). As summarized in the Introduction to this volume, this programme aimed to gather thick descriptions of learners' uses of technology and to understand their technology use in a holistic way. In all, nine research projects engaged over 200 learners in post-compulsory education in some form of extended dialogue (mostly using interviews and diaries) over periods of a few weeks to eighteen months. Over a period of 4–5 years, we have verified and clarified our ideas in order to gain an understanding of the factors that learners themselves perceive to be influential in learning effectively in this technology-rich age. Table 6.1 shows how the learners' experiences reported in these studies have been arranged into a developmental sequence. Figure 6.1 arranges this sequence as a pyramid, to emphasize that the attributes of effective learners are built up on a set of technology based practices – which in turn require appropriate skills and functional access to the relevant technologies.

**Table 6.1** Examples of Technology Use, Along With Enablers and Barriers, as reported by students in the JISC 'Learners' Experiences of E-learning' programme

| Examples of technology use at functional access stage | Examples of enablers | Examples of barriers |
|---|---|---|
| Access to networked computer with a range of software and networked services, e.g. via institutional membership Access to wireless/mobile and other digital devices, e.g. camera, phone Access to any specialist hardware or software required for learning | Course materials made available in electronic format (LeXDis) Resources that can be accessed anywhere via the institutional virtual learning environment (LEaD, BLUPS) Single sign-on access to a range of online services including email, VLE, online library resources (LEaD) | Restrictions on access to social networking technologies (E4L) Lack of facilities for those using audio support applications (BLUPS) Specialist software only being provided on fixed computers on site (LEaD) |

| Examples of technology use at skills stage | Examples of enablers | Examples of barriers |
|---|---|---|
| Using search engines to locate supplementary study materials (PB-LXP) Being adept at accessing and evaluating information in digital environments (Thema) Using specialist (domain-specific) tools (Thema) The ability to find and evaluate what's useful (Thema) | Support from family and friends to develop basic IT skills (STROLL) Learning to touch-type course and core modules in, for example, word processing (LEaD) Guidance and training on how to access key academic resources such as online journals, which is not confined to induction (BLUPS) Training in the use of library services and required digital tools available when it is needed (Thema) | Lack of 'technical literacy', e.g. anti-virus updates, backups, installing software updates (LEaD) Heavy workloads, lack of time to develop even basic skills (Thema) Staff not having the skills to use the technology appropriately (e4L) and inconsistency between staff (LEaD) Key information about, for example, IT training sent out at induction, an overwhelming time, and lost in all this information (STROLL, Thema) |

| Examples of technology use at practices stage | Examples of enablers | Examples of barriers |
|---|---|---|
| Downloading course materials onto a memory stick to support learning across several locations (PB-LXP) Choosing appropriate tools, e.g. Facebook, as a tool to share academic resources (Thema) Accessing additional course resources from other universities (BLUPS) Knowing when to 'e-' and when not to 'e-', blending the affordances of tools and interactions in the online and real worlds (Thema) Using strategies for resisting distractions from social tools while working (Thema) | Institutions need to provide flexibility and choice, acknowledging the many differences among learners (e4L) Materials available for downloading to PDA, facilitating short study bursts in multiple locations (PB-LXP) Recommendations from peers about technologies to use, e.g. Google docs to compile a report for a group project (STROLL) Accessing materials from other academic sites (BLUPS, STROLL, Thema) | Lack of confidence to explore new tools and resources (LEaD) Patchy wireless coverage limiting choices about where to study (Thema) Lack of tutor skills, e.g. having to print things out for tutor to read (BLUPS) Time pressures limiting ability to try out new tools, particularly for learners with disabilities (LeXDis) and international students (Thema) Difficulties in establishing network in new halls of residence or home, increasing isolation from home and family (LEaD, Thema) |

Note: STROLL: STudent Reflections On Lifelong e-Learning; BLUPS: Students' Blending Learning User Patterns; PB-LXP: Learners' experiences of blended learning environments in a practice-based context; Thema: Exploring the Experiences of Master's Students in Technology-Rich Environments; E4L: e-Learning for Learners; LeAD: Learner Experiences across the Disciplines; LeXDis: Diaabled Learners' Experiences of e-Learning. See http://www.voced.edu.au/docs/dest/TD_AG_80_02.pdf.

## Functional Access

At the base of the pyramid is the requirement to be able to access technologies, resources and services. Without reliable, convenient and cost-effective access, none of the other attributes of effective e-learners can be brought into play. It is now clear that the high ownership of personal technology amongst the majority of students does not equate to access. The value of the qualitative approach of the studies was clear as learners spoke of their ownership of laptops with broken screens or that were too old to be networked. Learners still express their need to access institutional technology, particularly networks, and have high expectations for institutions to provide them with the access they need (Hardy et al. 2009), such as:

> I am very, very highly dependent on the Internet and the networks that the university runs.
>
> (STROLL project, Jefferies and Hyde 2009: 125)

Where institutional provision and/or personal access to technology makes learning more convenient for some students, it is a necessity for others. The wide-ranging list in Table 6.1 shows the enablers and barriers to access mentioned by learners themselves, including access to portals, electronic resources in multiple formats, technical support for personal technology and the ability to integrate personal and institutional technology. Having *functional access* now involves ownership, mobility, access to networks of people as well

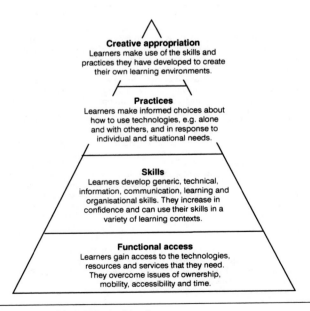

**Creative appropriation**
Learners make use of the skills and practices they have developed to create their own learning environments.

**Practices**
Learners make informed choices about how to use technologies, e.g. alone and with others, and in response to individual and situational needs.

**Skills**
Learners develop generic, technical, information, communication, learning and organisational skills. They increase in confidence and can use their skills in a variety of learning contexts.

**Functional access**
Learners gain access to the technologies, resources and services that they need. They overcome issues of ownership, mobility, accessibility and time.

**Figure 6.1** A Developmental Model of Effective E-learning

as information, and time to engage, along with what we might understand by accessibility. Candy (2004) describes these issues as the 'preconditions for participation'.

### Skills

At this stage learners develop generic technical, information, communication and learning skills. Certainly basic IT skills are important and include learning to touch-type and use a word processor, for example:

> When I started the course ... If the kids were at school I couldn't turn on the computer.
>
> (e4L)

However, the learner experience studies show that the range of skills needed by effective e-learners goes beyond technical IT skills. Learners also need to use specialist tools, to work in online groups, access and evaluate digital information, and collate what they have found. Macdonald (2008) explores these skills necessary for what she terms e-writers, e-investigators and e-collaborators. These are certainly skills that effective e-learners will have mastered, but they fail to reflect how the new technologies are changing the nature of learning and knowledge. 'E-create' takes the idea of e-writing into other media besides text. E-collation is an essential new skill that Macdonald misses, but that forms the centrepiece of Siemens' (2005) analysis of the 'connectivist' learner. Collation involves gathering of information nodes into new systems and networks, for example through tagging, mapping, modelling, editing and commenting, syndication, use of favourites and the social software versions of the same.

We note now that much of the dependence on Google and Wikipedia appears to be coming from prior educational experiences. Learners need opportunities to apply and practise their skills in different learning contexts, for different learning activities and objectives. Further specification of skills needs and how to develop them is picked up by Walker et al. in Chapter 15.

### Practices

At this stage learners become practised at using technology to meet a particular need. They develop flexible strategies in response to situational needs and mature in these choices and uses over time. Learners make informed choices about how to use technologies, choosing from a repertoire of possible approaches. Tools, skills, social contacts and learning approaches are mixed and matched to suit immediate requirements or as part of an evolving personal 'style' of technology use.

Making choices and decisions seems to be important and is explored further in later chapters (Seale and Bishop, Chapter 9; Benfield and De Laat, Chapter 13). Good choices were illustrated particularly by disabled learners who understand the affordances and properties of technology. Practices also evolve as learners become more aware of what they personally find helps their learning, for example:

> Podcast continues to be a great inspiration to the way I learn, I find it so helpful to listen to again and again.
>
> (Jefferies et al. 2009: 21)

Other choices might be taken with respect to where to study, for example:

> I avoid libraries as much as possible and find it difficult to find the materials I need, so I rely primarily on e-journals that I can download and read in the comfort of my own home. [...] I would personally rather be home in my slippers working with my laptop from the sofa.
>
> (Thema)

At this stage, learners develop personal strategies for getting work done, which might include not using technology:

> I simply unplug my Ethernet cord, keeping me from the internet altogether. Additionally, I sign out of Skype, gchat etc when I don't want those distractions.

### Creative Appropriation

When strategies become unconscious through practice, they could be said to be fully appropriated. At this stage the learner has 'creatively appropriated' available technologies and learning opportunities to meet his/her own goals. At this stage, personal attributes and styles come to the fore, as do personal motivations for learning, and beliefs about both learning and technology. Learners will have their own reasons for how they choose to spend their time, which technologies they use in which situations, how social they are in their learning, and how they manage and personalize the resources they need.

So, creative appropriation builds on the skills and practices already acquired. Here learners are taking control of their own learning, making suggestions for uses of technology that go beyond what is expected by their course or tutor, for example:

> Had a phone tutorial with my supervisor referring to a support document he emailed to me – I digitally recorded the tutorial and saved it as a digital file on my laptop. This has then been playing while I make the adjustments to the document.
>
> (Clarke 2009: 12)

Creative appropriation is underpinned by learners' conceptions of learning and technology, and their exploratory behaviour. Exploration, agile adoption, is driven by need, not provided by tutors. 'One of the group members was not able to make it today so what we did we were connected by using MSN Messenger so we were discussing notes. We were feeding back to the other person. (Jefferies et al. 2009: 16)

## Using the Model

Over the lifetime of the programme we found this model useful for visualizing messages from the research in developmental terms. We were aware of course that this was only one possible representation of the learners' experiences we were uncovering, and indeed we produced many others for different audiences and purposes. We believe that learners' own voices should be privileged, particularly in the contexts where their views have been collected and where they have a real stake in how those representations are used. We became increasingly aware, however, that this model might serve another need: promoting dialogue between staff whose main concern is the development of learners' academic practice, and staff whose main concern is the development of technology supported learning. We urgently need a model that speaks to both sides of the discussion, to help us rethink what learners need if they are to develop as effective lifelong learners in the digital age.

### *The Model as a Hierarchy of Needs*

One way we can have this discussion is to relate our model to Maslow's (1987) 'hierarchy of learning needs'. This posits that the highest goal of learning, which Maslow termed self-actualization, can only be strived for when more basic goals are being met. Without wanting to map our terms to Maslow's directly, we note that creative appropriation shares features with self-actualization, being concerned with how learners negotiate a new, more capable identity as a resource for acting in the world.

Given this, the model can be used to inform curriculum interventions that aim to make learners more capable of acting with purpose and effect in technology rich environments. We know from our research that staff tend to overestimate learners' technical abilities and underestimate the time required to cover basic proficiency when introducing new applications. The LLiDA project (Beetham et al. 2009) found innovators introducing Web 2.0 technologies and immersive environments such as Second Life, in the expectation that learners would use them to meet fairly high-level curriculum goals, only to find that they got 'stuck' on the affordances of the technology itself. The development pyramid helps us to situate our expectations of learners. Are we helping them to build functional access with technologies that may be unfamiliar, assessing their skills at a well-defined task, or demanding that they demonstrate complex practices such as collaborative knowledge-building in a fairly open-ended context? The higher up the pyramid our expectations, the more we need to ensure that learners are equipped with the capabilities they need at the foundational level. Incidentally, this approach can also help us to ensure assessment tasks and criteria are matched to our expectations.

### The Model as Learning Outcomes

The LLiDA study also identified the need for a new framework of digital literacies to which learning outcomes could be mapped across the curriculum. Participants in the study expressed frustration that provision to support learners was so poorly integrated. Study skills or academic literacies were often being addressed in one part of the institution, ICT skills in another, information skills in another – all typically outside of the core curriculum – while many essential aptitudes such as critical and media literacy, employability and citizenship were simply not considered relevant to learning by staff or students. The LLiDA report maps in some detail how different literacies are typically 'owned', described and inscribed into curriculum practices, where this is taking place. What follows is a simplification of this model.

Components of digital literacy, as identified by the LLiDA review, are:

- *Learning to learn*, 'study skills' for a digital age, for which learning outcomes are often defined in terms of: reflection, action planning, self-evaluation, self-analysis, self-management (time etc).
- *Academic practice* (an alternative conceptualization of general learning skills), for which learning outcomes are often defined in terms of: comprehension, reading/apprehension, organization, analysis, synthesis, argumentation, problem solving, research, inquiry, academic writing.
- *Information literacy*, for which learning outcomes are often defined in terms of: identification, accession, organization, evaluation, interpretation, analysis, synthesis, application.
- *Media literacy* (also 'visual', 'graphic', 'audio', 'filmic' etc literacy), for which learning outcomes are often defined in terms of critical reading and creative production.
- *ICT/computer literacy*, which is very variously defined, and often in terms of technologies that are already fading from use, but some learning outcomes might include: keyboard skills, use of capture technologies, use of analysis tools, use of presentation tools, use of social tools, personalization, navigation, adaptivity, agility, confidence.

While these can be useful for mapping elements of the curriculum, they do not include any indication of level or assessment criteria. In line with Bloom's

(1956) taxonomy of learning outcomes we suggest that the development pyramid could be used to identify the different levels students are expected to achieve in a range of literacy-related outcomes, i.e. functional access, skilful performance on specified tasks, complex practice in open-ended contexts, and creative appropriation.

Particularly at the level of creative appropriation, it is less relevant to think about component literacies and more important to consider the motivations and authentic activities through which learners are integrating their practices. For example, the LLiDA study identified three lenses through which all the other literacies were typically viewed by institutions: scholarship, employability and citizenship. For the institution these concern graduate attributes in the round, including issues such as participation, social justice and leadership, personal safety, ethical behaviours, managing identity and reputation, as well as how students are prepared for the knowledge economy and the world of work. For learners, these correspond to the most long term and personal of learning outcomes that we usually refer to in terms of developing lifepath and identity, self-efficacy (Zimmerman et al. 1992) and personal values.

## The Model as an Account of Learner Differences

The most consistent finding of the 'Learners' experiences of e-learning' programme has been the sheer diversity of the ways in which learners understand their learning with technology. As we have noted previously, while some learners feel disadvantaged by a lack of basic access to technology, others are making sophisticated choices among a range of technology-mediated learning strategies. With digital media and networks becoming more ubiquitous, many other differences that learners manifest – such as their social resources, their preferred times and places of learning, their skills of writing and communication, and their choice of solo or collaborative study – are taking on digital aspects. Technology use is no longer a single dimension of learner difference but is multiply inscribed into the different choices and modes of engagement that learners display.

We can explain these differences in many ways, for example in relation to prior experience, peer group influence, access to technology or individual traits and preferences. Green and Hannon (2007: 11) take the last approach, dividing learners into these types:

*Digital pioneers* were blogging before the phrase had been coined
*Creative producers* are building websites, posting movies, photos and music to share with friends, family and beyond
*Everyday communicators* are making their lives easier through texting and MSN
*Information gatherers* are Google and Wikipedia addicts, 'cutting and pasting' as a way of life.

But we also know that learner behaviour is highly dependent on context (Nicolas et al.), and that for sophisticated learners these 'types' are in fact practices that they can opt into or out of by choice. So rather than typologizing learners in fixed ways, a mode of analysis that has been significantly discredited in relation to learning styles (Coffield et al. 2004), the pyramid model allows us to assess individual learners' *current* stage of development, precisely in terms of the choices they can make. So to one learner, the use of pbwiki may be a technical skill to be mastered with help and support. To another, the use of one wiki application over another, or the decision to blog, tweet or edit a wiki page in response to a conceptual problem, is a strategic choice to be made on grounds of audience impact or personal style. Our focus is not then on the differences per se, but how the different technologies and strategies can become resources potentially available to all.

We must also be wary of seeing development as a one-way, one-route trip. The pyramid can be used to assess a range of different capabilities – for example the different literacies identified in the previous section – in recognition that learners do not develop all their capabilities equally or at the same rate. The fact that a cohort of learners may situate themselves in different parts of the pyramid with respect to different skills can be regarded as a problem of managing difference, or a resource for sharing kinds of expertise.

More radically, and with more learner-centred language, the model has the potential to be used by learners to diagnose their own digital literacy status and requirements. Rather than asking learners to rate their confidence in using specific digital tools, they could be asked to describe how they currently use these tools to support their learning. This leads us towards a fourth possible use of the model.

### *The Model as an Account of Learners' Conceptions of Learning*

We know that learner's behaviours and strategies are heavily influenced by their conceptions of e-learning (Ferla et al. 2009; Jungert and Rosander 2009), for example by prior experiences with the technologies they are using, by beliefs about their own competence and capability, by their motivation and engagement in the learning activity and by their relationships with their tutor and other learners. As conceptions of e-learning inform how learners experience e-learning, so they can also be self-reinforcing. In this volume, Goodyear and Ellis discuss the impact of positive and negative conceptions of e-learning, while Benfield and De Laat note that whether a learning space is perceived as informal/private or under academic surveillance has a profound effect on learner behaviour.

Conceptions, beliefs and expectations of learning are strongly influenced by prior experience, so good experiences of access, and confidence in their own skills and strategies, can help learners to develop positive beliefs about their efficacy in learning-with-technology situations. The LEaD project, for example, looked at expectations of technology use by new arrivals at Edinburgh University and found that they were conservative, in line with a conservative approach to study practice in general (Hardy and Jefferies, Chapter 8). For these learners to move beyond the practices that have served them well in school, they need to experience success in using new tools, where the focus is on high-level academic outcomes such as argumentation and research. The PB-LXP project, focusing on work-based students with very different experiences of formal education from the Edinburgh cohort, found that how learners perceived the value of ICT at work was the best predictor of the extent and diversity of their ICT use in learning (Edmunds 2009). These findings offer confirmation that access to technology is necessary but not sufficient to predict the level, quality or diversity of its use by learners.

The work we report on here has only scratched the surface of this fascinating issue: we now need to understand far more deeply how learners' expectations, conceptions and beliefs relate to the quality of experience they have, and their development as effective learners. In helping learners to express their beliefs about particular technologies – that they are an aspect of their personal style and identity at the top of the pyramid, or difficult to access at the bottom – we can see the model also having value as a research tool.

## Conclusions: From Entitlement to Enhancement

Educators and their institutions have a responsibility to ensure that students have functional access to technology and the skills to use it properly. Indeed, this responsibility is becoming enshrined in the policies of many national governments (Department for Culture, Media and Sport & Department for Business, Innovation and Skills 2009). We see the two lower or foundational levels of the pyramid as addressing learner entitlement, and as such they are relevant across all sectors of education and lifelong learning. The technologies available and the specific skills they demand of users will continue to evolve at speed. Learners need the capacity to update their skills, and to choose the technologies that work for them, in the tasks and contexts that occupy them.

In higher education, however, we need to think beyond the level of entitlement. Developing self-efficacy in learning means allowing individuals to take different pathways and express their personal or situational preferences for different modes of participation. Post-compulsory learning also focuses on how learners situate themselves in a particular discipline or in professional communities, which means specializing in certain approaches to knowledge building, certain combinations of media and certain technologies of scholarship or professional practice. Learners need to both inhabit and critique these modes.

## References

Beetham, H., McGill, L. & Littlejohn, A. (2009) *Thriving in the 21st century: Learning Literacies for the Digital Age (LLiDA project)*, Glasgow: Glasgow Caledonian University.

Bloom, B. S. (1956). *Taxonomy of Educational Objectives, Handbook I: The Cognitive Domain.* New York: David McKay Co Inc.

Candy, P. C. (2004) Linking thinking: self-directed learning in the digital age, Australia. Dept of Education, Science and Training (DEST). Available online at: http://www.voced.edu.au/docs/dest/TD_AG_80_02.pdf.

Case, J. & Marshall, D. (2004) Between deep and surface: Procedural approaches to learning in engineering education contexts, *Studies in Higher Education,* 29(5), 605–615.

Clarke, P. (2009) *Outline to illustrate patterns of six aggregated learner types, Blups project report,* Oxford: OCSLD.

Coffield, F., Moseley, D., Hall, E. & Ecclestone, K. (2004) *Learning styles and pedagogy in post-16 learning: A systematic and critical review,* London: Learning and Skills Research Centre.

Creanor, L., Trinder, K., Gowan, D. & Howells, C. (2006) *LEX: The learner experience of e-learning. Final report* (report under the JISC e-pedagogy 'Understanding my learner' programme), Glasgow: Glasgow Caledonian University. Retrieved 20 August, 2009, from http://www.jisc.ac.uk/whatwedo/programmes/elearning_pedagogy/elp_learneroutcomes.aspx.

Cuthbert, P. (2005) The student learning process: Learning styles or learning approaches? *Teaching in Higher Education,* 10(2), 235–249.

Department for Culture, Media and Sport & Department for Business, Innovation and Skills (2009) *Digital Britain Final Report.* Retrieved 12 October, 2009, from http://www.culture.gov.uk/what_we_do/broadcasting/6216.aspx.

Edmunds, R. (2009) *PB-LXP student survey: Summary Document,* The Open University. Retrieved 23 November, 2009, from https://mw.brookes.ac.uk/display/JISCle2m/Surveys.

Ellis, R. & Goodyear, P. (2009) *Students' experiences of e-learning in higher education: The ecology of sustainable innovation,* New York: RoutledgeFalmer.

Ellis, R., Goodyear, P., O'Hara, T. & Prosser, M. (2007) The university student experience of face to face and online discussions: Coherence, reflection and meaning, *ALT-J,* 15(1), 83–97.

Ferla, J., Valcke, M. & Schuyten, G. (2009) Student models of learning and their impact on study strategies, *Studies in Higher Education,* 34(2), 185–202.

Green, H. & Hannon, C. (2007) *Their space: Education for a digital generation,* Demos. Retrieved 15 September, 2007, from http://www.demos.co.uk/files/Their%20space%20-%20web.pdf.

Haggis, T. (2009) What have we been thinking of? A critical overview of 40 years of student learning research in higher education, *Studies in Higher Education,* 34(4), 377–390.

Hardy, J., Haywood, D., Haywood, J., Bates, S., Paterson, J., Rhind, S. and Macleod, H. (2009) *ICT & the student first year experience, project student views report.* Retrieved 30 April, 2009, from http://www2.epcc.ed.ac.uk/~lead/documents/.

Higgins, S., Wall, K., Falzon, C., Hall, E. & Leat, D. (2005) Learning to learn in schools. Phase 3 evaluation, year 1 final report, Newcastle: University of Newcastle. Retrieved 22 October, 2009, from http://www.campaign-for-learning.org.uk/logging/LogDownload.sp?ID=4075&DFile=%2Fcfl%2Fassets%2Fdocuments%2FResearch%2FPhase3Year1Report.pdf.

Jefferies, A. & Hyde, R. (2009) Listening to the learners' voices in HE: How do students reflect on their use of technology for learning? *Electronic Journal of e-Learning,* 7(2), 119–126.

Jefferies, A., Bullen, P. & Hyde, R. (2009) *Researching learners' journeys: STROLL, students' reflections on lifelong e-learning,* Hatfield: University of Hertfordshire.

Jungert, T. & Rosander, M. (2009) Relationships between students' strategies for influencing their study environment and their strategic approach to studying, *Studies in Higher Education,* 34(2), 139–152.

Kember, D. (1996) The intention to both memorise and understand: Another approach to learning? *Higher Education,* 31, 341–351.

Macdonald, J. (2008) *Blended learning and online tutoring* (2nd edition), Hants: Gower.

Margaryan, A. and Littlejohn, A. (2008) Are digital natives a myth or reality?: Students' use of technologies for learning. Retrieved 21 October, 2009, from http://www.academy.gcal.ac.uk/anoush/documents/DigitalNativesMythOrReality-MargaryanAndLittlejohn-draft-111208.pdf.

Marton, F. & Booth, S. (1997), *Learning and awareness,* Mahway, NJ: Lawrence Erlbaum.

Marton, F., Wen, Q. & Wong, K. (2005) 'Read and hundred times and the meaning will appear ...', Changes in Chinese university students; views of the temporal structure of learning, *Higher Education*, 28, 291–318.

Maslow, A. (1987) *Motivation and personality* (3rd edition), New York: Harper and Row.

Nicholas, D., Rowlands, I. & Huntington, P. (2008) *Information behaviour of the researcher of the future – executive summary,* London: JISC.

Savin-Baden, M. (2008) From cognitive capability to social reform? Shifting perceptions of learning in immersive virtual worlds, *ALT-J, Research in Learning Technology*, 16(3), 151–161.

Seale, J., Draffan, E.A. & Wald, M. (2008) *Exploring disabled learners' experiences of e-learning. LexDis project report*, Southampton: University of Southampton.

Siemens, G. (2005) *Connectivism: A learning theory for the digital age*, eLearnSpace. Retrieved 10 October, 2009, from http://www.elearnspace.org/Articles/connectivism.htm.

Thema (2009) Learner experiences of e-learning: Thema completion report. Retrieved 30 April, 2009, from https://mw.brookes.ac.uk/display/JISCle2/Projects.

Zimmerman B.J., Bandura, A. & Martinez-Pons, M. (1992) Self-motivation for academic attainment: The role of self-efficacy beliefs and personal goal setting, *American Educational Research Journal,* 29(3), 663–676.

# 7
# Expanding Conceptions of Study, Context and Educational Design

PETER GOODYEAR AND ROBERT A. ELLIS

## Editors' Introduction

This chapter links the study of students' conceptions of learning and learners' experiences of e-learning. Over a number of years, the authors have shown that students' conceptions of learning differ and they explain how they have investigated these differences in a number of theoretically driven, carefully designed studies. Here they show how their phenomenographic approach can be used to understand students' approaches to learning through online inquiry and face-to-face discussion in a problem based learning course. In particular they explore how students' conceptions are influenced by the context they find themselves in. They describe a model of 'teaching as design' that demonstrates how an understanding of students' conceptions can inform the design and evolution of learning environments.

## Introduction

University teachers and the people who work with them to design and manage higher education learning environments are having to reconcile the effects of a number of powerful forces. These include: (1) diversifying student needs and expectations; (2) increasing pressures on the time and intellectual energy of university staff; (3) rising expectations among employers, and in society more generally, about graduate capabilities; and (4) accelerating technological change.

Many university systems, including those in the UK and Australia, are under pressure from government to increase the proportion of people going to university, and to ensure that previously under-represented groups have access to higher education – not just by gaining admission, but with a reasonable chance of successful completion. Staff:student ratios have been worsening, while staff are also being urged to be more productive in research, more connected to business and the community, and more active in raising money. This leaves less time for teaching, yet there are more students and their needs are diverse, changing and sometimes uncertain. Moreover, it is not sufficient for universities to give everyone a chance to reach the standards of knowledge and performance displayed by last year's successful graduates. The skills, knowledge and personal qualities needed to survive and prosper in the twenty-first century do not align very well with current university curricula. Employers continue to grumble about the shortcomings of new graduates, and governments press universities to show how they are changing to meet twenty-first century needs. Moreover, technology is not a solved problem. Vice-chancellors and chief information officers who thought that buying a Learning Management System was going to be a sufficient strategic response are now seeing the educational technology world unravel again. The pervasiveness of digital technology, and the accelerating pace of change, is generating uncertainty at every level in the education system.

These four sets of forces – diversification, intensification, rising expectations and technological change – are placing such stresses on those involved in providing higher education that traditional teaching practices are fast becoming unsustainable.[1] But radical, sustainable change is hard to introduce. There is evidence of resistance by students to shifts in educational practice that reduce their opportunities for contact with their teachers. Large-scale, poorly designed, shifts to e-learning – for example – are generating student complaints, as well as government and media interest (see e.g. Ipsos MORI 2008; House of Commons 2009). In addition, the great majority of higher education practice continues to be insulated from the accumulating evidence base about 'good learning'.

These considerations lead us towards what might seem a surprisingly optimistic conclusion: *the times are right for a significant shift in how higher education gets done, and students will play a key role in shaping new learning practices and learning environments.* To do this in productive ways, students – and indeed everyone involved in their education – will need to develop a much clearer and more robust understanding of how to engage in knowledge work, and how to dynamically configure the resources needed to support their work. In the main part of this chapter, we summarize some of our recent research on how students conceptualize and approach learning, with a view to seeing how they might be helped to manage the evolution of their beliefs and practices. After that, we return to issues of sustainability in educational design, paying particular attention to the need for an expanded conception of student autonomy and self-regulation, with respect to learning activity and the contexts in which it takes place.

## Students' Experiences of Learning: The Research Approach

There are numerous ways of listening to what students have to say about their expectations and experiences of higher education. A number of these are illustrated in this book. They vary from quite loosely structured, almost naturalistic approaches – in which students talk in informal ways, using everyday language and setting the agenda for the conversation – to highly structured approaches, such as those that use validated rating-scale instruments and questionnaires. The relationship between theory and method also varies, with some approaches opting for a relatively open theoretical stance (as with 'grounded theory'), and others having a tighter coupling between theoretical commitments and instrumentation. More open and exploratory methods are highly appropriate in areas that are fresh to research. If research instruments are too tightly focused by theory, then some interesting phenomena remain invisible. However, theory-free observation is never possible, and sometimes the extra focus provided by theory brings things to light that might have slipped by in the complex whirl of data.

The research we will summarize here takes a quite highly structured, and theoretically committed approach to understanding aspects of students' learning experiences.

Following Marton and Booth (1997), Prosser and Trigwell (1999) and others, we adopt a *phenomenographic* approach: focused on understanding students' *experience*. Experience is a relational concept: neither objective nor subjective, but expressing a relationship between a person and a phenomenon. Every experience is someone's experience; every experience is an experience of something.

We are interested in students' experiences of study. More specifically, we have been looking at qualitative variations in the ways that students conceive of learning and in their approaches to some selected study activities. Conceptions of learning are revealed through what students say about what they think it is possible to learn in a specific situation: what learning means to them in that situation. Approaches to study have two components: strategies and intentions. In relation to specific learning situations, students tell us what they typically do (strategies) and why (intentions).

We have been researching learning situations with the following characteristics. First, they involve learning through discussion and/or learning through inquiry. Second, they take the form that is usually called 'blended learning'. By this we mean that the teachers concerned have designed tasks that integrate face-to-face and online activities. Examples we have studied include discussions that begin in face-to-face tutorial groups and continue online (see e.g. Ellis et al. 2006) and problem-based learning activities that involve interleaved face-to-face meetings and online inquiry (see e.g. Ellis et al. 2008). Third, they are *established* parts of courses taught by people other than us (the main researchers). These are not new courses, or ones in which we have a personal stake. Finally, all the data come from courses offered by 'conventional' universities, rather than ones that specialize in distance teaching.

We use three main data-gathering methods: semi-structured interviews, open-ended questionnaires and closed-ended questionnaires – using rating scales with sets of Likert items. Our semi-structured interviews normally involve 15–20 students from each course. The interviews are explicitly focused on a specific study situation, such as learning through taking part in an online discussion in their current course, and students are reminded at critical points in the interview that we are only interested in that specific study situation. We ask students about what they think it is possible for them to learn, and about how they approached their learning (what they actually did and why). These three parts of the interview generate talk about conceptions of learning, and approaches to study (strategies and intentions). Follow-up questions are used to get a clearer idea of what the student means by the key terms that they use (e.g. 'when you said "discussion really helps me question my own preconceptions", what did you mean by that?'). The interviews usually take 30–60 minutes, and are normally recorded and transcribed in full.

Our open-ended questionnaires have the same three-part structure as our in-depth interviews, allowing us to gather data from a larger number of students, but sacrificing the ability to ask follow-up questions. The closed-ended questionnaires use rating scales developed from themes identified in our analysis of the interview and open-ended questionnaire data, and again allow us to gather information about variations in conceptions and approaches from a much larger number of students. The open-ended and closed-ended questionnaires are usually administered at the end of lectures, and we normally get a high response rate.

Analysis of the transcribed interviews and open-ended questionnaire answers involves the following stages. Normally two and sometimes three members of the research team independently read and reread the transcripts. They each identify the different *kinds* of conception, strategy and intention in the data, with a view to constructing a manageably small set of categories that will represent the principal variations in the data with an appropriate balance between parsimony and representativeness. The researchers then meet to compare their category sets, using example transcripts to test their interpretations of the proposed categories, and work towards constructing an agreed single set of categories, known as an 'outcome space', for each of the three aspects of the students' experience: conceptions of learning, strategies and intentions.

The researchers then independently use the agreed categories to code up a sample of transcripts and/or open-ended questionnaire responses. They meet to compare results. (We normally get 75–90 per cent agreement prior to discussion; 80–100 per cent agreement after discussion.) Finally, quotations are selected from the transcripts to illustrate each of the categories of experience in each of the three outcome spaces.

This analysis normally produces two kinds of results. First, there are the outcome spaces, which give a sense of the kinds of variations in experience found within the group of students in the study. Second, we have usually been able to get end-of-course marks from the teachers involved, and have been able to locate students within each of the outcome spaces, and calculate correlations between their conceptions and approaches and marks.[2]

### Students' Experiences of Learning: Results

This section of the chapter is intended to give a flavor of the kinds of results we have been getting from the analyses described above. More detailed information about individual studies can be found in the Ellis et al. (2006, 2008) articles and also in our book (Ellis and Goodyear 2009).

CONCEPTIONS OF LEARNING THROUGH ONLINE AND FACE-TO-FACE DISCUSSION

Table 7.1 gives a sense of the kinds of variations in conceptions of learning that we have been discovering.

The conceptions form a hierarchy, in the sense that higher-level conceptions (like A) also embrace lower-level conceptions (like D). That is, students who see discussion as a way of challenging and improving their ideas, also see discussion as a way of collecting ideas. It is always a little risky to provide quotations to illustrate each of the categories, because it invites the reader to invent a slightly different category to suit the quotation. Bearing in mind that each category had to map onto quite a large number of interview and questionnaire excerpts, we offer the following to try to round out the category descriptions.

*Category A:* 'It [discussing] challenges my beliefs, which is always good … because a belief is something that is based on knowledge and experience and your understanding of the world, and if it is being challenged you are testing it … If my beliefs are challenged, I believe that my understanding of concepts is more complete.'

*Category B:* 'It sort of gives you different views of what people are getting out of the readings and stuff … it helps me, I guess, just because I am not

**Table 7.1** Conceptions of Learning Through Discussion

| Conception | Discussion as a way of |
|---|---|
| A | challenging ideas and beliefs to arrive at a more complete understanding |
| B | challenging and improving your ideas |
| C | collecting ideas |
| D | checking your ideas are right |

getting stuck in just this one mindset, it sort of makes me for a topic to go deeper, and just get other perspectives … I guess it gives me an appreciation that people do see it differently, that it's not clear-cut. It's one thing having my opinion, and it will mean different things to different people.'

*Category C*: 'It elaborates the readings even more like it sort of expands the readings out a bit … when you go to the tutorials and you express your ideas, it sort of makes them valid to yourself. Like you sort of remember it a bit more by the end of the tutorial … you just get to learn a bit more about the other people's ideas.'

*Category D*: 'Getting the teacher's point of view … it's good being able to talk and make sure you are really learning what you are supposed to be learning. It is just sort of reassuring.'

Category D is particularly worrying for those university teachers who would like to be able to make more use of online discussion as a way of supporting more active, engaged forms of learning. If significant numbers of their students believe that it is the teacher's job to say what is right and wrong then (1) the teacher is going to have to spend a *lot* of time moderating online discussions; and (2) without a teacher presence, some students will take the view that online discussions are a waste of time. (Looking across several studies, we found 10–30 per cent of students falling into the lowest of the categories of conception of learning.)

There is some evidence to suggest that conceptions of learning, and epistemological beliefs more generally, are relatively stable across contexts. But that line of argument is under increasing attack from researchers who believe that what students say about knowledge and learning is highly dependent on context. For example, Hammer and Elby (2002) have modelled epistemic beliefs as sets of fragmentary personal epistemic resources (ideas about knowledge) that are activated in a specific context. Different contexts may help activate different sets of epistemic resources. This is very different from thinking of personal epistemology, including conceptions of learning, as a coherent, stable network of interdependent beliefs. For one thing, it suggests that contexts can be designed so as to make it more likely that helpful epistemic resources will be activated. Indeed, Hammer and Elby show how students shift from 'teacher should tell us the right answer' to 'all ideas are open to improvement' conceptions – and act accordingly – when the educational context encourages them to do so.

## APPROACHES TO LEARNING THROUGH ONLINE INQUIRY AND FACE-TO-FACE DISCUSSION

When it comes to the attainment of desired learning outcomes, what students say they believe has less of an effect than what they actually do. Our data about how students approach their study activity, and why, bring us closer to the action. One of our studies investigated a problem-based learning (PBL)

**Table 7.2** Approaches to Researching Problem-based Scenarios Online

| Category | Approach |
|---|---|
| A | Researching PBL scenarios online to develop an understanding of professional resources necessary for diagnostic reasoning |
| B | Researching PBL scenarios online to understand problem scenarios in order to perform well |
| C | Using online databases to find information related to PBL scenarios |
| D | Using online databases to find answers to PBL scenarios |
| E | Using online databases for PBL scenarios only when they are easy to use |

course in which students' work was structured into a series of fortnightly group problem-solving tasks. Each of these involved meetings to discuss the nature of the problem, decide what needed to be learned in order to make progress on the problem, and review and present group solutions. In between these face-to-face meetings, students carried out online inquiry work and also used various online tools to coordinate their activity. Part of the rationale of PBL is to shift students from being relatively passive consumers of information – typically transmitted in lectures – towards being more actively engaged in inquiry, and taking more responsibility for managing their own learning. Sadly, our data show that students are quite capable of making highly strategic responses to active learning tasks. Table 7.2 summarizes the relevant data about the students' approaches to study.

The categories in Table 7.2 were generated in the way we described in the 'research approach' section, above. Using the established nomenclature of phenomenographic research, category A can be seen as a *deep* approach; category B as a *strategic* approach; and categories C to E as *surface* approaches (Ellis et al. 2008). Deep approaches are consistent with an intention to achieve a robust, personal understanding of the ideas and methods involved. Strategic approaches are concerned with getting the best trade-off between marks and effort. Surface approaches occur when students only engage with the most immediately apparent requirements of a task – typically, surface approaches reveal a failure to understand the educational intentions of the teacher. Of the 166 students in this study, only 16 per cent could be classified in the deep category, 19 per cent were placed in the strategic category, and the remaining 65 per cent were classified as adopting one or other of the surface strategies.

We can use some of the students' own words to give the flavor of the extreme categories.

*Category A:* 'Yeah when I'm searching at home I'd probably use a lot more on-line resources then text resources ... it will be either on-line versions of the Therapeutic Guidelines, the MIMS on-line, AMH, and again probably using Google for some broad information. Looking up health government health websites like 'Health Insight' or other organizations such as one called the 'Family Doctor'. And also myself, I look up original papers for Medline and … usually if there's something in particular that I know there's probably been research on, and that's probably a contentious issue, I'll use those so I can back up general information that you've found elsewhere.'

*Category E:* 'Initially I use[d] the library website like the MedLine, PapMed [sic] or the journal. But after a few classes I found that using Google search is more easier, it's more easy than like usually there are more things to look at and also the thing is more appropriate – more general. Whereas the PapMed and MedLine usually regarding to research. I know these websites have very good evidence to support the things but it's just too scientific to read – too boring to read.'

There are some well-tested explanations in the literature for why students fail to adopt a deep approach. These include an overloaded curriculum – students experience an excessive workload – and over-reliance on formal examinations and other tests of rote learning (see Prosser and Trigwell 1999, for a summary). The points we want to make here are (1) merely adopting a high-level pedagogy, like PBL, which is strongly associated with the benefits of active learning, can still result in students taking a surface approach; and (2) attention to the detailed design of the course is necessary, including providing scaffolding for students to engage with the challenges of PBL in appropriate ways. Such scaffolding can take a variety of forms, including the use of online tools that guide the students' workflow, and offer supportive scripts for key passages in the work (see e.g. Dillenbourg and Hong 2008).

### Students' Experiences of Learning: Summary Points

We have only been able to give a taste of the data and insights flowing from our research over the last five years. We want to highlight the following key messages from the research.

First, we would argue that looking for variations in how students conceive of learning (knowing and coming to know) does more than prove that such variations exist. It helps teachers and students understand the range of helpful and unhelpful ways in which learning and knowing can be thought about, and how these align or fail to align with some culturally valued knowledge practices (Goodyear and Ellis 2007).

Second, we think the data strengthen the case that many common higher education practices – including overloaded curricula, over-reliance on formal examinations of decontextualized knowledge, privileging the assessment of individuals over the encouraging of group work – encourage students to think and behave in ways that are of little use outside the academy.

Third, we would claim that introducing 'active learning' is no guarantee that students will shift away from surface and strategic approaches to study. If the macro-environment, or details of the work they have to do, are not carefully aligned to promote deep learning, then many students will fail to recognize, or will subvert, the best intentions of their teachers.

We now need to return to our opening questions about how knowledge about students' conceptions of learning and approaches to study can help with the design of learning environments that are more likely to be able to help the ever-diversifying needs of the incoming cohorts of students.

Our argument is as follows. Students' conceptions of learning and approaches to study are not immutable personal characteristics. They emerge from an interplay between student and context. 'Context' needs to be interpreted in a broad, inclusive way – we will introduce the idea of an 'activity system' to capture this expansive notion of context. What teachers *say* to their students about 'good learning' has little effect if their words are not backed up by salient features of the learning context – especially, but not exclusively, the assessment regime. The introduction of new technologies and new kinds of study activity, such as PBL, make the context much more complex than it used to be – they add complexity and uncertainty to the activity system. Managing complexity and uncertainty, while also helping align the activity system with sound pedagogical principles, is a very difficult task. It demands a careful kind of planning – a *design-based* rather than a *traditional* approach. When teachers are designing, they need to balance tensions between scaffolding and autonomy. The activity systems they help create and manage must *scaffold but not stifle* students' improving abilities to manage their own learning and shape their own learning environment. We now unpack some of these ideas, starting with the shift to teaching-as-design.

### Teaching-as-design and Issues of Sustainable Innovation

The pressures we mentioned at the start of this chapter cannot be handled for much longer by individual teachers working alone, however innovative they may (temporarily) be. Moreover, universities are not configured to deal appropriately with increasing student numbers, diversifying needs, the raised aspirations of employers and society, and the uncertainties brought about by accelerating technological change. Nor can solutions be expected to come from our students, however media-savvy they may be. It is not just our own evidence that suggests students conceive of, and approach, some twenty-first century challenges with 19th century ideas – see Ellis and Goodyear (2009) for an extended analysis.

Teachers, indeed everyone involved professionally in supporting students' learning, need to hear and value the voice of student experience. But if that voice is uncertain and conservative, how can it help our systems create and improve learning environments that align with the needs of the twenty-first century and with the best of what we know from research on student learning?

To answer this question, we need to introduce the idea of teaching-as-design, expand the notion of student autonomy, and sketch a vision of design as an ongoing, participatory process of continuing improvement.

Figures 7.1 and 7.2 help explain what we mean by 'teaching-as-design'.

Figure 7.1 refers to a shift in visions of teaching and learning. On the left we have teaching seen primarily as a process of explaining ideas: teaching as performance and exposition. The canonical form is the lecture; the site is the lecture theatre; the core values are clarity and passion. The role for the learner is to be an attentive member of the audience. Learning involves listening, note-taking, subsequent rehearsal, and preparation for tests of the ability to recall. (This is something of a caricature, but captures some key features of much contemporary practice.) Moving to the right, in Figure 7.1, we see a shift towards active learning, where the learner is encouraged to be more deeply engaged in a wider variety of learning activities and to take more responsibility for managing their own learning. The types of activity become more diverse – project work, inquiry-based learning, practical classes, discussion groups and so on – and the worksites become more diverse too. The teacher's role shifts to one of learning facilitator: someone who monitors and helps manage learning activities as they unfold. Good teaching, on this view, involves a sensitivity to learners' needs, the ability to spot emerging problems, and a knack for providing just the right level of guidance. The shift can be captured in a cliché: from the sage on the stage to the guide on the side. What's missing from Figure 7.1 is another important strand, perhaps a more important strand, in the work teachers have to do when learning takes on a more active quality.

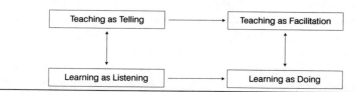

**Figure 7.1** From the Sage on the Stage to the Guide on the Side ...

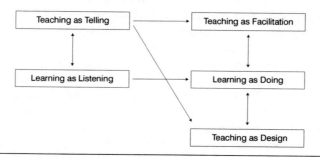

**Figure 7.2** ... To the Team With a Scheme (and Teaching-as-design)

In Figure 7.2, we label this teaching-as-design. Teaching-as-design includes all the planning work involved in setting good learning tasks, creating supportive learning environments and helping students share their efforts in learning teams or learning communities. It is most effective and sustainable when done by teams rather than lone teachers (Goodyear 2000, 2005).

The next move in our argument creates a place for an extended interpretation of learner autonomy, seen as exercising the capacity to take greater control of one's own learning. Classic accounts of learner autonomy focus on metacognition and self-regulation – the ability to manage one's own learning activity (see e.g. Vermunt and Rijswijk 1988). We want to extend that notion, to take into account the situated nature of learning and the distributed nature of cognition (Greeno 2006; Salomon 1993). We do this by extending the remit of teaching-as-design to encompass entire *activity systems*. In the context of learning in higher education, we use 'activity system' to mean:

- students, teachers, everyone else with a professional responsibility for supporting student learning (Deputy Vice Chancellor (Education) to lab technicians);
- learning tasks, learning activities;
- tools, knowledge objects and other resources (digital, physical, hybrid; off campus and on);
- learning places (digital, physical, hybrid; off campus and on);
- rules, regulations, policies, procedures and other formal requirements;
- divisions of labor (e.g. group work; communities of inquiry).

*All* the people listed in the first point above are actively engaged in creating and developing the (small number of) activity systems in which their work is set.[3] This fact is not widely or frequently acknowledged. Indeed, the work that students do to configure their own learning places and learning relationships is rarely recognized, or given any particular importance. If we take seriously the idea that knowledge work is socially and physically situated, then creating convivial learning places and effective learning relationships is just as important to becoming an autonomous knowledge worker as are the inward-focused talents associated with metacognition and self-regulation.

Taking a perspective on design that gives a central place to activity systems has a number of implications. Not least, it questions the dubious practice of *resetting the system* at the start of each academic year. (The fact that we throw away our students' work each year gives them a very clear message about how much we value it.) The increasing use of wikis and group-based knowledge-building tasks is one, still rather rare, example of how some teachers are using student-produced knowledge objects to enrich the environment for later cohorts of students. But practice in this area is still quite varied and there are fewer examples in which such knowledge-building work is central to the ongoing life of a learning community (see Benfield and De Laat, Chapter 13). We want to argue that a *broader* notion of enriching the activity system should come to take a much more important place in the practices of higher education. Students ought to get recognition for the contributions they make to the tools and resources, working methods and procedures, and all the other aspects of the intellectual and social capital available to their learning community. Technical expertise, broad and deep understanding, *and* the ability to co-create productive environments for knowledge-work are high on the list of social and economic desiderata.

The next question is *how* students can participate in this extended notion of the design and evolution of key components of activity systems, especially if they come in to higher education with much too restricted notions of learning, study, knowledge and the nature of legitimate peripheral participation. We glimpse the beginnings of an answer in teachers' use of student feedback. If feedback is essentially summative, and is squeezed into a narrow set of meanings referencing workload, the quality of lectures and/ or progress towards ill-defined graduate attributes, then it is of limited use, especially to the students who generated it. But if the full range of students' contributions to enriching their activity systems is properly and clearly valued, then feedback shifts from being too little and too late to being a continuous conversation – not just with the teacher (who has too little time for everyone and everything), but with everyone involved in evolving the activity system. It is in such *extensive* conversations, we believe, that fragmented conceptions of learning and surface approaches to study will wither and die.

This raises the stakes for teaching-as-design. On a simple view, a teacher's design work should focus on discrete learning tasks aligned with explicit learning outcomes. (For example, if students need to understand continental drift, get them to control a 4D animation.) Design becomes more complex when multiple learning outcomes have to be met – as when each learning activity has both specific and generic learning outcomes. An example might be where a learning activity is meant to help students understand continental drift, but also become better at group work. Finding appropriate trade-offs and synergies are classic challenges for design. But our conception of students and teachers (and others) co-operatively evolving activity systems stretches things even further. For example, it means that design work needs to focus on inter-cohort issues, such as the ways in which knowledge objects produced by this year's students will become resources for next year's students; tools found useful by this year's students are recommended to next year's students and so on. Design inspired by a proper sense of sustainability should not tolerate the routine throwing away of things to which students have attached value.

## Conclusion

This argument would now benefit from some further research. We have shown how students vary in the ways that they conceive of what can be learned, and how, in different educational situations. There is some evidence to suggest that their conceptions of learning and approaches to study are not fixed personal traits, but emerge in interaction with a context. This may point to the existence of sets of epistemic and other mental resources, differentially activated in different contexts. We are suggesting that students also have various ways of conceiving of the educational utility of tools, resources, spaces and even of other people. What they say about these things will vary, from person to person and from context to context. By helping students take a more active part in shaping and reshaping the contexts in which they work – defined broadly, as whole activity systems, or more narrowly, in terms of individual tools or artifacts – we can also help nudge their sense of what learning is, and how to become better at it, in more productive directions. That, at least, is the suggestion – and it needs some testing in practice.

## Notes

1 We do not mean to set up a 'straw man' by using the phrase 'traditional teaching practices'. Rather, we allude to a process whereby an individual teacher's ways of teaching are mainly shaped by their personal experience of being taught.
2 We don't have space to go into the correlations between end-of-course marks, conceptions of learning and approaches to study in this chapter. In general, we have found modest but statistically significant positive correlations between more elaborate conceptions of learning, deep approaches to study, and end-of-course marks. See Ellis & Goodyear (2009) for more information.
3 To make this concept of activity system workable, and easier to understand, we suggest you think of an activity system mapping onto a programme of study, or onto an academic department. Think of something larger than a single course module or unit of study, but smaller than a whole university. Once that's pinned down, you can start to deal with the complexity that comes from recognizing how various, numerous, interwoven and influential are the nested spaces in which learning occurs.

## References

Dillenbourg, P. & Hong, F. (2008). The mechanics of CSCL macro-scripts. *International Journal of Computer-Supported Collaborative Learning,* 3(1), 5–23.

Ellis, R. & Goodyear, P. (2009). *Students' experiences of e-learning in higher education: the ecology of sustainable innovation.* New York: RoutledgeFalmer.

Ellis, R., Goodyear, P., Prosser, M. & O'Hara, A. (2006). How and what university students learn through online and face-to-face discussions: conceptions, intentions and approaches. *Journal of Computer Assisted Learning,* 22(4), 244–256.

Ellis, R., Goodyear, P., Brillant, M. & Prosser, M. (2008). Student experiences of problem-based learning in pharmacy: conceptions of learning, approaches to learning and the integration of face-to-face and on-line activities. *Advances in Health Sciences Education,* 13(5), 675–692.

Goodyear, P. (2000). Environments for lifelong learning: ergonomics, architecture and educational design. In J.M. Spector & T. Anderson (Eds.) *Integrated and holistic perspectives on learning, instruction and technology: understanding complexity* (pp. 1–18). Dordrecht: Kluwer Academic Publishers.

Goodyear, P. (2005). Educational design and networked learning: patterns, pattern languages and design practice. *Australasian Journal of Educational Technology,* 21(1), 82–101.

Goodyear, P. & Ellis, R. (2007). The development of epistemic fluency: learning to think for a living. In A. Brew & J. Sachs (Eds.) *Transforming a university: the scholarship of teaching and learning in practice* (pp. 57–68). Sydney: Sydney University Press.

Greeno, J. (2006). Learning in activity. In K. Sawyer (Ed.) *The Cambridge handbook of the learning sciences* (pp. 79–96). Cambridge: Cambridge University Press.

Hammer, D. & Elby, A. (2002). On the form of a personal epistemology. In: B. Hofer & P. Pintrich (Eds) *Personal epistemology: the psychology of beliefs about knowledge and knowing* (pp. 169–190). Mahwah, NJ: Lawrence Erlbaum Associates.

House of Commons Innovation Universities Science and Skills Committee (2009). *Students and universities*. London: House of Commons.

Ipsos MORI (2008). *Great expectations of ICT: how higher education institutions are measuring up*. Bristol: JISC.

Marton, F. & Booth, S. (1997). *Learning and awareness*. Mahwah, NJ: Lawrence Erlbaum Associates.

Prosser, M. & Trigwell, K. (1999). *Understanding learning and teaching: the experience in higher education*. Buckingham: SRHE/Open University Press.

Salomon, G. (Ed.) (1993). *Distributed cognitions: psychological and educational considerations*. Cambridge: Cambridge University Press.

Vermunt, J. & Rijswijk, F. (1988). Analysis and development of students' skill in self-regulated learning. *Higher Education, 17*(6), 647–682.

# 8

# How Learners Change
## *Critical Moments, Changing Minds*

JUDY HARDY AND AMANDA JEFFERIES

## Editors' Introduction

This chapter combines findings from two major studies of the learner experience (the STROLL and LEaD projects) to examine the issue of change and transition. The aim is to help us understand the difficulties learners face on transition into higher education and at other critical points in their learning journey. Despite finding evidence of high ownership and prior experience of digital technologies on arrival, we see that learners are conservative in their views of the role of technology in support of learning. They value a blend of online and face-to-face teaching and easy access to online information relevant to their studies. In their first year, learners report increases in confidence, some new skills development in using technology, and show a determination to make the best use of technologies on offer. Monitoring such progression through periods of transition could be one of the ways in which we can conceptualise the differences often noted between learners in the way they express their experiences of technology use.

## Introduction

I knew the University has a lot of resources…but I couldn't believe it when I saw how much computers and the Internet are used in each course.

(Edinburgh, Male, Physics)

It's a bit different to what we did at school…we just used to Google everything and use search engines to find out as much information as we could.

(Edinburgh, Female, Physics)

In 2007, JISC/Ipsos MORI published a survey into the expectations of learners aged 16–18 who were anticipating study at tertiary level in UK universities (JISC/Ipsos MORI 2007). Its outcomes confirmed what a number of previous writers had already expected (e.g. Oblinger and Oblinger 2005), namely that this incoming generation of university students now expect to use technology to support their studies in a way that had not been seen in previous generations. Indeed, in the preliminary work prior to the launch of the recent UK Committee of Inquiry into the Changing Learner Experience (CLEX), it was suggested that: 'Students are in the forefront in the use of new technologies, and their experience and expectations have far reaching implications for institutions of higher education' (JISC 2008).

Nevertheless, a follow-up survey into learners' experiences in higher education the following year (JISC/Ipsos MORI 2008) showed that, although technology is widely perceived to offer real benefits for learning and teaching, its potential impact is not yet fully exploited by higher education institutions. The CIBER group's 'Google generation' report (CIBER 2008: 12) also pointed to an apparently easy but somewhat superficial engagement with technology by young learners, which did not necessarily support an in-depth engagement with their learning. They noted that: 'internet research shows that the speed of young people's web searching means that little time is spent in evaluating information, either for relevance, accuracy or authority'.

These findings were echoed in the CLEX final report (2009), which highlighted the need for higher education institutions to work in partnership with learners to explore the ways that technology can be used to support learning and teaching.

Many students arrive at university with a wide repertoire of IT-related skills already formed, largely derived from their prior personal and social uses of technology (Nicholson et al. 2005), and there is little room for doubting that this generation of learners is becoming more competent in using digital technologies to access information to support their learning. However, we do not yet understand how students' expectations and skills on arrival influence their uses of technology at university. We know that the transition to independent study at university is a critical time for all students. A recent study into the emotional impact on students of the transition into higher education highlighted the need for students to construct a new 'learning identity' that is appropriate for the particular learning environment that they encounter at university (Christie et al. 2008), while the bewilderment and anxiety experienced by some new students has been aptly termed 'learning shock' (Griffiths et al. 2005). There is some evidence that this sense of disequilibrium may be more acute for women (Jackson 2003) and it has also been noted that the ease with which students adjust to learning at university is influenced by their expectations prior to arrival, an effect that may persist well beyond the early months or even years into their university study (Jackson et al. 2000).

The ways that technology can be best used to support learning is clearly only one facet of this major life change, but in today's digital world, its impact should not be underestimated.

Most university students are expected to use a range of institutional technologies, such as email, portals and virtual learning environments (VLEs), to support both their academic studies and their interactions with administrative functions. For some, this may be complemented by personal use of non-institutional technologies such as blogs, social networking sites and instant messaging, a point noted in a recent report on students' transition to higher education in Scotland:

> E-learning approaches require the transition to a different mode of learning for school leavers and mature students alike... Students need to adjust to the technological environment, which integrates online technology through VLEs with the use of personal technologies and interaction with staff and fellow students through this medium.
>
> (Whittaker 2008: 23)

In a companion report on students' experiences in their first year at Scottish higher education institutions (Johnston and Kochanowska 2009: 35), it was suggested by some students that 'improved use of technology' to support their learning would be of benefit, however, this was tempered by a preference for a mixed-mode approach, together with a recognition that not all staff are equally comfortable using technology in their teaching. Despite this, there is relatively little research to date on the ways that technology can be used to help smooth this transition and facilitate the construction of an appropriate learning identity.

## Background and Context

In this chapter we present the experiences of students who took part in the JISC funded STROLL and LEaD studies (STROLL 2009; LEaD 2009) as they reflect on their own uses of technology both personally owned and institutionally provided through a time of transition and change at the start of university life and through their early years of study there. We explore the role of technology within the context of the students' learning experiences as a whole and the differing experiences of change encountered by students as they settle into university study and reflect on their personal transitions and developing maturity in learning. The methodological approaches used in these studies are described and discussed in detail elsewhere (Jefferies et al. 2009; Hardy et al. 2009a, 2009b; see also Conole et al. 2006). The overall shape of the research was based on two underlying principles. Firstly, to take a learner-centred approach, whereby the learners' own views and opinions are central to the study. Secondly, to adopt a holistic approach in which learners' use of e-learning is set within the context of their learning experiences as a whole. The data collection methods included extensive use of self-reflective student diaries, recorded as video or text, together with questionnaires and focus group discussions.

The University of Hertfordshire has embraced the use of advanced technologies to support its students and management and in particular with its managed learning environment (MLE), known as StudyNet. All students in the Hertfordshire study described below had access to StudyNet. This purpose built in-house intranet was first introduced at the university in 2001 and is now fully embedded in the university's study environment. StudyNet provides access via the personalised student or staff portal to the websites for programmes of study and individual courses. These hold information about the content of individual study sessions (lectures, seminars etc.) and provide access to, for example, online journals as well as collaborative tools such as discussion fora, virtual groups, wikis and blogs. It is from this background that fifty-four students volunteered for a longitudinal study using a diary methodology that would encourage their reflection on studying through times of transition and change within an environment which embraced the use of technology. While all students were clearly expected to make extensive use of the online facilities of the MLE, the diary reflections would identify whether this was seen as a positive support for their learning or whether the requirement to access the technology now seen by many academics as an essential skill was in fact an unnecessary imposition for students whether new to the university or already settled in. The diary reflections were completed for a week at a time at six-monthly intervals and captured the students' reflections across at least two academic years.

The majority of courses at the University of Edinburgh follow a campus-based model of teaching and learning based on a traditional lecture plus tutorial approach. The use of e-learning to enhance students' learning experience and to promote wider access is actively supported and encouraged by the university, with well-established e-learning support services providing VLEs, wikis, e-portfolios and formative and summative assessment tools together with technical and pedagogical advice. The centrally managed VLE WebCT/Blackboard is used by most courses, however, in the College of Medicine & Veterinary Medicine the bespoke VLEs EEMeC & EEVeC are used. Most e-learning services, together with other online services such as email, course and timetable information, online library etc. are accessed via the staff/student portal 'MyEd', which supports a single sign-on authentication model. At Edinburgh, twenty-four students were recruited from three degree programmes: physics, divinity and veterinary medicine. Early years' courses in all of these disciplines have a well-established online presence, marrying both online and real environments in a blended-learning approach. They have also begun to gain experience in embedding Web 2.0 tools such as weblogs and podcasts to support more traditional teaching methods. These tools, and the courses in which they are being piloted, emphasise a shift away from the transmission of knowledge towards a more bi-directional and collaborative approach.

Diaries were chosen in both studies as a method to encourage student reflection at critical moments in the academic year. The authors believe it is important to take such a learner-centred approach, thus placing learners' own views and opinions firmly centre stage and setting their use of e-learning within the context of their learning experiences as a whole, rather than taking a course-centric view of student activity. The use of diaries as a research methodology in education has not been widely recorded, although audio diaries were used in the JISC LXP project, where Conole et al. (2006: 13) noted that 'Diaries can provide rich data about the day-to-day events and contain a realistic account of the activities undertaken by the learners.'

Diaries provide an opportunity for learners to reflect on their experiences outside the direct intervention of an interviewer and can be completed at the learner's own leisure and at their own pace. Video was chosen as the preferred medium because it has the potential to provide a rich source of information that cannot be fully captured via audio or text diaries (Noyes 2004).

At Hertfordshire, students' reflections were compiled over a period of five days at a time and they were offered a choice of technologies or none for completing their diaries. Webcams and camcorders proved a popular choice, with an overall average of 58 per cent opting for a visual diary and 38 per cent opting for an audio only diary. None of the Hertfordshire students opted for a written diary as their first choice but some had to complete theirs in the form of an online blog when problems with using technology arose while they were away from the university on work placements.

At Edinburgh, students recorded reflective diaries over the course of the academic year 2007/08. Again, they were encouraged to record at least one diary entry as a video; however, there was no compulsion to use this approach so as not to exclude those who felt uncomfortable using video, or who were not technically confident. Participants were therefore free to use other methods such as audio, blogs, email, text documents or simply pen and paper. In practice, most diaries were recorded as either video or text, in addition to a small number of handwritten entries. Each diary entry had a particular theme and referred to a specific period of time, however, they were relatively freeform and unstructured and students were free to record comments and reflections on any aspects of their studying and learning.

Both studies have provided a rich source of qualitative data from the students' reflections, were was then analysed using a variety of means. All the Hertfordshire diaries were first transcribed into text documents and then highlighted according to the research themes. At a later stage they were imported into NVivo7 and coded. The qualitative data allowed for an investigation of words and phrases across participants and for a comparison across the diary stages. The Edinburgh diaries were organised and coded using NVivo8, with key sections of video transcribed into text.

## The Student Experience

There are, of course, many reasons why the transition to university is such a significant event. Class sizes, especially in the early years, may be well in excess of two hundred and there are limited opportunities for direct interaction between students and lecturers, yet students are expected to acquire the skills needed to become autonomous independent learners. Added to this is the increasing requirement for students to interact with unfamiliar and complex online systems for both course-related and administrative tasks, often from the first day they arrive or even earlier. At the University of Edinburgh, students' expectations on arrival regarding the use of technology to support their learning were generally high; however, it is also clear that they had widely differing experience of IT prior to arrival:

> I rarely used the Internet for studying during high school. My schoolwork didn't really involve much extra reading outside of the textbooks that the school distributed.
>
> (Edinburgh, Female, Veterinary Medicine)

> We had extensive computer training at my school from when we were eleven, and we had our own school intranet which was very similar to WebCT, we had our own school one.
>
> (Edinburgh, Female, Veterinary Medicine)

Not surprisingly, technology was firmly embedded into the social lives of many incoming students and both universities reported extensive engagement with social networks, such as Facebook; mainly, but not exclusively for personal rather than study use. However, there are important variations that should not be overlooked. Not all students embraced the use of technology to support learning. For those entering higher education as mature students especially, the high use of materials that are only available online registered as a matter of some surprise.

> I'm a mature student so my learning before university was very limited especially in the technology used so… the variety of technology that can be used to aid learning is probably the biggest difference.
>
> (Hertfordshire, Male, Philosophy & Psychology)

Despite variations in prior experience and outlook, it is clear that for many students the extent to which technology pervades all aspects of university life was somewhat unexpected. A survey of 1,345 incoming students at the University of Edinburgh, found that although over 90 per cent of new undergraduates brought a laptop to university, only around 30 per cent of them planned to carry their laptops on campus (Hardy et al. 2009b). In comparison, at Hertfordshire just 74 per cent of the STROLL project students reported owning a computer while the others, in particular the campus-based first years, relied on the extensive provision of computing facilities through the institution's own learning resources centres that are open 24 hours a day (Jefferies et al. 2009).

Well if there's one piece of technology that I could absolutely not do without it would most probably have to be my laptop or just a computer because I didn't have a laptop in my second year and it was difficult for me because I wasn't living on campus, I live a fifteen minute walk away.
(Hertfordshire, Female, Computing & Business)

As the academic year in which the research was undertaken progressed, the availability of online resources and the use of technology by teaching staff were increasingly considered beneficial by the students, with the important proviso that they should offer 'added value'. In other words, students expressed a desire that online resources should complement and enhance more traditional resources (lectures, paper notes, textbooks etc.) rather than simply provide an electronic repository for static information.

Lecturers did eventually put everything on WebCT following encouragement [by the students]. One was very good and put a good selection of different things – podcasts, connections to internet sources, further reading, as well as her own power points and lecture notes. But it was very lecturer dependent.
(Edinburgh, Male, Divinity)

You can visualise things a lot better if you can see animations on the web, you can visualise a concept better if you can see things moving rather than just static pictures in a textbook.
(Edinburgh, Male, Physics)

Furthermore, the majority of students reported some new IT skills development over the course of the year. This was often tied directly to ways that technology was used with a particular course; for example, prescribed use of discussion forums, blogs or wikis. Although there has been an increase in the use of online collaborative technologies such as wikis with students in higher education (Cubric 2007), this type of technology was generally unknown by the Hertfordshire students as a support for learning prior to entering university (Jefferies et al. 2007). The use of such collaborative technologies for learning was reported by students as an extension of group based learning developed after their first year of study.

This is my second year and my learning has changed to doing more group-based learning.
(Hertfordshire, Male, Computer Science)

I used Google Docs to compile a document with others as we contributed together online.

(Hertfordshire, Male, Business Studies)

Not surprisingly, students' use of technology was not limited to institutional online resources and activities. Leaving to one side the ubiquitous use of Google, Google Scholar and Wikipedia, one popular use of non-institutional technology was to facilitate interaction with other students, both online and face-to-face, for example, to ask questions or to organise study groups.

I find it really helpful to go over material with other students, whether I'm organising that through IT discussion boards or just emailing a person I know on the course.

(Edinburgh, Female, Divinity)

I use a lot of MSN and forums to communicate with fellow students and teacher, where I can ask questions and discuss with my colleague.

(Edinburgh, Male, Veterinary Medicine)

I used the class discussion feature on StudyNet to ask for help on a few of the questions I could not grasp but someone already had the same problem as me so I just read through the thread they had posted.

(Hertfordshire, Male, Computer Science)

There are some words of caution, and in particular practical issues such as ease of access and usability of online systems should not be neglected. In fact, most students used a mixture of paper and online activities in their studies. The proportion of each varied considerably, although overall paper was preferred by most Edinburgh students and online activity preferred by Hertfordshire students. However, many felt that a balance of activities was the key.

Although I feel equally reliant on both, if it came to a definitive choice, I just could not cope without electronic sources and materials!

(Edinburgh, Male, Physics)

Electronic resources should aid and not replace paper but all the time the two should work in harmony ...

(Edinburgh, Male, Divinity)

My learning has changed mainly because it's gone from physical to digital...from using pencils to do my drawings to using different mediums like Photoshop, Flash and my pen tablet.

(Hertfordshire, Male, 2D Animation)

In terms of students' expectations and the types of technologies that they use, some of the Hertfordshire students echoed the same comments as those from Edinburgh regarding the fact that their prior reliance on paper and writing changed to an increased use of online materials and the use of word-processing, especially for their assignments.

> I think nearly everything is IT focused now, certainly everything you hand in has to be word processed, a lot of resources are now online.
> (Hertfordshire, Male, Social Work)

> The biggest change in learning I experienced will be because it's been such a huge gap between present education as a student and my previous one ... just how technology has moved on so far from research done in the library with books with no online facilities, now [it's] at the click of a finger.
> (Hertfordshire, Female, Multimedia Technology)

The MLE at Hertfordshire (StudyNet) is widely used and has been praised by students as being a 'one-stop shop' where they can access online everything related to their studies (Thornton et al. 2004). This opportunity to use the MLE to support their learning was one of the key changes noted by Hertfordshire students from their previous study experiences.

> The biggest change in learning was the use of StudyNet, anything you want basically to do your course was on it, it has been so helpful.
> (Hertfordshire, Female, Digital & Lens Media)

> I feel Study Net is a great inspiration in the learning process. At college if I missed a class I would very rarely get the opportunity to catch up on what I had missed.
> (Hertfordshire, Male, Computer Science)

Many students reflected on their increased confidence in using technologies as they settled into university life and within a year had exhibited a willingness to try out technologies they had not previously encountered.

> My use of technology has changed dramatically over the past year. I am definitely using it more to support my learning now than I was a few months ago.
> (Hertfordshire, Female, Law)

> I am much more comfortable with using different technologies now.
> (Hertfordshire, Female, Multimedia Technology)

In both studies a blurring was noted between the use of technologies for personal time and study time. Furthermore, students accepted, without voicing complaint, the fact that they would be using personal technologies to support and access their learning instead of relying on provision by the university of all the necessary technology.

> Last year I didn't have my Mac laptop, I was running a PC desktop, this has benefited my learning 10 fold.
> (Hertfordshire, Male, Artificial Intelligence & Psychology)

The Mini Disc and laptop are only ever used for revision and learning and the PC, iPod and mobile are all used for a mixture of both learning and relaxing.

> (Hertfordshire, Female, Computing & Business)

However, the confidence of students in using varieties of different learning technologies beyond the MLEs varied; for example, some students could not use the integral webcams in their PCs for recording videos. Nevertheless, many voiced a desire and a determination to be online and to make best use of the opportunities, with students reporting enthusiastic use of podcasts from seminars and lectures that were recorded and made available by staff.

> Technology is a big part of my life, both in working and playing the first thing I do in the morning is to switch on my TV and my computer because I have to check my e-mails.
>
> (Hertfordshire, Male, International Business)

> I find it so helpful to listen to podcasts again and again.
>
> (Hertfordshire, Female, Philosophy)

> I wouldn't say technology's changed as much as I have developed using it.
>
> (Hertfordshire, Male, Computer Science)

Towards the end of their first year, Edinburgh students were asked what advice they would give to next year's incoming students and to the university. None of this advice would come as a surprise to people involved in the provision of ICT support, but the tips offered reflect the central position that technology occupies in students' studying. Advice for students included: bring a laptop, check email frequently, learn to touch-type, be proficient with MS Office packages and familiarise yourself with the online resources available. Advice for the university included: improve IT provision, provide help for students who have their own computers, standardise the availability of online resources across courses and provide a variety of resources. The increased maturity of the students is also evident from their awareness of the need for balance, both between online academic and social activities and between different approaches to learning and studying.

> Encourage lecturers to be more adventuresome… Offer a mixed approach as students learn differently and want choice. Such as paper or book, computer or internet, hand out or WebCT. This would fit the comfort of the student learning style.
>
> (Edinburgh, Male, Divinity)

## Supporting Students Through the Early Days: Lessons to Draw From These Experiences

The transition to university as reported by these students is momentous, not just in terms of the critical move to independence in living and studying, often away from their home environment, but in terms of the range and types of technology to which they are introduced and the dominance of technology for supporting their learning. This is apparent regardless of whether they are studying at an 'ancient' or 'new' university. Provision of technology at school level for the typical university entrant is varied, with some students already used to a virtual learning environment whereas others' experiences of computers and ICT is more for leisure than learning. Hence students arriving at university have a wide range of experiences and skills in the ways that technology can be used to enhance their own learning. The variety of types of technology and the importance of an MLE can both be identified as significant points of change in their experience, and understanding how to use technology is part of this transition. Students who have concerns about the available technologies will quickly seek help from friends, family or the university's resources. (It is worth pointing out that at both the universities where the research took place, extensive ICT support is made available and none of the students in these studies expressed difficulty with accessing or understanding how to use basic MLE technologies.)

We found that with the growing maturity and confidence that comes with time and familiarity, students often moved on to explore the use of additional technologies that they had not previously encountered. This was coupled with an increased expectation that technology will enhance their overall learning experiences in the future. It may be the case that holding a similar positive attitude will, more than any other single aspect of managing the transition to higher education, ensure students' growth and stability. This view is supported by recent research into the experiences of taught masters students at Oxford University (Thema 2009: 6), where it was noted that 'students who adopt a flexible approach to their new environment appear more likely to succeed in making the adaptation...'. The importance of both students' expectations and their reactions to the use of technology for learning and teaching was also emphasised by Creanor et al. 2006 (2008: 36), who found that 'From the outset, many learners display emotional reactions to e-learning which often impact on their attitudes and levels of motivation.' Does this reflect some degree of arrogance or superficiality on the part of students in terms of their attitudes to studying? We suggest that, on the contrary, the opinions given by students are careful reflections and hence are more likely to be considered comments on how they survive and flourish within a university environment. This is illustrated by comments from one mature student (who was fifty-one at the start of her studies) on her reliance on her family to assist with downloading material for her.

Support was available, I just didn't realise how much use it would be or how much I actually needed it...My children helped me download podcasts and record them so I can listen to them in the car on my way to university.

(Hertfordshire, Female, Radiography)

Yet eighteen months later she had transformed into a confident student who relished the use of technology, for example, '...Podcast continues to be a great inspiration to the way I learn.'

Competence and confidence at using technology do not necessarily have to be prerequisites for entering university, but the experience of studying in the twenty-first century suggests that the range of technology skills acquired are vital for supporting successful learning.

Of course, students do not form a homogenous group, so any conclusions about their journey to becoming autonomous learners, and the ways that this can be supported by technology, are inevitably complex. Although the majority of young peoples' personal and social lives are transparently immersed in technology and many are confident IT users, this does not necessarily translate into the skills needed to use technology to support independent academic study effectively. This point has been emphasised in two recent reports (CIBER, op. cit.: CLEX, op. cit.), both of which highlight a significant gap in the digital literacy skills needed for academic study, and these issues are explored in Part 3 of this volume. Furthermore, despite the transparency with which technology is embedded into many students' lives, it should not be forgotten that there is still a small minority of students who, at the point of entry to university, are either not confident with technology or do not recognise its potential value for studying. It is important, therefore, that universities engage with students from a very early stage, possibly even before arrival, in order to help smooth this transition. As the student population becomes more heterogeneous and diverse, and possibly less well prepared to study effectively using technological tools, it is likely that this will become increasingly important.

Irrespective of their prior experiences, the use of technology for learning and teaching is viewed positively by many students and rapidly becomes a valued and integral part of their academic study. However, the term 'e-learning' does not hold a great deal of meaning for them – there is simply learning (and teaching), with technology used to support and enhance this in a variety of ways that meet their personal needs and preferences. It is evident that students value the 'tried and tested' methods of lectures, tutorials, labs etc. and have a strong desire for face-to-face teaching with technology used to supplement and enhance this. Where the opportunity exists, students prefer a situation offering both online learning materials and face-to-face tuition rather than an 'either/or' choice between online learning and face-to-face learning. Furthermore, students are not generally pushing for novel or innovative uses of technology, although they do have high expectations in terms of reliability, ease of access and consistency of use across their courses. This intrinsic cautiousness suggests that an incremental approach to the introduction of new technologies might be best and also serves to highlight the importance of explaining 'up front' both the reasons for using a particular technology and its potential benefits.

The ever-changing digital landscape, an increasingly diverse student population and the continued move towards mass higher education and lifelong learning all pose challenges for teachers in higher education. It will be essential to keep students' own views and opinions central to future research in this field, in order to continue to meet the needs of both today's students and the students of the future. As students mature through their learning journey they increasingly consider using technology strategically to support their personal learning requirements.

> I have come to reflect yet again on the technology which plays such an essential role in my education...
> (Edinburgh, Female, Veterinary Medicine)

## References

Christie, H., Tett, L., Cree, J., Hounsell, J. & McCune, V. (2008). A real rollercoaster of confidence and emotions: Learning to be a university student, *Studies in Higher Education*, 33(5), 567–581.

CIBER (2008). Information behaviour of the researcher of the future. University College London. Retrieved 10 June, 2009, from http://www.jisc.ac.uk/media/documents/programmes/reppres/gg_final_keynote_11012008.pdf.

Committee of Inquiry into the changing Learner Experience (CLEX) (2009). Higher education in a Web 2.0 world. Report of an independent committee of inquiry into the impact on higher education of students' widespread use of Web 2.0 technologies. Retrieved 19 May, 2009, from http://clex.org.uk/CLEX_Report_v1-final.pdf.

Conole, G., de Laat, M., Dillon, T. & Darby, J. (2006). LXP: Student experiences of technologies – final report. Retrieved 19 June, 2009, from http://jisc.ac.uk/media/documents/programmes/elearningpedagogy/lxp_project_final_report_nov_06.pdf.

Creanor, L., Trinder, K., Gowan, D., & Howells, C. (2006). LEX: The learner experience of e-learning. Final report (report under the JISC e-pedagogy 'Understanding my learner' programme). Glasgow: Glasgow Caledonian University. Retrieved 20 August, 2009, from http://www.jisc.ac.uk/whatwedo/programmes/elearning_pedagogy/elp_learneroutcomes.aspx.

Creanor, L., Trinder, K., Gowan, D. & Howells, C. (2008). Life, learning and technology: Views from the learners, *Journal for Learning and Teaching in Higher Education*, 2, 26–41.

Cubric, M. (2007). Wiki-based process framework for blended learning. In A. Désilets and R. Biddle (Eds.) Proceedings of the 2007 International Symposium on Wikis, Montreal, Canada, New York: ACM.

Griffiths, D.S., Winstanley, D. & Gabriel, Y. (2005). Learning shock: The trauma of return to formal learning, *Management Learning*, 36(3), 275–297.

Hardy, J., Haywood, D., Haywood, J., Bates, S., Paterson, J., Rhind, S. and Macleod, H. (2009a). Techniques for gathering student views of their experiences at university. Retrieved 4 July, 2009, from http://www2.epcc.ed.ac.uk/~lead/documents/Main_LEaD_Report_final.pdf.

Hardy, J., Haywood, D., Haywood, J., Bates, S., Paterson, J., Rhind, S. & Macleod, H. (2009b). ICT and the student first year experience, project student views report. Retrieved 4 July, 2009, from http://www2.epcc.ed.ac.uk/~lead/documents/Methodology_LEaD_Report_final.pdf.

Jackson, C. (2003). Transitions into higher education: Gendered implications for academic self-concept, *Oxford Review of Education*, 29(3), 331–346.

Jackson, L.M., Pancer, S.M., Pratt, M.W. & Hunsberger, B.E. (2000). Great expectations: The relation between expectancies and adjustments during the transition to university, *Journal of Applied Science,* 30(10), 2100–2125.

Jefferies, A., Quadri, N. & Kornbrot, D. (2007). Investigating university students' prior experiences of technology and their expectations of using technology in their studies. In S. Wheeler and N. Whitton (eds) 'Beyond control: learning technology for the social network generation.' Research Proceedings of the 14th Annual Association for Learning Technology Conference ( ALT-C 2007), Nottingham, pp 201–211.

Jefferies, A., Bullen, P. & Hyde, R. (2009). *Researching learners' journeys: STROLL, student reflections on lifelong e-learning,*University of Hertfordshire. Retrieved 5 July, 2009, from http://www.jisc.ac.uk/media/documents/programmes/elearningpedagogy/strollanalysis. pdf.

Jenkins, H. (2006). *Convergence Culture: Where Old and New Media Collide.* New York: NYU Press.

JISC (2008). Independent inquiry will look at how the 'Google Generation' could drive change in higher education. Retrieved 19 May, 2009, from http://www.jisc.ac.uk/news/stories/2008/02/ changinglearnerexperience.aspx.

JISC/Ipsos MORI (2007). *Student expectations study.* Key findings from online research and discussion evenings held in June 2007 for the Joint Information Systems Committee. Retrieved 19 May, 2009, from http://www.jisc.ac.uk/media/documents/publications/ studentexpectations.pdf.

JISC/Ipsos MORI (2008). *Great expectations of ICT. How higher education institutions are measuring up.* Retrieved 19 May, 2009, from http://www.jisc.ac.uk/media/documents/ publications/jiscgreatexpectationsfinalreportjune08.pdf.

Johnston, B. & Kochanowska, R. (2009). *Quality enhancement themes: The first year experience. Student expectations, experiences and reflections on the first year,* Retrieved 17 August, 2009, from http://www.enhancementthemes.ac.uk/documents/firstyear/StudentExpectations.pdf.

LEaD (2009). Learner experiences of e-learning: LEaD completion report. Retrieved 30 April, 2009, from https://mw.brookes.ac.uk/display/JISCle2/Projects.

Nicholson, S., Macleod, H., Haywood. J. (2005). *E-Learning: Who is leading whom, and where might the road be going?* 3rd International Conference on Universal Access in Human - Computer Interaction (UAHCI).

Noyes, A. (2004). Video diary: a method for exploring learning dispositions, *Cambridge Journal of Education,* 34, 193–209.

Oblinger, D.G. & Oblinger, J.L. (Eds.) (2005). Educating the Net Generation. Boulder, CO: Educause. Retrieved 10 June, 2009, from http://www.educause.edu/educatingthenetgen.

STROLL (2009). Learner experiences of e-learning: STROLL completion report. Retrieved 30 April, 2009, from https://mw.brookes.ac.uk/display/JISCle2/Projects.

Thema (2009). Learner experiences of e-learning: Thema completion report. Retrieved 30 April, 2009, from https://mw.brookes.ac.uk/display/JISCle2/Projects.

Thornton M., Jefferies, A., Doolan, M., Parkhurst, S., Alltree, J. & Jones, I. (2004, September). How was it for you? An evaluation of student learning experience following the introduction of an MLE in one English university, Paper presented at the BERA Conference, UMIST, Manchester.

Whittaker, R. (2008). Quality enhancement themes: The first year experience. Transition to and during the first year. Retrieved 10 October, 2008, from http://www.enhancementthemes. ac.uk/documents/firstyear/Transition%20-%20Final.pdf.

# 9
# Listening With a Different Ear
## *Understanding Disabled Students' Relationships With Technologies*

JANE SEALE AND NICK BISHOP

## Editors' Introduction

This chapter draws on research concerning disabled students' experiences of learning with technology. The learners' voice is emphasised in all the chapters, but in this chapter the researcher and student have come together to write a chapter that shows vividly the benefits of their participatory approach to research. In terms of the development of frameworks that can help us understand the complexity of the learners' experiences, the concepts introduced here of 'digital agility' and 'digital decision making' add depth to our understanding of effective e-learners. These agile users of technology showed both familiarity and confidence with technology, and this enabled them to customise their technology to suit their purposes, employ a wide range of strategies and make informed decisions about which technology to use in which circumstances, including decisions of non-use. Both the research approach adopted here and the detailed descriptions of technology are useful beyond the scope of looking at the experiences of disabled students.

## Introduction

In this chapter, we will review what is currently known about disabled students' experiences of technology in post-compulsory education, and the theories and concepts used to try and explain these experiences. We will then present the findings from a JISC funded study of disabled students' experiences of e-learning (LEXDIS) and Nick's experiences as a disabled student at university. We will use these findings and experiences to present new insights into the technology experiences of disabled students. In particular we will argue that disabled learners, like many other learners, are agile users of technologies, capable of embracing technologies on their own terms. Where disabled learners may differ from other learners is that they often have to make difficult decisions about their technology use; decisions that are influenced by a vast array of factors such as time, resources, access, support and most importantly their desires and needs. The identification of the two phenomena of 'digital agility' and 'digital decision making' highlights the strengths of disabled students and confirms the belief of many disabled students that thinking solely in terms of what disabled students cannot do is not necessarily that helpful or informative. Instead, we need to try and understand in more detail the complex relationship that disabled learners have with their technologies.

### What Do We Know About Disabled Students' Experiences of Technology?

The results of past studies that have explored the general learning experiences of disabled students in higher education have provided a small amount of information regarding their e-learning experiences. They reveal, for example, that disabled students are using general and specialised technologies to support their learning (Mortimore and Crozier 2006) but that they experience some difficulties. Difficulties include:

- barriers to using publicly available information technology facilities such as lack of specialised software on PCs and unfavourable or inaccessible location of facilities (Fuller et al. 2004);
- frustrations with the efficiency of the funding and assessment procedures for obtaining assistive technology (Shevlin et al. 2004; Goode 2007);
- lack of support or training to enable disabled learners to become 'fluent users' of assistive technologies (Shevlin et al. 2004).

Results from a small number of studies in the UK that have specifically explored the technology experiences of disabled learners support these findings. For example, Draffan et al. (2007) in a survey of the use of and satisfaction with assistive technology by dyslexic students in UK post-secondary education highlighted the variability of technology provision. Cobham et al. (2001) conducted two UK surveys of students who were supplied with equipment under the Disabled Students' Allowance (DSA) and concluded that training levels for using assistive technologies were unsatisfactory. Whilst there are frustrations for disabled learners in terms of access, provision and support, they are generally very satisfied once they are able to obtain and use assistive technologies to support their learning (Draffan et al. 2007; Fidler 2002).

## Theorising About the Technology Experiences of Disabled Learners: An Access and Barriers Discourse

Theorisation of disabled learners' experiences of technology has been largely influenced by broader debates regarding digital inclusion. In the context of education, digital inclusion is broadly understood as a phenomenon whereby marginalised people, in this case disabled people, are able to access and participate meaningfully in the same learning activities as others, through use of digital technologies. As a concept, digital inclusion is frequently linked to social inclusion and the digital divide. Unequal access to technology can serve to widen existing social inequalities; whilst equal access can help to reduce marginalisation (Castells 2001; Warschauer et al. 2004; Selwyn 2006).

The focus of digital inclusion has until recently been on increasing access to technologies and improving the ability of people to use them (Selwyn and Facer 2007). Consequently, the process of digital inclusion has been conceptualised as creating gateways, opening doors and letting people in. Practitioners working with those identified as digitally excluded are therefore encouraged to identify barriers that keep these gateways and doors shut, for example, not having access to technology or not knowing how to use technology.

In the context of disabled students in post-16 education and their relationship with digital technologies, the access and barriers discourse from the digital inclusion literature is repeated, but through a narrower 'accessibility lens'. A particular focus of attention has been the inaccessibility of virtual learning environments for disabled students (e.g. Newland et al. 2004). In a review of accessibility issues in higher education, Seale (2006) noted that although disabled students may have access to computers and the Internet, they may not necessarily have access to accessible online learning resources and activities. This provides evidence for what Burgstahler (2002) described as the 'second digital divide'.

We will now go on to give an overview of the methods and results of the LEXDIS project. The participatory methods adopted by the project attempted to give voice to disabled learners' experience and in doing so illuminate the e-learning experiences of disabled learners in a way that previous studies have not done. The power of the voice that has been revealed through these methods also encourages us to listen with a different ear. This has revealed new insights into how digital inclusion can be understood and conceptualised, which has important implications for practitioners.

### The LEXDIS Project

The LEXDIS project was a JISC (Joint Information Systems Committee) funded project, situated within its 'E-Learning Pedagogy programme'. Research was carried out at the University of Southampton. By exploring in detail the e-learning experiences of disabled students, the LEXDIS project sought to increase our understanding of the complex relationship between students and technologies. The related objectives of the study were to:

- explore and describe how disabled learners experience and participate in technology-rich, e-learning environments;
- investigate the strategies, beliefs and intentions of disabled learners when using technology-rich environments;
- identify factors that enable or inhibit use of technologies.

In order to meet these aims, the project adopted a participatory framework where participation was defined as:

Involving disabled learners as consultants and partners and not just as research subjects. Where disabled learners help to identify and (re)frame the research questions; work with the researchers to achieve a collective analysis of the research issues and bring the results to the attention of each of the constituencies that they represent.

(Seale et al. 2008a: 11)

Ethical approval for the project was obtained through the ethics committee of the University of Southampton, School of Education. An integral element of the ethical approach to the project was to enable participants to decide whether and how to anonymise their contributions. Each student chose the name they wanted to be associated with their contributions, and it is these names that are referred to in this chapter when presenting extracts and quotes.

There were thirty-one student participants in the project. The disabilities of the group were varied, with some declaring more than one disability, but the most commonly declared disability was dyslexia (see Table 9.1). The majority of students were aged twenty or under.

**Table 9.1** Range of Disabilities Represented Across the Thirty-one Participants

| Disability | Frequency |
|---|---|
| Specific learning differences (e.g. dyslexia) | 14 |
| Blind | 1 |
| Visual impairment | 3 |
| Hearing impairment | 3 |
| Wheelchair user and dexterity issues | 4 |
| Mobility/dexterity issues | 3 |
| Autistic spectrum/Asperger's | 1 |
| Mental health difficulties | 3 |
| Other | 3 |

Results from the LEXDIS project confirm issues that we already know about regarding access and barriers, but also reveal new insights into the digital agility and digital decision making of disabled learners in relation to their use or non-use of technology, and how they used technologies to support their learning.

## LEXDIS Results

### Confirming What We Know About Access and Barriers

Analysis of the data revealed issues regarding access and barriers that have been identified in other research. Participants identified six main accessibility issues: 1) e-learning applications do not interact well with assistive technologies; 2) navigability of library websites; 3) navigability and usability of Blackboard; 4) problems opening and manipulating PDF files; 5) learning environments that influence whether or not student can access preferred assistive technologies; 6) difficulties scanning non-standard symbols or text.

Several students shared their frustrations regarding access and accessibility issues:

> I find the university of Southampton library website extremely hard to use, actually. There's far too much information there that you really don't need. Instead of having quick links all in one place, they are spread out on different pages and you have to go searching for things. You've got to login to each and every single thing separately. You can't transfer information from one end to the other, for example from WebCat into TDnet, even if you cut and paste it. You just don't get it. Then it logs you out, because it thinks you're not doing anything with it, even though you're using it and typing into the boxes. It drives me absolutely mad. [laughing]
>
> (Guenevere)

Despite sharing frustrations, many participants were still able to say that they liked or could see the benefits of the technologies they were using:

> I really like Blackboard, but I think that there is an awful lot on there, and it could be made a lot easier to use. The navigation is difficult. My lecturer might say: 'We've put up this, on this subject', and then I won't know which section it's in. I'd have to go into each section and open each document section to find it. [...] There was an Inter-professional Learning forum, but that was really difficult to use. It didn't tell you whether or not you had read the Postings (the ones previously), so you had to just keep looking through to see if there's anything new. It got really tedious.
>
> (Stacey)

This confirmation of access and accessibility issues for disabled learners is important in terms of challenging any complacency there may be regarding the presumed success of disability legislation and supposed simplicity of implementing accessibility guidelines. The LEXDIS project has, however, also revealed new information, which suggests that access and accessibility issues cannot be considered in isolation from wider personal and contextual issues.

## Providing New Insights Regarding Digital Agility and Digital Decisions

Detailed analysis of the LEXDIS data revealed results that suggested that disabled learners can be incredibly 'digital agile', but find themselves making complex 'digital decisions' regarding their technology use.

### Digital Agility

Results revealed that the 'digital agility' of the disabled students was an important factor that aided their studies. Evidence for the digital agility of students included being extremely familiar with technology, using a wide range of strategies and having high levels of confidence in their own ability to use technology.

Evidence for how familiar disabled students were with technology was drawn from a number of related findings. For example, all the students customised their computer in some way, particularly toolbars and menu items and the print size on screen. The majority of students used instant messaging participated in discussion forums, knew how to use social networking sites, and uploaded videos or photos onto the Internet. All the students used search engines such as Google, accessed online learning materials of some kind, used word-processors and spreadsheets and contacted tutors using email.

This familiarity with technologies meant that many students in the project were able to talk very knowledgeably about the strengths and weaknesses of specific technologies in terms of design, usability, cost and availability as well as the implications of these factors for their own strategy development and technology use. In studies where disabled students are invisible in the reporting of data, students have typically been described as sophisticated 'digital natives' of the 'Net Generation' (Oblinger 2003). The findings from the LEXDIS project regarding familiarity with technology enable us to not only extend this description to disabled students, but to add depth to the description.

The LEXDIS project identified thirty-one different types of strategies that students were adopting and devising when using technology to support their learning (see Seale et al. 2008b for further details). The most common types of strategy adopted by students tended to be related to computer or information access and ways of coping with written work. These strategies therefore involved the use of both specialist assistive technologies (e.g. Inspiration or Dragon Dictate) as well as more generic technologies (e.g. mobile phone or

Google). Interestingly, students perceived many of their strategies as being common or basic when in fact they were indicative of the agile and considered way in which they were approaching the use of technologies; for example using free alternatives to standard assistive technologies that may be provided under the DSA (Disabled Students Allowance) scheme.

Based on the range and creativity of strategies that the disabled students employed, we would suggest that they have the kind of 'sophisticated awareness' that Creanor et al. (2006) described when they talked about effective learners being prepared to adapt activities, environments and technologies to suit their own circumstances. This contradicts somewhat the arguments of Parker and Banerjee (2007: 6) who, in making comparisons with non-disabled students, argued that disabled students were less able to develop meta-cognitive 'self-regulated strategic approaches' to using learning technologies to help them meet academic goals. Whilst we do not deny that some students will have different strategic abilities to others, we believe the results regarding strategy use are important in terms of reminding us that a deficit-based approach to understanding disabled students' use of technologies may not always be that helpful.

Participants' confidence in their ability to use technology was generally quite high. For some, high confidence levels appeared to be linked to comfort levels and familiarity. For others, confidence manifested itself in not being afraid of the technology, or in a preference for learning how to use technology through trial and error:

> I've had quite a lot of experience with it by now. It's generally quite easy to use. It doesn't faze me.
>
> (Sarah P)

> I'd just use it – trial and error. I'd possibly ask my peers, but as I'm quite good with computers, I can just get stuck in [...] Most of the time I would probably just have a play.
>
> (Ben C)

Trial and error approaches are probably most successful when students have the confidence to know what to do when something they try doesn't work (not being 'fazed', as Sarah P said). It could be argued that it would be more effective for students to be trained how to use technologies, so they don't need to rely on trial-and-error approaches when something doesn't work as expected. However, the LEXDIS results suggest that for technology training to be effective it might need to recognise and utilise the skills (e.g. strategy use), abilities (e.g. confidence) and preferences (e.g. trial and error) that disabled students bring to training sessions.

## DIGITAL DECISION-MAKING

Results suggest that LEXDIS participants were making a wide range of choices or 'digital decisions' regarding technology use. Whilst the nature of these digital decisions was varied, some interesting results were revealed with regards to the decisions students made not to use technologies. Furthermore, the complexity of the 'digital decisions' that disabled students in the LEXDIS project were making appeared to be reflected in the way disabled students approached decision making.

The results from the LEXDIS project revealed that students loved and hated technologies in equal measure and were able to express preferences for using certain technologies over others based on detailed knowledge of the strengths and weaknesses of particular technologies compared to others. There were, however, three striking examples where students made decisions not to use technologies: 1) deciding not to use social networking tools; 2) deciding not to use assistive technologies; 3) deciding not to access technology-related support systems.

An exploration of the reasons why disabled students might make decisions regarding non-use of technology (and related support) suggests that the circumstances around 'digital decision making' can be quite complex. For example, the two most frequent reasons given by participants for not accessing support (e.g. training to use assistive technologies) were having a preference for trial and error and being too busy to access support. For many students, being too busy to access support was possibly linked to the nature of their courses, for example whether or not they were vocational in nature or had a large placement element, suggesting that the 'study-fitness' of technology influences to some extent the decisions that disabled students make:

> When I got all my software in autumn last year, and they said: 'you need to have your training on this' [...] I did feel like I was doing 2 courses and that was, frankly, too much. I had to stay with my old bad habits because I just didn't feel I had the time to take out to learn something new to help me. It was a vicious circle, really.
>
> (Stephanie, studying for a physiotherapy degree)

This finding, combined with those of Draffan et al. (2007) who found that almost 25 per cent of the disabled students they surveyed turned down the opportunity for training because they felt confident about their IT skills, support the arguments made by Selwyn (2006) that non-use should not be automatically equated with digital exclusion without first attempting to understand the many factors that influence non-use. From the results of this study we have hints of a potentially complex picture, whereby both lack of resources (time) and available resources (IT skills) influence decisions regarding non-use.

As we have seen from results presented so far, a wide range of factors appear to influence students' decisions about technology use, and the circumstances surrounding these decisions can sometimes be complex. This complexity is further reflected in two separate, but related, approaches to decision making: using general criteria or questions to make judgements about the benefits of technology and using specific 'critical' criteria to make decisions based on a cost–benefit analysis.

In making decisions about whether or not to use technology, some students adopt approaches to their decision making where judgements about the potential benefits are qualified against general criteria or questions. For example Andy L asks himself: 'is this the right tool for the job?':

> The thing that I came to do some time ago was there isn't this thing 'all or nothing' – you either have technology or you haven't. I use my computer. I use my word processing on the computer, but I still draw my mind-maps on paper because it is easier and quicker for me. I am a firm believer in using whatever tool that is appropriate for the job. Sometimes that is the technology, but not always.
>
> (Andy L)

Some students in the LEXDIS study appeared to be adopting a cost–benefit analysis approach to their decision making, where judgements regarding potential benefit were qualified against specific and quite 'critical' criteria. For example, nine students talked about their decisions being influenced by time considerations, six students mentioned cost as a deciding factor and two mentioned perceptions of risk. Time, however, seemed to be particularly critical in relation to decisions made regarding use of assistive technologies and social networking applications. Students were aware of the benefits or pleasures that use of these technologies might bring them, but were making a decision about whether the benefits (learning or social) outweighed the costs in terms of time taken away from study.

> I have got Dragon 8 voice recognition software, which is OK but it takes ages to get used to and I haven't got the time. [...] And, that's why I never really got to grips with Dragon 8 too much, because it was quite good, but I didn't have the time. It was only now and then that I had an essay, and when I did have it, I had to get on and do it. I didn't really have time to learn it [...]
>
> (Sarah B)

Time is a critical criterion when making decisions, because answers to questions such as 'how much time will I have to commit to learning to use this technology?' and 'can I afford to divert this time away from studying?' might override answers to questions such as 'is it the right or appropriate technology to use?' or 'does it work?' The approaches to decision making identified here and the complexity of factors that influence these decisions suggest that disabled students are capable of the kind of 'strategic fluency' identified by Parker and Banerjee (2007) as important for disabled students. Whether such fluency guarantees successful learning outcomes, needs to be explored in more detail, however.

In the next section, Nick will share his experiences of using technology to support his university studies. Nick outlines how using technology at university was an absolute necessity for him. Although he describes himself as a competent or agile user of technologies at university, the decisions he made about when and how he used technology were influenced by a range of factors.

## From a Student's Perspective: Nick

During my studies at Southampton, I gained a first-class honours degree in modern history and politics. I have recently completed a postgraduate diploma in journalism studies at Cardiff University.

Throughout life, computers have been hugely important tools for me. My disability, cerebral palsy, means that I use a wheelchair full-time and have particularly limited mobility in my limbs. I do not have the dexterity to write by hand. So I have used a computer in learning environments and at home since I can remember.

At university, I could access a huge amount of electronic learning material, including lecture handouts and vast databases of journal articles. I was also introduced to a number of assistive technologies, such as voice dictation software, which I had never known about at school. Without these new resources, I do not think it would have been physically possible to continue in higher education. The volume of work that degree students must complete means it is particularly crucial that learning is easily accessible to all.

The electronic learning offered at university was a big change from school days. Back then, while we had a few textbooks, most learning materials were paper sheets: worksheets, photocopied pieces from books or newspapers etc. When trying to study from this mountain of material, it was impossible to simply flip through the pages. Indeed, my lack of dexterity meant that most of them ended up on the floor.

### How Technology Helped Me in My Learning

At university, I was still given a forest of paper to read. But my tutors also used an additional approach, which bypassed the need for hard learning materials. My tutors posted electronic files on a university portal, Blackboard. They also pointed us towards useful information on the web.

Electronic learning was just so much easier. The accessibility of the material meant that I could turn pages instantly, and I could highlight or bookmark parts that I need. My learning was revolutionised.

Moreover, at university, I could combat the deluge of inaccessible material. Any sheets that were given out in a lecture were often produced on a computer. So, I could use a scanner to make the information electronic – converting it into editable electronic text.

Learning from books had been a struggle at school. It was impossible to type notes from books while holding the volume open. I simply hoped that I retained enough information to jot down a few key points at the end – a strategy that would have proven completely inadequate at degree level. During my undergraduate course, I learnt to take notes from books using voice dictation software; I talked into my computer as I read the book. Again, at university I was afforded a solution that was previously unknown to me. With so many books on my shelf, voice dictation has proven to be a critical asset.

Nowadays, I rely on using a second computer monitor. It is essential for displaying notes and plans while writing assignments. No longer is an article or essay plan cluttering up my laptop screen, or clumsily strewn over a bookstand. It can be clearly set out in front of me on another monitor.

Prior to starting university, taking notes during lectures was a worry for me; I knew my typing would not be fast enough to keep pace with my lecturer. However, in higher education, a trained note taker is available, who types my notes in electronic format. I can also record the lecture, just in case I have any queries about the notes.

At university then, I had access to a lot of technologies that have enabled me to cope with the heavy demands of university study. These tools have proven vital. Electronic materials for learning are indispensable; a Word document has few logistical difficulties. Assistive technologies have been crucial aids in order to cope with the abundance of 'hard' materials. So, I could not manage at university without things like scanners and voice dictation software.

### Strategies and Decisions

During my studies, I have become a very flexible learner. In different circumstances, I will select different strategies. One day, I might choose to annotate a book using voice dictation. Another day, I might decide to scan relevant pages, so I have a copy of the original source. Choosing the most suitable strategy is not a clear-cut decision. It depends on the accessibility of each solution, the importance of the material I am using and the amount of time I have to spend on it. I need several methods of learning in order to manage effectively with the pressures of higher education.

However, at this point it has to be said that many of these strategies are far from ideal. For example, using voice dictation is often tricky. The accuracy of its interpretation is far from perfect, and it requires a lot of patience to get things right. Using a scanner to convert material into electronic text is also a lengthy, drawn out procedure.

I consider myself to be quite a proficient technology user. It is not due to a lack of competence that these processes take so much time, and it is certainly not due to lack of practice. It is mostly due to the sheer volume of hard materials that need to be turned into electronic format. This process is immensely wasteful, and eats into time when I could be working. I still have swathes of handouts and notes that were left unread, primarily because I did not have the time to feed them all through my scanner.

### Technology Use is a Necessity, Not a Preference

For me, use of technology is not just a preference; it is, far more often than not, a necessity. So it is frustrating that there is still a limited capability for students to learn electronically. In my opinion, educational institutions should not look upon increasing the accessibility of learning as a burden. It is not the student's disability that is the problem. It is the inaccessibility of a lot of learning material. Learning materials should, of course, be accessible to all.

In my opinion, as a student with considerable mobility and dexterity difficulties, I am a different type of learner to most others. I am far more reliant upon, and more willing to embrace, electronic learning materials. I hesitate to say that my traits apply to 'disabled learners' as a whole. There is such a broad range of disabilities that each student will have their own needs and preferences. However, I would still maintain that it is conceptually useful to distinguish between learners who have disabilities, and those who do not. Sometimes, a student's disability will mean there is a pressing need for them to use a different type of learning method than others. A blind student may be dependent on electronic learning materials and Braille; his able-bodied peers can simply read the original paper copy if they must. Among disabled students, alternative methods of study are often imperative.

### Conclusion

In this chapter we have used results from the LEXDIS project combined with Nick's personal experiences to present what we consider to be a more rounded picture of disabled learners' experiences of technology in post compulsory education. This picture has revealed aspects of students' experiences that challenge us to listen to, think and respond in different ways. In particular we are challenged to think through the implications for online provision of materials and the support available to use these materials. Some specific recommendations for future practice include:

1. Increase the level of provision for online materials: Despite the fact that many disabled students comment on issues of accessibility and ease of use of some of the online materials, this method of sharing resources is vital for those who cannot handle paper based materials easily. Scanning and using optical character recognition to cope with paper based materials takes time and the results are not always sufficiently accurate for easy reading with text to speech or Braille translation.

2. Raise awareness and understanding regarding accessibility issues, particularly within virtual learning environments: Offering teaching staff the ability to adapt the virtual learning environment (typically, Blackboard) to their own personal specifications may be causing navigational concerns for students who have to spend longer on task to find items and work within the various different VLE courses they are required to use, due to differences and inconsistencies in structure and organisation across courses.

3. Increase the level of awareness for the use of alternative formats: There remains a lack of awareness regarding the impact that inaccessible teaching and learning resources can have on disabled students. Even the most basic PDFs and PowerPoints can cause problems if they cannot be read on the screen with speech output or accessed via the keyboard. This does not mean that innovative teaching materials using interactive online applications should be avoided but rather that alternatives may need to be on offer that can provide a similar learning outcome.

4. Be prepared to recognise the digital literacy skills that many disabled students have: Build on these by providing more opportunities for improved learning outcomes through an increased choice of multimedia tools and resources. The LEXDIS online strategy database may provide a useful insight into possible options (http://www.lexdis.org/). The database is searchable using short descriptions of the type of difficulties that may arise in an e-learning situation. The results of the search reveal a range of strategies (many of which involve alternative technologies) that disabled students have used to deal with or avoid the difficulty.

5. Design and develop learning opportunities and support systems that recognise the significant factors that influence disabled students' use of technology, particularly time: Many disabled learners cite 'TIME' as a real issue that influences their decisions about whether to use technology and whether to seek support to use technology. Therefore, 'just-in-time' learning seems one of the most appreciated types of support.

# References

Burgstahler, S. (2002). Distance learning: the library's role in ensuring access to everyone. Library Hi Tech, 20(4), 420–432.

Castells, M. (2001). The Internet galaxy: reflections on the Internet, business and society. Oxford: Oxford University Press.

Cobham E., Coupe, C., Broadbent, E. & Broadbent, S. (2001). Evaluation of the process of identifying the provision of assistive technology, study strategies and support for students with disabilities in higher education and the value of this intervention on their education and their lives. The Skill Journal, 69: 4–11.

Creanor, L., Trinder, K., Gowan, D. & Howells, C. (2006). LEX: the learner experience of e-learning. Final report (report under the JISC e-pedagogy 'Understanding my learner' programme). Glasgow: Glasgow Caledonian University. Retrieved 20 August, 2009, from http://www.jisc.ac.uk/whatwedo/programmes/elearning_pedagogy/elp_learneroutcomes.aspx.

Draffan, E.A., Evans, D.G. & Blenkhorn, P. (2007). Use of assistive technology by students with dyslexia in post-secondary education. Disability and Rehabilitation: Assistive Technology, 2(2): 105–116.

Fidler, R. (2002). An evaluation of the use of specialist support services by dyslexic students at a higher education institution. Retrieved 20 April, 2006, from http://www.roehampton.ac.uk/dyslexia/skilljournalarticle.doc.

Fuller, M., Healey, M., Bradley, A. & Hall, T. (2004). Barriers to learning: a systematic study of the experience of disabled students in one university. Studies in Higher Education, 29(3): 303–318.

Goode, J. (2007). 'Managing' disability: early experiences of university students with disabilities. Disability & Society, 22(1): 35–48.

Mortimore, T. & Crozier, W.R. (2006). Dyslexia and difficulties with study skills in higher education. Studies in Higher Education, 31(2): 235–251.

Newland, B., Pavey, J. & Boyd, V. (2004). Disabled students and VLES. Accessibility issues in learning environments and research technologies project. Retrieved 15 July, 2009, from http://www.bournemouth.ac.uk/alert/guidelines/word/alert_allVLEguidelines.doc.

Oblinger, D. (2003). Boomers, Gen-Xers and Millennials: understanding the new students. Educause Review, July/August: 37–45.

Parker, D.R. & Banerjee, M. (2007). Leveling the digital playing field. Assessment for Effective Intervention, 33(1): 5–14.

Seale, J.K. (2006). E-learning and disability in higher education: accessibility research and practice. Oxford: Routledge.

Seale, J., Draffan, E.A. & Wald, M. (2008a). An evaluation of the use of participatory methods in exploring disabled learners' experiences of e-learning. LEXDIS methodology report to JISC. Retrieved 15 July, 2009, from http://www.lexdis.ecs.soton.ac.uk/project/reports.

Seale, J., Draffan, E.A. & Wald, M. (2008b). Exploring disabled learners' experiences of learning, LEXDIS final report to JISC. Retrieved 15 July, 2009, from http://www.lexdis.ecs.soton.ac.uk/project/media/LEXDIS_ProjectReport_Dec08final.doc.

Selwyn, N. (2006). Digital division or digital decision? A study of non-users and low-users of computers. Poetics: Journal of Empirical Research in Culture, Media and the Arts, 34(4–5), 273–292.

Selwyn, N. & Facer, K. (2007). Beyond the digital divide: rethinking digital inclusion for the 21st century. Retrieved 15 July, 2009, from http://www.futurelab.org.uk/resources/documents/opening_education/Digital_Divide.pdf.

Shevlin, M., Kenny, M. & Mcneela, E. (2004). Participation in higher education for students with disabilities: an Irish perspective. Disability & Society, 19(1), 15–30.

Warschauer, M., Knobel, M. & Stone, L. (2004). Technology and equity in schooling: deconstructing the digital divide. Educational Policy, 18(4): 562–588.

# 10
## Strengthening and Weakening Boundaries
*Students Negotiating Technology Mediated Learning*

LAURA CZERNIEWICZ AND CHERYL BROWN

### Editors' Introduction

We have seen that it is often differences and contradictions in research findings that challenge us to devise explanatory frameworks. The previous chapters in this part show how such differences might be explained by the influences of learner development, context and individual differences. Once again, we have chosen to highlight work that demonstrates a rigorous approach to exploring these problems. In this chapter the authors use the Bernsteinian framework of boundaries to help them interpret data from six years of survey-based research. They demonstrate how to use this combination of empirical research and a theoretical lens to explore complex issues including: boundaries between, in and out of the curriculum; social and academic uses of technology; and physical and virtual learning environments. Finally, they challenge us to use these findings to consider the new literacies and practices that learners are beginning to need, and which are explored in Part 3.

### Introduction

Current representations of student learning experiences within a technology mediated world are premised in the media, the literature and the blogosphere on notions of change – indeed of transformation, pertaining to modernist notions of development and improvement. Generally, the discourse of students' technology mediated learning experiences is of a 'greater good' with the concomitant discourse of change representing technology mediated change as a desired and desirable end. There is a dangerous slippage between these well-intentioned aspirations and a kind of single-minded evangelism, which quietly ignores the contradictions emerging from both empirically based research investigations and reported reflective practice. These kinds of blinkered views do not assist the aims of all those who seek to harness the affordances of technology in support of student learning.

Fortunately, there are also emergent contradictions and paradoxes being acknowledged and explored in the literature (see, for example, Traxler 2009). This chapter presents the findings of a South African study of students' ICT-mediated learning, and offers a framework for describing and exploring the contradictions and paradoxes that were observed. This provides a way of capturing ambiguities and allows for two seemingly opposite trends to be occurring concurrently.

## The Research and Its Framework

The observations in this chapter are based on six years of multi-phased research into more than 10 000 university students' access to and use of information and communication technology (ICT). The project has different dimensions: a survey of 6577 students conducted in 2004 amongst six universities in one South African region and a second survey in 2007 of 3533 students among six universities in four other regions. A mixed-method approach was adopted including a quantitative analysis of the fifty-eight question survey, and a qualitative analysis of the questionnaire's open-ended questions and eighteen related student interviews. In addition, a 2008 survey of 4226 users of the learning management system (LMS) was undertaken at our own institution and, in 2009, 466 students from four other universities were also surveyed. These surveys have formed the basis of a nested approach, leading to telephone interviews and focus groups being undertaken at the time of writing.

At the outset of the project, we sought to set the scope and delineate the parameters of the investigation tightly. Thus we set out to focus on a pedagogy of formal learning in a defined curriculum; defined learning spaces (i.e. on campus and off campus, virtual and physical); students' academic activities rather than their social ones; and access to resources (including physical, personal and contextual resources).

Reflecting on the work to date, we realised that these assumptions were at times confirmed, although sometimes in surprising ways. At the same time, the assumptions were also challenged, as the findings turned out to be more fuzzy than we had anticipated. Thus we focused our attention on the respective categories delineated by our assumptions and to issues of distinctiveness, permeability, porousness and inconsistency. In the light of these considerations, we found Bernstein's work useful for framing the discussion; his work provides an orienting framework. Thus, we use the term boundaries in the Bernsteinian sense of the relationship or border between two different categories or contexts. For Bernstein a stronger boundary is tightly closed and non-porous – difficult to cross. A weaker boundary is more permeable. What is compelling about the Bernsteinian notion of a boundary is that it is not a polarised representation, rather boundary strength is relative. Boundary strength (or weakness) is conceptualised along a continuum rather than as a binary.

The starting point is that 'there is always a boundary. It may vary in its explicitness, its visibility, its potential and the manner of its transmission and acquisition. It may vary in terms of whose interest is promoted or privileged by the boundary' (Bernstein and Soloman 1999: 273).

The Bernsteinian framework also provides a way of describing the what and who of pedagogy, through the concepts of classification and framing. Classification describes relations between and the degree of maintenance between categories, including the boundaries between agents, spaces and discourses (the 'what' and 'who' of pedagogy). Classification refers to the degree of strength between contexts or categories, and is expressed as being stronger, where boundaries are explicit and categories are insulated from one another, or weaker, where there is integration, or where the boundary is weak or blurred. Framing refers to the strength of control 'from above' within those contexts or categories. It therefore provides a way of describing the 'how' of pedagogy.

This chapter approaches ICT-mediated student experiences through the lens of boundaries and shows how boundaries are being strengthened, weakened or reconstituted. Boundaries, as explained, are delineators of categories and contexts. The form and strength of those boundaries are inevitably associated with power, although 'strong' does not connote 'good' nor does 'weak' connote 'bad'. The power relations intertwined with boundaries are often complex and subtle.

In the sections following, we draw on our findings to show in which instances boundaries are strengthening and when they are weakening, bearing in mind that there are contexts where examples of both may exist.

## Strengthening Boundaries

The first dimension where boundaries are strengthening is that of the digital divide, or indeed a digital chasm, as broadband exacerbates existing divides and introduces new ones (Brown and Czerniewicz 2009). On campus/off campus divides and social class distinctions are deepened by class-based personal access in private homes. Issues of access are pertinent to student experiences because they shape what is possible (Czerniewicz and Brown 2005).

The second dimension where boundaries are being strengthened by ICTs is in pedagogical relationships; pedagogy being the interaction of student, teacher and curriculum content (Yates 2009). A central delineation is the strength of the boundary of lecturer–student pedagogic identities, i.e. the relation between the agents. It is this boundary that is claimed to be weakened in such mantras as 'the guide on the side', born of the claim that the introduction of ICTs is shifting teacher–student power relations.

However, in our work we have observed that students' experiences continue to be largely shaped by teachers and institutions. Teachers set the formal curriculum and determine both the times and places where and when teaching takes place; they still determine assessment tasks and assessment criteria. Institutions have generally not changed their assessment criteria to align them with emergent ICT-based pedagogical practices. Indeed in pedagogical terms, ICTs are being used to strengthen existing boundaries and support existing power relations. Thus there are examples of ICTs being used to cement long-standing pedagogical roles rather than challenge them. Students welcome the presentation of content in class and comment for example, 'I enjoy it if lecturers use PowerPoint in class' [S2-J-295] and are grateful when material (including answers) are provided online, as in '[I like] answers for classwork that lecturers put on [LMS name] & e-mails they send us to keep us updated & for old exam papers' [S2-J-295].

These and other comments are positive in tone, suggesting that the use of technology to support traditional transmission modes is considered useful by students. Interestingly, very few students talk about using ICTs as a reason not to participate in lectures. In fact, the students we studied strongly value the face-to-face interaction of lectures and see ICTs as playing a supportive rather than replacement role despite many lecturers' concerns to the contrary. This comment is typical, 'I would be strongly averse to using [LMS name] exclusively because I think face-to-face interaction is very important in a learning environment' [S3-A-2564].

We have not observed instances of boundaries weakening in terms of pedagogical relations; indeed the relations between teachers and students appear to be as they ever were, with ICTs mainly being used to strengthen or replicate traditional teaching activities. Our research has provided no indication of educators changing their roles thanks to the introduction of technologies, indeed no sign of the student–teacher power relationship being challenged at all.

The third dimension where we observed strong boundaries remaining intact is between social and academic activities. This contrasts with commentary from elsewhere (for example Riddle and Howell 2008) that students in a digitally mediated world interweave their various activities as part of everyday life. It is often argued that students move between the academic and non-academic or social aspects of their lives and that they undertake them simultaneously and seamlessly.

In our study we observed that the boundaries between the social software and the academic learning management systems remain strong. We found that the uptake of social software in South African higher education is low:

71 per cent of students hardly ever publish their own online content and 42 per cent hardly ever upload resources to the Internet. In relation to learning, 71 per cent of students hardly ever keep course-related blogs and 60 per cent hardly ever share course resources online. Such findings underline that the 'knowledge power' remains with the teachers.

What is especially important is that these strong boundaries between academic and social tools appear to be as a result of students' preferences and choice. Some students consider the two to have different purposes and strengths, as in 'I consider [our LMS] to be an academic resource. Other social networking sites are better suited to non-course activities' [S3-A-1273] and '[our LMS] is not for non-course activities – it frustrates me when people use the chat room like MSN or Facebook. It is strictly to do with varsity work' [S3-A-3975]. Students are also conscious of the problems of time wasting in merging the two, as in '... if I started to use MXIT [cell phone chat], I would just Mix all day and all night. So I don't want to go in there, into that habit ' [I1-F-1].

These examples of contexts where boundaries remain strong (or are becoming relatively stronger) suggest that in many ways higher education may not be being disrupted by ICTs quite as much as is imagined (or feared).

**Weakening Boundaries**

At the same time, there are dimensions of the student experience where boundaries are weakening and existing power relations do appear to be being disturbed. The first instance is in aspects of the curriculum whereby course content is always scaffolded, adjusted, selected and ordered. While it has always been possible for students to access resources outside the curriculum and to read ahead for example, widening access to ICTs, especially through the web but also through online databases, means that curriculum boundaries are changing. This is the first dimension where we see boundaries weakening; in the past, 'in the curriculum' and 'out of the curriculum' were clear concepts – now the boundaries between what is 'in' and what is 'out' of the curriculum are becoming porous in various ways, because of ICTs.

The most obvious challenge to the traditional curriculum and to local control of content is with regard to preselected content that has traditionally been in the hands of teachers. Students are able to disregard content selected by others and take control of content choice. This is experienced both positively and negatively. Positive experiences of this boundary weakening means that the students' experiences can be enriched, especially advantageous when students have poor teachers. Thus a student from a previously disadvantaged South African university comments: 'But when you go to Internet, you'll find that ... maybe in Britain, maybe in Oxford University, they are doing the same stuff as you are doing. And you can get tutorial questions based on that ...'

[I1-F-6], and another says that she 'can get more information about certain projects that you can't get from lecturer, tutor etc.' [S2-G-11357].

At the same time, our findings draw attention to how overwhelmed students can feel. This question was not probed for specifically, yet a number of comments revealed how daunted the student can be. Thus,

> when I'm using an internet you know that's where I get some frustration. I only know some [of] the addresses, 3 of them you know while other people know more than I know and from there actually sometimes I don't get what I want from the internet.
>
> [I1-H-15]

and 'not all information is 100 per cent accurate – books are more reliable, I think' [S2-H-1807], and

> I feel a lot better when I actually went out and found books for research. For instance ... going on line... you have to find the right site and once you do find the right site your information might not be all there so personally I feel that I do a lot better without computers.
>
> [I1-I-21]

In addition to these examples, which point to shifts in content selection, ICTs have seen boundary weakening with regards to pacing. This occurs when course notes and presentations are provided ahead of time. While a version of this was previously possible, the increased ease of access may provide students with increased confidence and sense of status, as in 'The use of sites like Dti and the news at SABC 3 and labour.net.com, help me keep ahead on my studies. I am able to read ahead, and sometimes challenge my lecturers on subject matters that I read about' [S2-G-3093].

These weak boundaries allow students to prepare better for classes, as in 'the great thing about it is getting your notes before class and preparing beforehand' [S2-H-1388], and to review work presented in lectures at their own pace later, as in 'Use of ICTs helps in understanding things that one did not get in the lecture, through revisiting PowerPoint slides presented in class' [S2-F-1010]. They are also given opportunities to keep up when traditional avenues fail: 'So they say they're going to give us textbooks. But they didn't ... we only got it after June. So we rely on Internet to get that book ... we were just like on the Internet the whole semester' [I1-F-7].

In addition, even in contexts where webcasting is not the norm, students can record and share lectures, making it possible to hear the exact lecture at a later stage and weaken the temporal strength of content presentation. 'He explains so fast. So I just record sometimes when I feel that I'm tired ... my brain cannot concentrate anymore, and if they [other students] want, they sometimes come to get it' [I2-H-3].

Learning environments have been previously understood to be static, stable and location specific. Thus lectures take place in lecture halls, seminars in smaller rooms on campus and homework or independent work in the library or off campus. Virtual environments are relatively recent, and even more recent is the wireless access that makes it possible for them to be accessed in formal learning locations. How does this play out? ICTs are weakening the boundaries of learning environments in ways in that learning becomes less location specific, as noted by 'ICTs makes it easier, your work is more mobile. Work is not restricted to university or home' [S2-I-2914] and '[I like] easy access to information, abundance of advice and choice of sources, mobility of access' [S2-I-2680].

Wireless hot spots are not yet the norm in South African universities but cell phone ownership and access is ubiquitous, profoundly changing the student ICT-mediated experience in terms of access, connectivity, learning environment, presence, temporality and locatedness. Thus boundaries are being weakened to the point of being reconstituted. Learning spaces especially are being reconstituted as students use cell phones for access and use in unanticipated ways. Thus access is being determined by connectivity not by location. These experiences are increasingly common. 'You can access it [the LMS] anywhere even from your cell phone' [S3-A-3490] and 'You can use your phone via google. Maybe I don't have time for a computer. Or maybe it's late, and the assignment must be submitted. Then I use my phone' [I1-F-5]. Such experiences challenge the authoritarianism of time and space.

At the same time as our earlier observations, it must be noted that boundary weakening is also to be observed in terms of tools, and the purposes for which they were intended or designed. It is significant that while this does occur, only a small percentage of students report that they use social software such as Facebook and Flickr for academic purposes (3 per cent – 133 students and 4 per cent – 176 students respectively). Some suggestions as to why are evident in the qualitative responses. This may be because it is an easy avenue that students can control as in 'The lecturers don't extensively use [the LMS], so the students also use other forum such as Facebook and SMSs' [S3-A-3374] or that these tools offer global opportunities for learning as in 'I belong to a virtual community – where participants from around the globe have discussions and virtual conferences related to human rights' [S3-A-5812].

However, it appears that the boundary weakening is more pronounced in terms of how learning management systems are adapted for non-course related purposes rather than how social software is appropriated for academic purposes.

It is interesting that while most students prefer strong demarcations between social and academic activities and tools, there are a vociferous few who would prefer weaker boundaries in the form of increased integration, and say that they 'wish we had a university calendar including all social, activism, seminar, etc. events' [S3-A-2100] and 'It [the LMS] needs more social network features (Twitter-like status updates at the very least) so that one can develop an online academic community rather than the highly restrictive per-course communities at present' [S3-A-2403]. We need to know whether students indeed wish to break down the barriers between social and academic activities, or whether they merely wish to have more resources to enable social activities amongst the student community, effectively sustaining strong boundaries between the social and the academic. It is also important to find out who these students are, and whether they have shared characteristics that might explain their views.

Unexpectedly, although the learning management system is designed to support course-related activities, it has also been appropriated by students who use it for student activism and social responsiveness projects. Thus,

> Being a member of the Green Campus Initiative I have found [the LMS] extremely useful and very helpful in furthering our cause. The GCI [LMS] site is our primary means of communication and publicity to the student body. [The LMS] participation in Green Week was also extremely important
>
> [S3-A-2188]

And finally, while the majority of students show no indications of widespread ICT-enabled multitasking, a few do indeed provide examples of multitasking, an obvious example of boundary weakening where affordances of technology enable easy movement between online activities. Thus students talk socially and share work in chat rooms, and work and study almost simultaneously online:

> maybe you are chatting with someone in [nearest town] and you are asking them what life is like...and [at the same time] you can send them your assignment, and they can send it back. ...and you check it while you're chatting. And then you can re-do some things and send it back.

Also,

> because if you don't know anything, you can just go search, and you can type back to your assignment. As you are doing your assignment... it's encouraging. Because you can do something recreational on the computer to refresh your mind, and then go back to your work.
>
> [I1-F-7]

ICTs can make these types of activities seamless and can also occur in and across a range of teaching and learning spaces.

As observed here, boundaries are weakening in specific ways at the level of student experience. Such instances occur in very specific contexts; higher education culture is generally rigid and hierarchical. Thus, any weakening of boundaries at the level of each individual student is also bound to have some effect on power relations in the aggregate. Boundary weakening is therefore intrinsically caught up with the power dimensions of institutional culture.

## Discussion

The journey that students travel in higher education has always been challenging and confusing and technologies have always been one element of their travels. That there is a profound digital technological disruption in society occurring presently is not in dispute. What is not clear is how this is manifested in student experiences coming into and studying in higher education institutions. Academics inducting students into disciplines and into academic discourses have to (amongst other things) be mindful of the influences and mediating roles of ICTs and new social practices. Making sense of student experiences is not helped by grand claims, by easy generalisations or by homogenising presentations of student identities. It is also not helped by representations of academics as teachers who are somehow stingy with their knowledge or power hungry in relation to student learning.

The concept of boundaries provides one way of thinking about where and how the experiences of students we studied are shifting; it has provided a way of reflecting on our observations and of mapping where and how shifts are, or are not, occurring. We have seen that there are some clear trends (somewhat unanticipated), that there are simultaneous realities and that there are emerging and conflicting practices. We have observed boundary strengthening propping up both entrenched and new roles, and we have seen boundaries weakening in ways that both enhance and threaten, democratise and close down.

It is demanding to track how these shifts are occurring, and several notes of caution must be sounded. It is important to research and report what is actually happening and not to generalise beyond the observed cases. New technologies indeed have the potential to enable all sorts of new practices but these may be transient and changes may not percolate through deeply entrenched institutional cultures. It is important to report accurately exactly how much and how often these shifts are happening. There are instances where different practices are observed in small or occasional numbers, and receive a disproportionate amount of attention simply because they are unusual or interesting. These observations are too often generalised to a broader population. It is only a very small group of our students who are online producers, for example. The rest are sustaining existing demarcations. Rather than making claims about all students, it would be more useful to consider which students are behaving differently, in which conditions and why.

Evolving changes, weakening boundaries and unusual new practices are fascinating precisely because they are new and unexpected, and not surprisingly researchers are drawn to them. But they are not automatic harbingers of profound change to either student experience or to higher education itself. Sometimes, what appear to be new trends are fleeting and disappear. Oftentimes changes occur in specific conditions and configurations, for example in a specific disciplinary context.

It is important to be careful about what boundary shifts mean and what they imply. Quite often these shifts mean that existing activities continue to exist, fundamentally unchanged as activities, but through new routes or media. Thus, access to more information, as described above, may simply mean that there is more information available. This may not always be construed by students as a 'good thing', or even easy or helpful and it may introduce new problems, as is often noticed by those who write about the necessity for critical literacies alongside information literacies. Access to more information does not automatically challenge power relations within formal education, although in certain instances it might. As long as academics select and assess students on the curriculum content of their choosing, all the information in the world that students may have access to is not necessarily altering the prevailing power relations in higher education classrooms.

Of course, the weakening of boundaries may well suggest long-term changes. But boundaries weaken in different ways and in different constellations, and it is not possible to tell as the porousness increases, where cave-ins might occur; where genuine remediation is happening and where there will be complete reconfigurations. Weakening boundaries is not in itself a sign of authority being challenged. It may be a new form of authority. In addition, weakened boundaries suit students from some social backgrounds and not others, and are useful in certain conditions and not in others.

Boundaries can be constraints in the sense of being barriers or they can be opportunities in the sense that what is on the edge may lead to something new and valuable. Whichever meaning boundaries have, students, more than ever, will require the information and technological literacies to effectively engage with them, and the critical literacies to understand what they might retract and what they might offer.

### Acknowledgements

With grateful thanks for thoughtful feedback and stimulating conversations with Karl Maton (University of Sydney), Teresa Barnes (University of Illinois) and Kevin Williams (University of Cape Town).

## References

Bernstein, B. & Soloman, J. (1999). Pedagogy, identity and the construction of a theory of symbolic control: Basil Bernstein questioned by Joseph Soloman. *British Journal of Sociology of Education, 20*(2), 265–278.

Brown, C. & Czerniewicz, L. (2009, May). *The mobile Net Generation: beyond digital apartheid.* Paper presented at The Net Generation Symposium, Open University, Milton Keynes.

Czerniewicz, L. & Brown, C. (2005). Access to ICTs for teaching and learning – from single artefact to inter-related resources. *International Journal of Education and Development using Information and Communication Technologies, 1*(2), 42–56.

Riddle, M. & Howell, C. (2008). *You are here: students map their own ICT landscapes.* In Hello! Where are you in the landscape of educational technology? Paper presented at Ascilite, Melbourne, 2008.

Traxler, J. (2009, September). *Students and mobile devices: choosing which dream.* Paper presented at Association for Learning Technology Conference 2009, In dreams begins responsibility – choice, evidence and change, Manchester, UK.

Yates, L. (2009). From curriculum to pedagogy and back again: knowledge, the person and the changing world. *Pedagogy, Culture & Society, 17*(1), 17–28.

# Part III
## New Learning Practices

# 11
## The Changing Practices of Knowledge and Learning

### HELEN BEETHAM AND MARTIN OLIVER

### Editors' Introduction

This chapter opens the third and final part, which is concerned with new learning practices. Here Beetham and Oliver critically examine the claims that today's learners demonstrate a whole new set of learning practices. Rather, they conduct a review of how the context is changing for learners and what 'digital literacies' they will need to develop as a result. Beetham and Oliver confirm the powerful influence of the course and its tutors on the development of literacies and make recommendations about how educators should respond to these challenges.

### Introduction: From Information Skills to Digital Literacy

Use of the term 'digital literacy' to describe how effective learners work with information and knowledge – not limited to textual representations – is growing in currency (e.g. Martin and Grudziecki 2007; Lea 2009). In the UK, 'information literacy', 'media literacy', and 'digital literacy', are all central to government strategies for the future of the economy and citizenship (Department for Culture, Media and Sport & Department for Business, Innovation and Skills 2009), while the recent European Commission (EC) *Digital literacy* review calls explicitly for a shift of attention away from technical skills and towards concepts of literacy, criticality and judgement (EC 2009: 24–25).

Before considering what it means to apply the term 'literacy' to *digital* practices and capabilities, it is interesting to consider how the term 'literacy' itself stands in contrast to other terms such as 'skill' or 'competence'. Literacy can be said to involve:

- a *foundational* capability on which more specific skills depend;
- a cultural *entitlement* without which a learner is impoverished in relation to culturally valued knowledge;
- *representation,* involving culturally significant communications in a variety of media;
- *interpretation:* though based on public/shared forms, literacies involve these forms being internalised and made available for personal use;
- the need for *practice:* literacies are acquired through continuous development and refinement in different contexts;
- *socially and culturally situated* practices, often highly dependent on the context in which they are carried out, and on the actions and reactions of others;
- *self-transformation:* literacies (and their lack) have a lifelong, life-wide impact.

Literacies are developed personally – as in 'learning to read' – but also have a collective or social trajectory. As technologies of representation change, for example, new forms of collective knowledge practice such as texting or commenting on blog entries appear, and in turn support new personal strategies for sharing and making meanings.

To understand literacy as socially situated is not simply to suggest that learning with others is important to individual development, though this is undoubtedly the case. It is to insist that knowledge practice is social *before* it is personal, and that the most private habits of mind depend on shared tools and collective values. From this it should be clear that different meanings and values can be attached to 'the same' technologies and technical skills. This is one reason why researching knowledge practice from the learner perspective is so important. Learners arriving at college and university must occupy (at least) two knowledge cultures – the informal practices of their family and peer group, and the formal expectations of their academic school or institution – and both are changing rapidly under the influence of digital technologies.

Information literacy, defined as '[the ability] to recognize when information is needed and have the ability to locate, evaluate, and use effectively the needed information' (Spitzer et al. 1998; CILIP 2005) is the most widely recognised and defined of the capacities that learners require in the digital age. To date, however, the focus has largely been on individual discovery, analysis and application of information in the context of a specific task or problem. While these remain essential skills, they are no longer adequate for societies and cultures in which digital information is pervasive. For example, a recent review of the literature on literacies of the digital (Beetham et al. 2009), found the following terms being used implicitly or explicitly to move the terms of debate beyond the informational.

- *Multimodality*: Representations are now more commonly accessed via the screen than the page, and all media have the potential to be digitised, with profound implications for how we 'read' and access information (Kress and Bezemer 2009).
- *(Multi)media literacy*: Technical changes to the nature of media, including computer gaming, entail shifts in education towards a multimedia knowledge practice in which ideas of representation, production and audience are important (Buckingham 2007; see also Ryberg and Dirckinck-Holmfeld, Chapter 12).
- *Hypermedia, metamedia literacy*: A completely new capacity for meaning-making is called for when representations become multiply linked and layered (Landow 2006).
- *Sharing and collaboration*: Web 2.0 technologies, with their focus on collaborative knowledge building, shared assets, and conversation-as-knowledge-making, evince a breakdown of the distinction between knowledge and communication (Glister 2006). The recent launch of GoogleWave ('both a conversation and a document': http://wave.google.com/help/wave/about.html) is particularly interesting in this respect.
- *Connectivism*: Individual processing of information is giving way to the development of networks of trusted people, who share content and tools: the task of knowing is 'offloaded onto the network itself' (Siemens 2005).
- *Critical 'technoliteracies'*: The idea that learners can move beyond technical competence to take a critical stance towards the tools they are offered for knowledge-making is implicit in the development pyramid (Sharpe and Beetham, Chapter 6), and widely explored by writers in the critical education tradition (Kahn and Kellner 2005).
- *Ethical and political awareness*: Partly influenced by campaigns to protect children from danger online, and partly in reaction to them, there is an awareness across sectors of the need to help learners deal with personal and environmental risk in an information environment where private and public are being redefined (Facer and Green 2007).

Digital literacy, then, is a complex but highly relevant term for exploring learners' experiences of learning, and the directions in which learning may evolve in the near future. The JISC Learning Literacies for a Digital Age (LLiDA) project (Beetham et al. 2009) defined digital literacy as 'practices of effective learning' in contexts dominated by digital forms of information. In the following section, we explore the broad social and technical changes that are taking place in information and knowledge practice, and the new practices that are being demanded of learners as a result. In the third section, we collate evidence about the real, informal, social and personal practices of learners. Finally, we ask how colleges and universities should respond to these two challenges, and ask in what ways learners' informal knowledge practices are the basis of a new literacy for lifelong learning, and in what ways there are significant tensions between 'Web 2.0' knowledge practices and the demands of academic study.

## The Changing Context

We already inhabit technical, social, economic, cultural and educational contexts in which digital forms of information predominate. It makes sense to ask how learning provision should adapt to fit graduates for living and working in such contexts.

The nature of work is changing, not just for the growing numbers of graduates directly employed in the 'digital' industries (estimated at 1,500,000 in the UK) but for the 77 per cent of jobs (again this is a UK figure) that involve some form of ICT competence (eSkills UK 2008). Global digital networks are also having a profound impact on how organisations recruit the expertise they need. A recent report on *Education, Globalisation and the Knowledge Economy* (Brown et al. 2008) notes that British graduates are competing for highly skilled, high-value jobs on a global stage, in which graduates from emerging economies have several advantages. Along with the globalisation of knowledge work, this report identifies 'digital taylorism' or the trend towards division of labour in the service and intellectual industries, dissecting coherent professional roles into discrete projects or even tasks. In this paradigm, the high-level knowledge skills of synthesis and judgement, and 'permission to think', are reserved for a small percentage of the workforce. Middle class labour of all kinds is also becoming less secure as digital networks make it easier for tasks to be contracted out on a piecemeal basis, loosening the ties between employers and individual professionals. There is a greater requirement for workers to be independent, self-motivated and self-evaluating, as well as a tendency for individuals to move jobs and careers more frequently and to be in fixed-term or flexible contracts (Hellgren et al. 2008). Learning for life is no longer a policy buzzword but a requirement for individual economic well-being.

The texture of social life is also changing, with more and more people conducting and sustaining relationships via digital media. Many social interactions, from buying and selling to voting and registering for health care, are routinely conducted online. In its recent paper on 'Digital Britain' (Department for Culture, Media and Sport & Department for Business, Innovation and Skills 2009) the UK Government expresses an active intention to enhance this trend, and lists 'media literacies and IT skills' second only after access to the internet as a requirement for building a society of 'empowered and informed consumers and citizens'. Of course national boundaries are in some senses eroded by the new technologies, as individuals affiliate to distributed global communities (e.g. religious communities, country-of-origin communities, shared interest groups) in preference to geographically localised ones. But, to date at least, this trend is secondary to the use of participative technologies to enhance face-to-face relationships and engage more effectively in the locality.

As well as reconfiguring the nature of communities, and enabling new communities to emerge, connectivity means constant opportunities to participate in interactions with people not physically present (virtual presence), and to be attentionally absent from those who are (absent presence) (Kleinman 2004). Both opportunities affect how families and co-located groups of people interact with one another.

In both professional and personal spheres the nature of knowledge is changing, so that what counts as useful is increasingly biased towards what can be represented and manipulated in digital form. Many scientific and research enterprises now depend on data being shared in the almost instantaneous fashion enabled by the internet, while the sheer processing power available to researchers is ushering in new methods of investigation and, in places, whole new disciplines and genres of knowledge.

In a related fashion, communications and media are changing profoundly, with the new social media and gaming technologies being embraced by innovative educators (Martin and Madigan 2006; Lankshear and Knobel 2008), and simulations becoming widespread as tools for training and continuing professional development in subjects as diverse as catering, health and safety at work, medicine and law. In this space, the idea of multimodal literacy (Kress and Street 2006; Bezemer and Kress 2008), understood as a complex set of critical and social practices, has largely replaced the discourse of 'learning styles' (Honey and Mumford 1982; Kolb 1984), which tended to imply a fixed set of learner attributes. A critical engagement with ideas in different media, once an aspect of specialist courses such as media studies, is becoming understood as an essential skill for navigating the information age (Buckingham 2007).

Closely related to this last point, literacy practices themselves are changing. There are examples of cases where new literacy practices – such as gaming – have been used to support adults' development of basic and critical literacy skills (Kambouri et al. 2006). More fundamentally, though, writing has moved from a paper-based to a largely screen-based medium (Kress 2003), while texting – sometimes seen as a hybrid form between writing and transcribed speech – has arguably accelerated the casualisation of the written word. The vast availability of knowledge resources online, alongside tools for finding, repurposing, re-editing and re-presenting them, have profoundly changed the way in which writing is typically constructed (Cushman 2004), by professionals as well as by learners. Bricolage or 'patch writing' are terms for the practice of constructing new text around existing textual components (Bayne 2006). Graphical and video media are increasingly used to communicate high-value knowledge (Nicholas et al. 2008), so that the ability to decode images and moving images have become essential literacies for students across the disciplines. Audio technologies such as voice recognition, speech-to-text, podcasting and the ability to annotate audio files, are also undermining the central role of text. Why transcribe lecture notes or annotate an essay manually when an audio recording is just as portable – and almost as manipulable – as a text file?

Collective intelligence, amateurisation and pro-sumerism are terms that have been applied to the new ways knowledge is being constructed through social media. On sites such as Flickr, YouTube, SlideShare, blip.tv and GroundReport, professionally produced media artefacts rub shoulders with amateur uploads and with low-quality copies or fragments of themselves. Opinion and gossip circulate alongside professional news agency feeds and officially sanctioned government broadcasts, all equally available for reaggregation and repurposing by users. Facer and Selwyn (Chapter 2) have already discussed how the practices of social networking have repositioned users as co-producers of knowledge, with the emphasis on uploading, tagging, repurposing and redistribution rather than access and viewing. Other technologies supporting this paradigm shift are ubiquitous and easy-to-use recording devices – e.g. mobile phone cameras – alongside cheap or free editing tools, and Web 2.0 applications that allow users to build and enrich content together. Valued content is no longer (only) the creative production of a unique originator, or the painstaking outcome of established methods, the two stories that academic writing has always told about itself. Authorship and authority, evidence and hearsay, original and copy (and hence copy*right*), are complicated by the mashing and meshing of texts produced by others (Bayne 2006).

Finally, semantic technologies are accelerating an underlying trend for knowledge work to be distributed among human and non-human agents (search engines, data mining applications etc.) in complex networks of expertise (Cliff et al. 2009). If some of the more routine tasks of research, for example, can be carried out by intelligent search engines, human researchers can focus on developing higher level skills such as those involving critical evaluation and judgement. An important aspect of literacy becomes the capacity to work with expert, non-expert and non-human others, and to deal with hybrid knowledge.

In this rapidly changing context, it is increasingly difficult to specify the skills that learners will require even a few years into the future. At the same time as this uncertainty has beset the curriculum, the line between formal education and other kinds of learning and knowledge acquisition has become blurred. Online social networks and open content create vast new opportunities for individuals to learn outside of or alongside formal learning, challenging the unique role of educational institutions (Seely Brown and Adler 2008).

Institutions are responding to these challenges in different ways, for example by 'unbundling' previously integrated activities such as teaching, learner support, assessment, accreditation, research and development (Hine 2009), or by becoming 'edgeless' and so embracing the alternatives that threaten them (Bradwell 2009). What seems certain is that knowledge resources and opportunities to learn will continue to proliferate for those with the resources, technical access, competence and confidence to take advantage of them.

Even in educational contexts as currently defined there are profound changes in the ICT access and capabilities expected of learners. Institutional technologies are giving way to an expectation that learners will have personal access to networks and services, while virtual learning environments are being challenged by learner-configured spaces and personal learning environments (Wilson et al. 2007). In some respects these developments simply echo more general technology trends towards disaggregation and personalisation: complex, large-scale applications are making way for apps, widgets and services; trusted content sources are trumped by personal aggregators; and online articles or e-books are ignored in favour of blog entries and tweets as sources of up-to-date information. All these developments place much greater onus on learners to choose, use and manage their own technologies, develop their own practices and define their own trusted sources.

## Learners' Personal Knowledge Practices

If the changing context requires learners to demonstrate many new capacities, how (if at all) are they acquiring them? Many theorists see learners responding to the new technical and social opportunities with little help from the formal education system. Redecker (2009) describes how online social networking practices map onto theories of active learning in communities; Siemens (2005) finds evidence of connectivism and deep networking in learners' informal knowledge practices; Jenkins (2006) refers to participative practices as a new model for learning (see also Walker et al., Chapter 15); Ziegler (2007: 69, cited in Facer and Selwyn, Chapter 2) identifies social networking as having 'the capacity to radically change the educational system'. A recent UK project looked at the literacy practices of FE students' everyday lives, and concluded that these shared many features with Web 2.0 practices: multi-modality, shared forms, non-linearity, self-direction and creativity (Ivanic et al. 2007).

However, there is evidence that learners' social knowledge practices do not necessarily transfer to formal learning contexts in ways that support deep or lasting forms of learning (Cranmer 2006). There is also a growing body of research that is adding nuance to the 'Net Generation' discourse, and showing up some of the contradictions in the characterisation of young people as 'digital natives' (Luckin et al. 2009). Whilst new forms of media are clearly significant in shaping their thinking and knowledge practice, learners' engagement with digital media is complex and differentiated (Bennett et al. 2008; Hargittai 2009).

For example, studies in the UK funded by the JISC under its 'Learners experiences of e-learning' programme have confirmed that the internet is the primary source of information accessed by learners for the purposes of study (Creanor et al. 2006). However, detailed interviews with learners revealed many differences in approach, from sophisticated triangulation of internet references to a naïve faith in Google as a 'vast encyclopaedia'. We know that most learners read only the first page of results returned to them by a Google search, have little idea how to evaluate information for relevance, accuracy or authority (Williams and Rowlands 2007) and are generally uncritical about messages offered to them via online media (Ziegler 2007). The JISC programme confirmed other evidence that students – and their tutors – overestimate their ability to engage with information in a critical and literate manner (Kirkwood 2006).

The programme also confirmed that learners are powerfully influenced by their tutors and course requirements in choosing technologies for learning (Trinder et al. 2008; Bennett et al. 2008). Lea (2009), in a rich study of undergraduate literacy practices, also found that learners were organising their search for information around a narrow interpretation of course requirements, and especially assessment tasks. An associated finding from the JISC programme concerned learners' attitudes to risk in their digital practice. A small number of learners were 'agile' adopters of technology, exploring new applications and features, and personalising devices to suit their needs. Ryberg and Dirckinck-Holmfeld (Chapter 12) demonstrate what these agile or 'power' users of technology can teach educators about innovation. Yet we found – and other research consistently confirms – that these are a small minority of students (Hargittai and Walejko 2008).

While most students have encountered Web 2.0 technologies from a user perspective, knowledge co-creation such as contributing to wikis, tagging, sharing bookmarks, meme-ing and reviewing, and radically participative environments such as Second Life or GoogleWave, are options that most learners simply do not discover for themselves (Kennedy et al. 2007; Luckin et al. 2009). Learners are generally reluctant to engage in group learning activities unless they can see a clear benefit to their own outcomes. This should alert us to the fact that there are currents towards privatisation and consumerisation of knowledge in society, as well as towards openness and sharing. What is shared in social networks tends to relate to the personal: 'valued knowledge' tends not to be shared without induction into a specific community where purposes and values are also shared.

The JISC work did uncover a range of 'canny' approaches that characterise learners' strategic use of technology to help them meet the demands of study. These included various forms of informal collaboration, usually in spaces deliberately kept invisible to tutors and separate from academic spaces (Conole et al. 2007; see also Benfield and De Laat, Chapter 13 on learners' strategies for using technology 'around the task or under the radar'). 'Sharing the load' with other students was identified as a strategy partly of time management, as one or two members of a group would attend a lecture on everyone's behalf, and partly of shared reflection and analysis during the 'reporting back' process.

Students also reported repurposing of texts, both sourced from friends and accessed on the internet, though this strategy was often accompanied by anxiety about plagiarism. They had a range of media preferences for receiving information, with many positive experiences of using video and/or audio recordings that can be played back at a learners' own pace. This evidence, along with findings from a British Library study that 40 per cent of 16–19 year olds were accessing their resources through image searches (Nicholas et al. 2008), suggests that learners work with a wider range of knowledge media than the typical university or college course allows for.

Learners make choices about technology and media – indeed choice and consumption is a key frame through which they view the technology-mediated world. Alongside choice, ubiquity, accessibility, rapid feedback and ease of use are all features of learners' daily experience of technology, which they may transfer to expectations they have about knowledge and learning. However, there is little evidence of learners demanding more, or more radical, uses of technology in formal learning, and indeed some evidence in the opposite direction. A minority of 'digital refuseniks' are making wholesale choices to avoid the use of ICT for study, while other learners simply prefer paper for specific activities such as mind mapping or note taking (e.g. Hardy et al. 2009). This is borne out by a recent study of learners in schools, which found that children did not want their out-of-school use of technology to fundamentally alter the way that they engaged with information in school, even if computers could 'brighten' the experience for them (Sheehy and Bucknall 2008). The JISC studies also found a strong attachment to the 'reassurance' of academically approved sources of content, which again is confirmed by Lea's (2009) finding that the university and its curriculum were seen as the arbiter of authoritative knowledge.

To summarise, the jury is still out on whether there is a clear 'Google generation' effect in terms of knowledge practice: the picture is more complex than the buzzwords suggest. A JISC/British Library study found that researchers responded in similar ways to the online environment, regardless of their age and academic status (Nicholas et al. 2008), suggesting that digitally 'native' practices may be at least as contextual as they are generational. Our findings confirm that digital literacies are multiple, and personal, and that learners vary in complex ways.

One way of interpreting the findings about learners' facility with social technologies, and relative conservatism about the use of technologies in formal learning, is that they are straddling two different knowledge cultures. For example, we know that learners with experience of free content and open sharing sites can struggle with academic knowledge practices around originality, which manifests in 'accidental plagiarism' (Baggaley and Spencer 2005) or simple anxiety about how legitimately to reference others' work. Lea (2009) found that students who were relentlessly public with their social identities were very reluctant to manifest their academic identities in public ways. This finding confirms that learners make clear distinctions between their social and academic spaces; anecdotally they are less comfortable taking up a personal stance in relation to knowledge when they are asked to meet academic criteria of evidence and judgement. These contradictions throw up the question of how students develop and manage identities, and how they reach and express opinions, across the two cultural spaces.

It is important to distinguish potential clashes between different cultures of knowledge production from the powerful public discourse concerning the pitfalls of the information society, which focuses on its alleged superficiality, learners' inability to concentrate or to produce sustained argument, and the risks of identity theft and information overload (e.g. Derbyshire 2009). This discourse is the flip side of the celebratory rhetoric about learners' digital skills, which would have formal education running to catch up with a generation that learns everything it needs on the social web. The evidence points to a more complicated interrelationship of the two cultures, which in any case are not singular but multiple and contested. Academic knowledge practices are already deeply inscribed with technology, as we have seen, while most of the technologies of the web continue to originate in academia, and both cultures are shaped by common forces of standardisation, globalisation, marketisation and personalisation. From the perspective of this book, however, we are concerned with how learners manage the different practices they encounter at the interface between them.

### Conclusions: How Educators Can Respond

How can further and higher education respond to these challenges, changes and contradictions? Several responses are possible. For example, we could accept the challenge to traditional forms of academic knowledge presented by participatory cultures and rethink some academic practices of knowledge production, particularly around assessment and collaboration. At the same time, or alternatively, we could continue to assert some of the values of academic knowledge, while doing more to help students negotiate its demands. Unfortunately, the LLiDA study (Beetham et al. 2009) found few examples of universities responding strategically, either at the level of rethinking knowledge practices in the curriculum, or at the level of integrating support for students' digital literacies.

In responding to the needs of learners, educators should make few assumptions about their facility with technology. We have seen that even confident internet users often lack evaluative and critical skills; that even learners with many personal digital devices may have no idea how to use them to support their learning; and that even the 'Net Generation' can have low levels of ICT skill and a history of negative experiences with technology in school. In addition, further and higher education institutions are increasingly catering for adult learners who may have little or no experience of ICT in practice. The entitlement agenda requires that learners are not excluded from opportunity by a lack of digital access or capability (Becta 2009).

There are many reasons why informal uses of technology should not simply be incorporated into formal educational practice. The 'not in my space' attitude, while not universal, shows that many learners intuitively know that the meanings of digital spaces change when they are co-opted for formal learning tasks (Hemmi et al. 2009). It is not the technology that defines the practice but the surrounding context. Lankshear and Knobel (2006) discuss some of the problematic associations children may make with particular technologies, and propose rethinking the use of technologies for learning rather than simply adopting them. They argue, for example, that educational practice around technology should help learners become competent participants in real discourses, and should involve the creation of opportunities to negotiate different points of view so as to foster critical engagement.

Both the 'Learners' experiences of e-learning' studies and the LLiDA project found that learners can become more critical, evaluative, self-aware, self-confident, skilled and capable in the use of technologies, given the right support. We suggest that for most learners this should involve:

- authentic contexts for practice, including digitally mediated contexts;
- individual support for development, recognising learners' different prior experiences and practices;
- making explicit academic practices and expectations of meaning-making;
- anticipating and helping learners manage conflict between different practices and contexts.

The LLiDA report also identified a tension between delivering an 'entitlement' to basic digital literacy, and recognising technology practice as diverse and constitutive of personal identity, including individual styles of participation. Arguably, educators have a responsibility to help learners rethink their identities as well as build their skills, and give them space to develop into critical users and active citizens of the information age as well as capable knowledge workers.

If these conclusions point back to the need for a radical restatement of academic values, there are indications that values around knowledge and learning are already changing. Innovative educators are demonstrating how technologies can be used to engage critically and creatively with knowledge (Anderson 2007; Downes 2007). Thorpe (2002), for example, describes how the last three decades or so have seen a shift away from a characterisation of students as dependent on tutors, towards independence; from independence, through a consideration of prior knowledge to personal transformation; and from this consideration of self and identity to social and situated accounts of learning. Whereas the earlier accounts may still have seen knowledge as being contained, or at least controlled, by teachers, these latter accounts look for learning as a consequence of social participation and practice.

There are different traditions of meaning-making within the academy and professions, and these traditions might constitute the gap between information and knowledge that learners have to cross if they are to succeed in their chosen subject. One institutional strategy identified by the LLiDA study calls for students to develop an 'awareness of the provisional nature of knowledge, how knowledge is created, advanced and renewed, and the excitement of developing knowledge'. But academic staff in general have few opportunities to reflect on the impact digital technologies are having in their field, and those opportunities that exist, for example around curriculum validation and review, do not always foster an open and innovative approach.

The LLiDA study found examples of digital literacy support being embedded into the curriculum in professional and vocational subjects, especially where professional bodies are open to exploring how practice in their profession is changing. Less well embedded were notions of digital scholarship – the changing research practices of disciplines and how these need to be reflected in learning tasks and assessments. Disciplines also have ideas to contribute to generic notions of 'digital literacy'. How specific subject areas make meaning in digital contexts, analyse and collate data, and think creatively using digital tools, are potentially resources beyond the boundaries of subject teaching. Examples might be visual literacies in art, or critical media literacies in media studies. Recognising that different subjects can contribute expertise in different literacies for learning is a first step towards breaking down boundaries: recognising that learners have their own expertise to contribute is a step further.

One important strength of 'traditional' academic teaching in disciplines is that it recognises learning not as the collection of competences but as the emergence of an identity. Particularly in higher education, learning involves taking up a personal stance in relation to subject knowledge and expertise. In a digital age, learners need to practice and experiment with different ways of enacting their identities, and adopt subject positions through different social technologies and media. These opportunities can only be supported by academic staff who are themselves engaged in digital practices and questioning their own relationships with knowledge.

# References

Anderson, P. (2007). *What is Web 2.0? Ideas, technologies and implications for education*, Bristol: JISC. Retrieved 12 October, 2009, from http://www.jisc.org.uk/media/documents/techwatch/tsw0701b.pdf.

Baggaley, J. & Spencer, B. (2005). The mind of a plagiarist, *Learning, Media and Technology*, 30(1), 55–62.

Bayne, S. (2006). Temptation, trash and trust: the authorship and authority of digital texts, *E-learning*, 3(1), 16–26.

Becta (2009). *Harnessing technology for next generation learning: children, schools and families implementation plan 2009–2012*. Retrieved 12 October, 2009, from http://publications.becta.org.uk/download.cfm?resID=39547.

Beetham, H., McGill, L. & Littlejohn, A. (2009). *Thriving in the 21st century: report of the learning literacies in a digital age project*, London: JISC.

Bennett, S., Maton, K. & Kervin, L. (2008). The 'digital natives' debate: a critical review of the evidence, *British Journal of Educational Technology*. 39(5), 775–786.

Bezemer, J. and Kress, G. (2008). Writing in multimodal texts: a social semiotic account of designs for learning, *Written Communication*, 25: 166–195.

Bradwell, P. (2009). *The edgeless university: why higher education must embrace technology*, London: Demos.

Brown, P., Lauder, H. & Ashton, D. (2008). *Education, globalisation and the knowledge economy, TLRP commentary*. Retrieved 12 October, 2009, from http://www.tlrp.org/pub/documents/globalisationcomm.pdf.

Buckingham, D. (2007). Digital media literacies: rethinking media education in the age of the internet, *Research in Comparative and International Education*, 2(1), 43–55.

CILIP (2005). *Information literacy: definition*, London: CILIP. Retrieved 12 October, 2009, from http://www.cilip.org.uk/professionalguidance/informationliteracy/definition/.

Cliff, D., O'Malley, C. & Taylor, J. (2009). *Future issues in socio-technical change for UK education*, paper prepared for the Beyond Current Horizons Project, Bristol: DCSF/Futurelab.

Conole, G., de Laat, M., Dillon, T. & Darby, J. (2007). 'Disruptive technologies', 'pedagogical innovation': what's new? Findings from an in-depth study of students' use and perception of technology, *Computers & Education*, 50(2), 511–524.

Cranmer, S. (2006). Children and young people's uses of the internet for homework, *Learning, Media and Technology*, 31(3), 301–316.

Creanor, L., Trinder, K., Gowan, D. & Howells, C. (2006). *The learner experience of e-learning, final report of the LEX project*. Retrieved 12 October, 2009, from http://www.jisc.ac.uk/whatwedo/programmes/elearning_pedagogy/elp_learneroutcomes.aspx.

Cushman, E. (2004). Toward a rhetoric of new media: composing (me)dia, *Computers and Composition Online*, Spring 2004. Retrieved 12 October, 2009, from http://www.bgsu.edu/cconline/theory.htm.

Department for Culture, Media and Sport & Department for Business, Innovation and Skills (2009). *Digital Britain final report*. Retrieved 12 October, 2009, from http://www.culture.gov.uk/what_we_do/broadcasting/6216.aspx.

Derbyshire, D. (2009). Social websites harm children's brains: chilling warning to parents from top neuroscientist, *Daily Mail*, 24 February, 2009.

Downes, S. (2007). An introduction to connective knowledge. In H. Theo (Ed.) *Media, knowledge & education – exploring new spaces, relations and dynamics in digital media ecologies* Proceedings of the international conference, Innsbruck: Innsbruck University Press.

eSkills UK (2008). *Technology counts: IT and telecoms insights 2008*. Retrieved 12 October, 2009, from http://www.e-skills.com/Research-and-policy/Insights-2008/2205.

European Commission (2009). *Digital literacy: high-level expert group recommendations*. Retrieved 12 October, 2009, from http://ec.europa.eu/information_society/eeurope/i2010/docs/digital_literacy/digital_literacy_hlg_recommendations.pdf.

Facer, K. & Green, H. (2007). Curriculum 2.0: educating the digital generation. In S. Parker (Ed.) *Unlocking innovation: why citizens hold the key to public service reform*. London: Demos.

Glister, P. (2006). Digital fusion: defining the intersection of content and communications. In A. Martin & D. Madigan (Eds.) *Digital literacies for learning*, London: Facet Publishing.

Hardy, J., Haywood, D., Haywood, J., Bates, S., Paterson, J., Rhind, S. & Macleod, H. (2009). *ICT & the student first year experience: a report from the LEaD project*. Retrieved 12 October, 2009, from http://www.jisc.ac.uk/whatwedo/programmes/elearningpedagogy/lead.aspx.

Hargittai, E. (2009). An update on survey measures of web-oriented digital literacy, *Social Science Computer Review*, 27(1), 130–137.

Hargittai, E. & Walejko, G. (2008). The participation divide: content creation and sharing in the digital age, *Information, Communication and Society*, 11(2), 239–256.

Hellgren, J., Sverke, M. & Naswall, K. (2008). Changing work roles: new demands and challenges. In K. Naswall, J. Hellgren & M. Sverke (Eds.) *The individual in the changing working life*, Cambridge: Cambridge University Press, 46–66.

Hemmi, A., Bayne, S. & Land R. (2009). The appropriation and repurposing of social technologies in higher education, *Journal of Computer Assisted Learning*, 25(1), 19–30.

Hine, D. (2009). Unbunding the university, paper to the *Future of Technology in Education* Conference, University of London, 2 October, 2009.

Honey P. & Mumford A. (1982). *Manual of learning styles*, Peter Honey Publications.

Ivanic, R., Edwards, R., Satchwell, C. & Smith, J. (2007). Possibilities for pedagogy in further education: harnessing the abundance of literacy, *British Educational Research Journal*, 33(5) TLRP Special Issue, 703–721.

Kahn, R. & Kellner, D. (2005). Reconstructing technoliteracy: a multiple literacies approach, *E-Learning*, 2(3), 238–251.

Kambouri, M., Thomas, S. & Mellar, H. (2006). Playing the literacy game: a case study in adult education, *Learning, Media and Technology*, 31 (4), 395–410.

Kennedy, G., Gray, K., Judd, T., Waycott, J., Bennett, S., Maton, K., Krause, K.-L., Bishop, A., Chang, R. & Churchward, A. (2007). The Net Generation are not big users of Web 2.0 technologies: preliminary findings. Proceedings of ASCILITE Conference, Singapore, 2007.

Kirkwood, A. (2006). Getting networked learning in context: Are on-line students' technical and information literacy skills adequate and appropriate? *Learning, Media & Technology*, 31(2), 117–131.

Kleinman, L. (2004). *Connecting with the absent presence: pervasive technology use and effects on community*, paper to CHI 04, 24–29 April, 2004, Vienna, Austria.

Kolb, D. (1984). *Experiential learning: experience as the source of learning and development*, Englewood Cliffs, NJ: Prentice Hall.

Kress, G. (2003). *Literacy in the new media age*, London: Routledge.

Kress, G. & Bezemer, J. (2009). *Multimodal design: knowledge, communication and creativity*, paper prepared for the Beyond Current Horizons Project, Bristol: DCSF/Futurelab.

Kress, G. & Street, B. (2006). Multi-modality and literacy practices. In K. Pahl & J. Rowsell (Eds.) *Travel notes from the new literacy studies*, Bristol: Multilingual Matters.

Landow, G.P. (2006). *Hypertext 3.0: critical theory and new media in an era of globalization*, Baltimore, MD and London: The Johns Hopkins University Press.

Lankshear, C. & Knobel, M. (2006). *New literacies: changing knowledge and classroom learning*, Maidenhead and New York: Open University Press.

Lankshear, C. & Knobel, N. (Eds.) (2008). *Digital literacies: concepts, policies and practices*, New York, Berlin, Oxford: Peter Lang.

Lea, M.R. (2009). *Digital literacies in higher education: project report*, Swindon: Economic and Social Research Council.

Luckin, R., Clark, W., Logan, K., Graber, R., Oliver, M. & Mee, A. (2009). Do Web 2.0 tools really open the door to learning: practices, perceptions and profiles of 11–16-year-old learners, *Learning, Media and Technology*, 34 (2), 87–104.

Martin, A. & Grudziecki, J. (2007). DigEuLit: concepts and tools for digital literacy development, *Italics*, 5(4), 249–267.

Martin, A. & Madigan, D. (Eds.) (2006). *Digital literacies for learning*, London: Facet Publishing.

Nicholas, D., Rowlands, I. & Huntington, P. (2008). *Information behaviour of the researcher of the future - executive summary*, London: JISC.

Redecker, C. (2009). *Review of learning 2.0 practices: study on the impact of Web 2.0 innovations on education and training in Europe*, JRC European Commission, Scientific and Technical Reports.

Seely Brown, J. & Adler, R. (2008). Minds on fire: open education, the long tail, and learning 2.0, *Educause Review*, 43(1), 16–32.

Sheehy, K. & Bucknall, S. (2008). How is technology seen in young people's visions of future education systems? *Learning, Media and Technology*, 33(2), 101–114.

Siemens, G. (2005). *Connectivism: a learning theory for the digital age*, eLearnSpace. Retrieved 10 October, 2009, from http://www.elearnspace.org/Articles/connectivism.htm.

Spitzer, K., Eisenberg, M.B. & Lowe, C.A. (1998). *Information literacy: essential skills for the information age*, Syracuse, NY: ERIC Clearinghouse on Information and Technology.

Thorpe, M. (2002). From independent learning to collaborative learning: new communities of practice in open, distance and distributed learning. In: M. Lea & K. Nicoll (Eds.) *Distributed learning: social and cultural approaches to practice* (pp. 131–151), London: Routledge.

Trinder, K., Guiller, J., Margaryan, A., Littlejohn, A. & Nicol, D. (2008). *Learning from digital natives: bridging formal and informal learning*, report for the Higher Education Academy. Retrieved 12 October, 2009, from http://www.academy.gcal.ac.uk/ldn/LDNFinalReport.pdf.

Williams, P. & Rowlands, I. (2007). *Information behaviour of the researcher of the future; work package ii: the literature on young people and their information behaviour*, London: CIBER, UCL. Retrieved 12 October, 2009, from www.ucl.ac.uk/slais/research/ciber/downloads/GG%20Work%20Package%20II.pdf.

Wilson, S., Liber, O., Johnson, M., Beauvoir, P., Sharples, P. & Milligan, C. (2007). Personal learning environments: challenging the dominant design of educational systems, *Journal of e-Learning and Knowledge Society*, 3(2), 27–38.

Ziegler, S. (2007). The (mis)education of Generation M, *Learning, Media and Technology*, 32(1), 69–81.

# 12

## Analysing Digital Literacy in Action
### *A Case Study of a Problem-oriented Learning Process*

THOMAS RYBERG AND LONE DIRCKINCK-HOLMFELD

### Editors' Introduction

The chapter by Ryberg and Dirckinck-Holmfeld brings a welcome European perspective to the debate on digital natives and digital literacy. The authors echo other contributors in warning against the assumption that young people come to formal education with their technological, critical and creative skills largely formed. At the same time they celebrate the creative media and knowledge practices demonstrated by a group of young Danish students, who were brought together in an open-ended, problem-based, authentically high-stakes setting. The authors argue for a critical rather than a functional definition of digital literacy, and use Buckingham's (2006) framework to analyse the literacies evidenced in their case study. They conclude that if education institutions are to recognize and harness young people's experience with technologies as cultural forms, they must move towards more problem-based and open-ended pedagogic settings, with the focus on authentic tasks in which technologies are a natural part of the learning environment.

### Introduction

In recent years there has been a growing interest in the technology use, attitudes and skills of the so-called digital generation or Net Generation (Oblinger and Oblinger 2005). Many qualitative studies and larger-scale surveys indicate that young people are intensive users of technologies, have relatively good ICT skills, and can be very creative and competent when experimenting with digital media – in particular at home and in informal contexts (Holm Sørensen et al. 2002; Facer et al. 2003; Lenhart, Madden and Hitlin 2005). The emergence of so-called Web 2.0 technologies and practices has further fuelled the debate. In particular, these practices are hypothesized to better afford learners' control of their own learning, while also facilitating more collaborative modes of learning and work. These ideas resonate well with modern thinking about educational practice, and are in line with political initiatives whereby terms such as 'innovation' and 'knowledge creation' have become central (Crook and Harrison 2008). At national policy level, in much of Europe, there is a movement away from thinking about education as the mass production of skills, towards educational models that favour critical thinking, problem solving and the ability to transform information into new knowledge. The perceived affordances of Web 2.0 harmonize well with these ideals, and as a result it has been claimed that young people have become self-directed 'digital native' learners (Prensky 2001), who engage with advanced knowledge creation practices through their informal use of technology.

While it is evident that young people gain rich experiences and skills through their informal use of technology (Holm Sørensen 2002a, 2005; Holm Sørensen et al. 2007; Ito et al. 2009), several studies also find nuanced uses of technology among young people, and more varied levels of critical and academic skills than suggested by concepts such as 'digital natives' (Bennett et al. 2008; Kennedy et al. 2008; Jones and Ramanau 2009). These studies suggest that we should be careful in assuming that young people will automatically develop advanced learning capabilities and critical, academic skills through their informal use of technology, use that is most often motivated by social and entertainment purposes (Clark et al. 2009). The study by Clark et al. (2009) suggests that there is 'digital dissonance' between the learning potential of Web 2.0 as envisaged by researchers and innovative practitioners, and the actual Web 2.0 practices that the majority of young people engage with. These practices are often less sophisticated than the 'digital natives' hypothesis would predict, and are characterized by 'passive interaction' rather than creative co-production. Following on from this, Clark et al. find that many young people lack 'an understanding of ways in which such technologies can be used critically and creatively to support their learning' (ibid: 68). In line with a range of other studies, the authors therefore argue that educational institutions play an important role in ensuring that young people develop the skills necessary to become critical users and producers of digital media, and to support their own learning.

However, educational institutions have been slow to find ways of engaging with the technologies that are such a central part of young people's everyday lives (Buckingham 2006; Kennedy et al. 2008; Jones and Ramanau 2009):

> [...] the school institution appears to be slow to realize the potential of collaborative, communicative interactions, and the open and flexible potentials of learning 'beyond the classroom walls'. Institutions need to consider the implications of elements such as social networking and mobile devices, which are part of young learners' everyday 'life worlds', and to see that what is needed is a supportive negotiated response

through which the institution guides the learner towards a more critical, reflective appropriation of these technologies.

(Clark et al. 2009: 68)

This points to the need for more flexible educational approaches that can help bridge the gap between the technology practices young people engage in outside school and the critical skills and literacies demanded in the classroom (Facer et al. 2003; Buckingham 2006). This is what Buckingham (2006) terms 'digital literacy'.

> [...] digital literacy is much more than a functional matter of learning how to use a computer and a keyboard, or how to do online searches. [...] As with print, they also need to be able to evaluate and use information critically if they are to transform it into knowledge. This means asking questions about the sources of that information, the interests of its producers, and the ways in which it represents the world [...]
>
> (Buckingham 2006: 267)

But what are these skills and literacies, and how can we develop more flexible pedagogies to better connect experiences from home and school? To address these questions, we analyse a case where eight young people, aged between thirteen and sixteen, worked intensively for three days on an open-ended problem defined as 'how to reduce poverty through the use of technology'. Although they did not use so-called Web 2.0 tools to collaborate, their work involved the use of multiple technologies and the production of various media. The final outcome of their work was a highly multimodal and well-argued presentation including video, animation, oral presentation, graphs, pictures and music (Ryberg 2007; Ryberg and Dirckinck-Holmfeld 2008).

In many respects the case we describe is quite unique, and contains aspects that may not easily transfer to a typical formal context. Nevertheless, we believe there are good reasons to study and analyse practice in such intensive, experimental contexts, particularly when we consider the fact that there are relatively few successful examples from within the formal school system (Crook and Harrison 2008; Clark et al. 2009). We consider that the pedagogical approach adopted is of general interest, and that the case sheds light on how 'digital literacy' unfolds in action, and how it can be understood and analysed.

We begin by outlining the background to the case and by presenting our research and pedagogic design. We then provide a brief summary of the learning process, which leads to a discussion of digital literacies and skills. We further explore this by providing examples of the young people's activities during the symposium and discussing those in the light of our digital literacy analysis. Finally we reference other studies and experiments from the Danish context to explain why the pedagogical approach we adopted was particularly suited for these skills to unfold and flourish.

### Background to the Case Study

The 'Power Users of Technology' project (http://powerusers.edc.org/) was a research initiative emerging from the hypothesis that young people might be learning and solving problems in new ways due to their intensified use of technology. It was designed to explore and question the concepts of the Net Generation (Oblinger and Oblinger 2005) and digital natives (Prensky 2001). It took place in August 2005 in San Juan, Costa Rica. During the symposium six teams of young 'power users' from different countries worked on a series of open-ended challenges that they had chosen. On the final day they presented their findings to researchers, practitioners and business people attending the event. Throughout the symposium the authors followed and supported the Danish team, who had chosen to work with the problem of 'how to use technology to reduce poverty in the world'.

Our research design focused on qualitative methods and encompassed intensive participatory observation and documentation of their work. Data collected during the symposium included approximately twenty hours of video data, field notes and the materials students had worked with or produced (digital and handwritten notes, documents and files). Finally, we conducted eight individual semi-structured interviews during the event (Kvale 1996), and two group interviews after.

Before the symposium we met with the young people and their parents to inform them about the project, including what data would be collected, how it would be used and the scope of the research. Although we obtained written consent that we could use the data collected for research purposes and academic publishing, we also approached the young people later to confirm this consent. All names in the presented data material (except researchers and facilitators) have been replaced with random English names.

It was agreed that each of the teams should work with global challenges inspired by the UN 2015 millennium goals, but apart from this each research team had the freedom to orchestrate and organize the learning processes according to their own wishes. Our pedagogical design was founded on a problem-oriented approach, whereby we wanted the learning and inquiry process to be driven mainly by the young people. This was inspired by the pedagogical touchstone of Aalborg University, the 'Aalborg PBL Model' (Kolmos et al. 2004) or 'Problem Oriented Project Pedagogy' (Dirckinck-Holmfeld 2002). One of the main differences between this model and other interpretations of PBL is that the problems are not defined by a 'teacher' but continuously negotiated and decided by the 'students'. Likewise, learners identify and decide on the theories, methods and tools that can help them address the problem, with help from supervisors and through inspiration from the lectures available that semester. Our main aim was therefore to create a relatively open setting for the young people to act in, rather than designing sequenced events or controlling in detail what they should learn and how they should organize their work. We did, however, arrange for a lecture on poverty and contact some potential expert witnesses to be interviewed. Prior to the symposium we organized workshops where the students could work on defining their problem and discuss possible methods for studying poverty. In addition, we provided them with a number of tools: four tablet PCs, a Mac notebook, a mini-disc recorder and two video cameras.

While a lot of effort was put into defining and choosing the challenge to work with, the students had relatively vague ideas and conceptualizations of poverty when they arrived in Costa Rica. Neither were they entirely sure how to define and address their problem. Their work began on 7 August (in the evening) when they started to create interview guides, and it was concluded on 10 August when they presented their findings to the symposium attendees. The main arguments in the presentation focused on 'taxes' and 'education'. In particular, education was presented as a means to provide civic engagement and reduce poverty, but many other issues were drawn in as causes of, or solutions to, poverty (e.g. corruption, lack of secondary education, and Intel Clubhouses as an opportunity for young people to improve their ICT-skills and desire to learn).

The format of the presentation was highly multimodal, combining many different media and resources. It contained music, pictures, animation, video extracts from the interviews (some of them subtitled), and different graphs with statistical information about poverty. On the screen behind the students while they presented, a slideshow with pictures of 'poor people' was displayed, while their main PowerPoint presentation was projected onto another screen. All of these means supplemented their oral presentations and were collated, adapted or produced entirely by the students themselves. The graphics in their animation were hand-drawn and animated in PowerPoint, while the photographs were found on the web, edited and de-saturated to create the effect they wanted. The graphs were repurposed from a PowerPoint presentation used by the local researchers in their lecture on poverty. The interviews were video recorded and later transformed into small clips, which were used as part of the presentation. In this way the entire presentation was a complex multimodal 'patchwork' composed to communicate their conceptualizations of poverty and their solutions to this problem.

The presentation was also a complex work of conceptualization as they collated facts, discussion issues and ideas from many different sources, and synthesized these into a coherent argument (Ryberg 2007; Ryberg and Dirckinck-Holmfeld 2008). For the purpose of this chapter, however, we are more interested in how they used, adopted and produced media than in how they composed their arguments.

### Digital Media Literacies and Skills

In this section we do not intend to present an overview of the literature and discussions on digital literacy as they have unfolded (though see Beetham and Oliver, Chapter 11, for more background on this). Rather, we focus on a particular interpretation put forward by Buckingham (2006), which we use as a point of departure in discussing the examples from our case. We have chosen this framework because it is strongly rooted in notions of critical literacy, and because it specifically aims at bridging 'formal' literacies and experiences from cultural practices outside school. Therefore it is better suited for analysing existing practice than the 'radical' new literacy frameworks such as those proposed by Jenkins et al. (2006).

Buckingham's conceptual framework consists of four essential components of media literacy: representation, language, production and audience (Buckingham 2006: 267–268). Representation concerns the ability to critically assess and reflect on issues such as authority, reliability and bias, to notice whose voices are being heard, and whose are silenced. Language concerns the ability to understand the 'grammar' of various forms of communication and the codes and conventions of different genres. Production entails a fundamental understanding of who is communicating to whom, and why, which also encompasses awareness of commercial interests and influences. Finally, the notion of audience concerns an awareness of one's own position, both in terms of being targeted by communications and in terms of participating in communications as a critical recipient, active cultural consumer and co-producer. Buckingham (2006) argues that these four essential components can be used as a general framework for producing more specific categories such as web literacy or gaming literacy. Furthermore, he stresses that these dimensions should not only be understood as analytical skills of 'reading' media, but also in relation to more productive activities of 'writing' media. We use these four aspects of critical digital literacy to analyse and discuss examples from our case.

### Examples From the Case

In the following we focus on the young people's production of, and reflections on, various elements of their presentation. Initially, we look at their preliminary thoughts on the presentation, as these illustrate well their varied knowledge of different genres and communicative means.

The following two extracts (Extracts 12.1 and 12.2) come from the first full day of work. On the previous night the students had worked in smaller groups creating interview guides and discussing ideas for the presentation.

Here they are discussing two ideas they have generated, the first a role play involving the audience, and the second an interactive animation based on a film or cartoon. In relation to the latter they are discussing how to create a narrative representation of the interviewees' stories. One suggestion is a 'matchstick man' animation and another includes recording the interviews and using them to document their points.

While they are quite keen on the idea of the role play, they later agree that it might be too difficult to carry through successfully. This conclusion arises from a longer discussion that reflects their awareness of the language or requirements of that particular type of presentation. Some of the problems they anticipate and discuss are initially raised by Neil, who mentions time and complexity as potential barriers. At the same time, though, they discuss how open or closed the descriptions of the 'situations' might have to be, and conclude that a very open approach might generate too many scenarios, which could prove difficult to moderate and meaningfully synthesize.

The idea of creating the presentation as a 'role play', while not pursued to realization, is interesting from the perspective of the students' ability to reflect critically on their own role as producers. The idea of positioning the symposium participants as active co-producers shows a complex awareness

**Extract 12.1** Discussing a Role Play – Extract From Discussions on 8 August 2005

| | |
|---|---|
| Neil: | Yeah, but we talked about ehm what do you call it, involve the audience in that role play, maybe in groups do a role play (7.0) |
| Jack: | A role play? (1.0) |
| Others: | Yes, Yeah (2.0) |
| Jack: | That's nice |
| Neil: | That's fun |
| Angie: | Do everybody know what it was that we talked about? |
| Laura: | No |
| Angie: | Alright ... fine |
| Neil: | It is ... |
| Angie: | Then you better explain it (2.0) |

| | |
|---|---|
| Neil: | It is just a suggestion for a role play, but I don't know if it will be too complicated, now that we don't have much time to do it all (1.0) but it was something like dividing people into some groups that ehm (1.0) that each should represent parts of society where they could themselves be confronted, in their groups ... they could be confronted with some of the problems there are when they are in that situation they have been put in ... then we would first have to write ... explain to them their situation in advance (1.0) and then from those information they have about their (1.0) role life that ehm then choose some things and then we should summarise afterwards which consequences their choices would have for those social groups ehm. |
| Laura: | Which social groups might that be for an example? |
| Neil: | But ehm it could be for example an ... I don't know, what do you call it, a peasant or what do you call it a plantation owner with his family with kids that need an education and all, and then a big businessman that might be importing bananas from the US, and I don't know. |

**Extract 12.2** Extract From Discussions on 8 August 2005

| | |
|---|---|
| Angie: | We had ehm me and Samuel we talked about we would do what we have all talked about, such a, yeah movie – either with matchstick men or with real persons ehm to you know ... to show, to give some examples if they break their leg then it is good that we pay taxes for the poor, because then they don't have to pay ... with taxes they can manage ... and if we didn't pay taxes then it would be somewhat difficult because they would not have the money to pay the bill and things like that ehm I think that would work out very well (1.0) I don't know (3.0) |
| Diana: | I know we also talked about |
| Jasper: | [inaudible] |
| Diana: | We talked about at some point in time to compare it to Denmark, but wouldn't that become a little toooo ... |

(They discuss the possibilities of comparing Denmark and Costa Rica in terms of taxes and welfare system)

| | |
|---|---|
| Jack: | Well if it's the thing about taxes we want to illustrate then we don't necessarily have to use countries because it is almost like we put somebody in a bad light. |
| Neil: | That is true. |
| Laura: | Yeah [inaudible] |
| Jack: | If it is taxes we want to highlight we don't need to mention countries (2.0) |

of the audience of their own production. By inviting participants to occupy different subject positions and actively produce different voices – each of which might represent certain 'biased' or 'positioned' responses to the problem of poverty – they demonstrate a complex awareness of both the problem and the communicative context. For example, through conversations with a young local guide – a political science student – they became aware that a poor Costa Rican farmer and a rich business person might interpret trade agreements very differently.

The students were also aware of their own position and bias as producers, as we see in the second extract, where they discuss the other ideas for the presentation. This time it is Diana who initiates the idea of comparing Costa Rica and Denmark, while simultaneously questioning it by adding 'but wouldn't that become a little toooo ...'. Jack takes up this theme later when he comments that they don't want to put anybody in a bad light or make comparisons between particular countries. While Diana does not finish her sentence, her unease signifies a growing concern about their own particular Danish or Scandinavian perspective. Being culturally embedded in a Danish welfare system with high taxes, a high degree of income equality and a high level of investment in social services (free health care, school, university, social security etc.) they tended to view the Scandinavian societal model as the best way of resolving the issue of poverty. However, they became increasingly aware of, and sensitive to, their own 'Scandicentric' cultural bias, and would remind each other that different values and societal models existed. They did not abandon their belief that taxes, welfare, economic equality and access to

**Extract 12.3** Movies or Animations? Extract From Discussions on 8 August 2005

| | |
|---|---|
| Angie: | You could also, we could also do it like, we do some kind of movie right, then it starts with a normal picture of one of those persons we meet today and then their name and job are there, and things like that ... here comes his story or something like that, right ... and then we create a story ... then we create some story about him breaking his leg or something like that ... 'Woah' something right ... and we do that with matchstick men, but there will just be some picture of him from the start. |
| Jack: | You could also do that with a movie, that is to ... I mean, instead of doing these, I mean, narratives with movies, then you can create ... we are going to have some interviews from all of this? |
| Sophia: | Yeah, we have to use it for visualisation ... hey. |

| | |
|---|---|
| Jack: | Yeah yeah so if we are going to do some interviews it is a damn good idea doing those with a movie because it doesn't take as much time either, and then people can better understand it. |
| Angie: | Yeah. |
| Jack: | Instead of us standing there reading something aloud for example. |
| Angie: | So we could do something (gestures) a combination of it all? |
| Jack: | Yeah, where we incorporate many different things. |

education were important in resolving poverty, but they became more aware that such a system depends on a high level of trust and a low level of corruption to be realizable in practice.

In this way they became more aware of the importance of their own cultural perspective and position in producing knowledge.

The final extract exemplifies the multimodal and performative ways in which they expressed their thoughts. From these extracts, and the final presentation itself, it is clear that aspects such as performance, narrative, story, 'visualization' and 'action' are important to them. These are reflected in their decision to create multimodal narratives through animation or moving pictures, rather than static montages. Jack's comment about 'standing there reading something aloud for example' underlines that they feel it is important to capture the audience in a more engaging way. This is further stressed by a comment Laura made a little earlier in their conversation:

I just think it was a good example you gave Jack – when you sit and watch the news you don't wake up until you see those small ... small where they have done something animated [inaudible] with plenty of colour and sound.

As well as focusing on movement and narrative, they are keen to include different modes of expression, whether animated or acted out in the form of role plays. It should be stressed that discussions of the best forms of presentation were tightly interwoven with discussions of the problem area, and they were concerned to find an appropriate balance between form and content. Diana, for example, raises a concern about the attempt to integrate too many 'different things':

Diana:    Yeah, but also because one of the things we wrote yesterday, Neil and me, was that we must keep in mind the connecting thread, because else you won't be able to follow. Then it will just be all kinds of different things like ok
and then …

Jack:    No no no we of course have to maintain the connecting thread and that is also why at all times we have to look at our problem definition, these are just the means to make it look easy … I mean to, I'll just try again … they are the means so it becomes easier to see.

Laura:    Yeah.

Sophia:    To understand.

The means of presentation were not employed for the sake of creating a multimodal tapestry, but rather as a way of getting the message across by capturing the interest and attention of the audience, and 'connecting' ideas in the flow of media. In the following analysis we consider two examples from their final presentation in more detail, which illustrate both their use of media and their playful familiarity with popular cultural elements.

### Laughing and Crying – Pathos in Action

The final presentation began with the young people sitting silently on the stage in a half-circle, accompanied by Eric Clapton's 'Tears in Heaven'. A slideshow with black and white pictures representing poverty was projected onto a big screen behind them. The emotional appeal of this opening was very strong and intended to underline the gravity of the subject. The pictures were all found on the web and then resized, cropped and de-saturated to create a 'sadder' atmosphere, as one of them expressed it. The pictures were then put into a timed, looping PowerPoint show. The introduction could equally well have been an infomercial from the Red Cross or Amnesty International, as it mimicked the 'pathos appeal' and adopted many of the codes and conventions employed in this particular genre. In other words, the students were consciously adopting the language of the genre, to achieve a particular emotional response from the audience.

The other example uses humour rather than pathos to bring about an audience response. This was accomplished through an animated PowerPoint featuring 'Rich George' and 'Poor Fernando'.

Very briefly summarized, the animation shows what happens to two characters who each break a leg in 'the land of no taxes'. Poor Fernando is unable to pay for medical treatment and 'must go home one-legged. Poor guy!' A contrasting animation shows how the outcome could be different if George and Fernando lived in a country where taxation supports health care.

George hurts his leg ... OUCH!   Fernando also hurts his leg ... Poor guy!

**Figure 12.1** Rich George and Poor Fernando

In these drawings one can find references to the general language of cartoon animation, where a broken leg is really broken, rich people have dollar signs on their briefcases, and poor plantation workers hold bananas in their hands. Also worth noting is how students used their own popular cultural frame of reference to support their work with the animation. While drawing the characters, they named them after two fictive characters (Brother Salsa and Chris) from popular Danish TV and radio shows. Another reference that was not visible in the final drawings was the use of little rhymes to identify the animation files: 'hænder der ligner ænder' (hands that look like ducks), 'fattig mand med dyr tand' (poor man with expensive tooth). These rhymes were inspired by the absurd humour in the two popular programmes, and shows how they used familiar cultural references playfully to support the serious and unfamiliar task of representing poverty.

**Discussion: Skills, Literacies and Pedagogy**

It seems fair to say that these young people were digitally literate in many ways. They were able to reflect critically on their own roles as producers, and to produce a multimodal presentation drawing on different rhetorical strategies (humour, pathos). They used diverse means of communication successfully, including video interviews, graphs, animations and the pathos-laden performance that served as an introduction.

These are not technical skills in a narrow sense. While they depend on mastering technologies with a relatively high level of skill, they are equally dependent on having the competences to construct a coherent narrative, collaborate, organize a complex work process, and harness various forms of expression to a rhetorical purpose. This echoes the point made by Buckingham (2006: 267) that digital literacies are critical rather than simply functional in nature. We should be cautious, then, about decomposing literacies into smaller self-contained skills or 'technical' operations such as searching for information, finding pictures, creating graphics, word-processing or video editing. These operations become relevant only when they are harnessed to the students' analytical, creative and critical capacities, and the application of these to a particular problem of real concern.

The learning process was open-ended and problem oriented, and the collaborative work involved was largely self-organized by the participants. The pedagogical design and planning consisted of arranging some learning opportunities, rather than deciding in any detail how and what should be learned. Arguably the whole setting where the students were selected as 'power users', brought to Costa Rica and asked to perform with other teams in front of a large audience, had an important impact on their motivation. However, we would argue that equally important factors were the exploratory approach, the problem orientation, granting them control and providing them with various technologies (Ryberg 2007).

These are factors that have also been emphasized by others. For example Holm Sørensen (2002a, 2002b) argues that young people favour acting, producing, creating, collaborating, exploring and controlling the processes with which they engage. Facer et al. (2003) argue that these traits are what characterize young people's use of technologies outside of school, when they engage in what they term 'authentic learning experiences'.

> That is what was so different in children's learning at home; their learning was authentic in that it was involved, albeit in different degrees, with knowledge creation. [...] We believe that the skills associated with knowledge creation are central to learning in the information age and this is the challenge that children who are already computer literate are posing for the education system.
>
> (Facer et al. 2003: 39–40)

As Facer et al. (2003) and Holm Sørensen (2002a, 2002b) suggest, there are many differences between the experimental, playful, exploratory and collaborative learning that is possible in 'authentic' settings, and the traditional pedagogy of the classroom. In the classroom, teaching is often – though not always – organized in clearly defined time slots, and the teacher typically directs the interactions. This setting may be particularly problematic when teachers seek to work meaningfully and productively with the new media, as suggested by Clark et al. (2009) and Crook and Harrison (2008). Authentic tasks, with technology embedded naturally into collaborative activities, are important for learners' motivation and for developing the necessary skills (Holm Sørensen 2002a; Facer et al. 2003; Holm Sørensen et al. 2007). In line with the conclusions from these and other studies, we would argue that educational institutions should be supporting more exploratory and problem-oriented learning processes.

While the case we have presented is not representative or easily transferred to a formal school context, we believe that the pedagogical approach has wider currency. This is borne out by experiences from a large Danish research project.

> The 'ICT in New Learning Environments' project shows that students bring their informal learning forms into the school context. This happens particularly when the school has undergone physical alterations and when its organisation of learning and teaching are also restructured, with project-based learning becoming an important part of the school work and with the media available in the learning environment.
>
> (Holm Sørensen 2005: 1)

In arguing for a stronger focus on problem-oriented and project-based activities in schools, and more collaborative, critical and reflective appropriation of technologies in the classroom (Holm Sørensen 2002a, 2005; Holm Sørensen et al. 2007), we do not mean to underplay the role of teachers or formal schooling, or to overemphasize young people's capacity to learn from informal contexts. The studies we have discussed warn against overestimating the technological, critical and creative skills of young people. However, they also suggest we should not dismiss young people's technical skills or their experience with technologies as cultural forms and important aspects of their everyday life. While we cannot pinpoint the origin of the literacies displayed by the young people in our case study, which might be rooted in formal or informal learning experiences, we have outlined a setting and approach in which these literacies can flourish. We have also demonstrated how Buckingham's (2006) framework can be used to help analyse and understand these literacies in action.

## References

Bennett, S., Maton, K. & Kervin, L. (2008). The 'digital natives' debate: A critical review of the evidence. *British Journal of Educational Technology*, 39(5), 775–786.

Buckingham, D. (2006). Defining digital literacy. What do young people need to know about digital media? *The Nordic Journal of Digital Literacy*, 1(4), 263–276.

Clark, W., Logan, K., Luckin, R., Mee, A. & Oliver, M. (2009). Beyond Web 2.0: Mapping the technology landscapes of young learners. *Journal of Computer Assisted Learning*, 25(1), 56–69.

Crook, C. & Harrison, C. (2008). *Web 2.0 technologies and learning at key stages 3 and 4: Summary report*. Research Report. BECTA. Retrieved 19 October, 2009, from http://partners.becta.org.uk/upload-dir/downloads/page_documents/research/web2_ks34_summary.pdf.

Dirckinck-Holmfeld, L. (2002). Designing virtual learning environments based on problem oriented project pedagogy. In L. Dirckinck-Holfeld & B. Fibiger (Eds.) *Learning in virtual environments* (pp. 31–54). Frederiksberg C: Samfundslitteratur Press.

Facer, K., Furlong, J., Furlong, R. & Sutherland, R. (2003). *Screenplay: Children and computing in the home*. London & New York: RoutledgeFalmer.
Holm Sørensen, B. (2002a). Børnenes nye læringsforudsætninger – didaktiske perspektiver. In B. Holm Sørensen, C. Jessen & B.R. Olesen (Eds.) *Børn på nettet - Kommunikation og Læring* (pp. 17–42). København: Gads Forlag.
Holm Sørensen, B. (2002b). Digital produktion – nye æstetiske former og produktionsmåder under udvikling. In: B. Holm Sørensen, C. Jessen & B.R. Olesen (Eds.) *Børn på nettet – Kommunikation og Læring* (pp. 43–66). København: Gads Forlag.
Holm Sørensen, B. (2005). Informal learning – power users of information and communication technology. Paper presented at the Power Users of Information and Communication Technology International Symposium, San Juan, Costa Rica: EDC.
Holm Sørensen, B., Jessen, C. & Olesen. B. (2002). *Børn på nettet – Kommunikation og læring. Børns brug af interaktive medier – i et fremtidsperspektiv*. København: Gads Forlag.
Holm Sørensen, B., Danielsen, O. & Nielsen, J. (2007). Children's informal learning in the context of schools of the knowledge society. *Education and Information Technologies, 12*(1), 17-27
Ito, M., Baumer, S., Bittanti, M., Boyd, D., Cody, R., Herr, B. & Horst, H. (2009). *Hanging out, messing around, geeking out: Living and learning with new media*. Cambridge: MIT Press.
Jenkins, H., Purushotma, R., Clinton, K., Weigel, M. & Robison, A. J. (2006). *Confronting the challenges of participatory culture: Media education for the 21st Century*. Chicago, IL: MacArthur Foundation. Retrieved 19 October, 2009, from: http://www.projectnml.org/files/working/NMLWhitePaper.pdf.
Jones, C. & Ramanau, R. (2009). *Collaboration and the Net Generation: The changing characteristics of first year university students*. In C. O'Malley, D. Suthers, P. Reimann & A. Dimitracopoulou (Eds.) Computer Supported Collaborative Learning Practices Conference Proceedings. Rhodes. Retrieved 19 October, 2009, from http://cscl2009.blogspot.com/2009/04/collaboration-and-net-generation.html.
Kennedy, G.E., Judd, T.S., Churchward, A., Gray, K. & Krause, K-L. (2008). First year students' experiences with technology: Are they really digital natives? *Australasian Journal of Educational Technology, 24*(1), 108–122.
Kolmos, A., Fink, F.K. & Krogh, L. (2004). *The Aalborg PBL model - progress diversity and challenges*. Aalborg: Aalborg University Press.
Kvale, S. (1996). *InterViews: An introduction to qualitative research interviewing*. Thousand Oaks, CA: Sage Publications.
Lenhart, A., Madden, M. & Hitlin, P. (2005). *Teens and technology. Youth are leading the transition to a fully wired and mobile nation*. Washington: Pew Internet & American Life Project. Retrieved 15 August, 2007, from http://www.pewinternet.org/pdfs/PIP_Teens_Tech_July2005web.pdf.
Oblinger, D. & Oblinger. J.L. (2005). *Educating the Net Generation*. Washington, DC: Educause. Retrieved 19 October, 2009, from http://www.educause.edu/educatingthenetgen/.
Prensky, M. (2001). Digital natives, digital immigrants. *On the Horizon, 9*(5), 1–6.
Ryberg, T. (2007). *Patchworking as a metaphor for learning. Understanding youth, learning and technology*. PhD thesis, Department of Communication and Psychology, Aalborg University. Retrieved 19 October, 2009, from http://www.ell.aau.dk/fileadmin/user_upload/documents/publications/ell_publication_series/eLL_Publication_Series_-_No_10.pdf.
Ryberg, T. & Dirckinck-Holmfeld, L. (2008). Power users and patchworking. An analytical approach to critical studies of young people's learning with digital media. *Educational Media International, 45*(3), 143–156.

# 13
## Collaborative Knowledge Building

GREG BENFIELD AND MAARTEN DE LAAT

### Editors' Introduction

Collaborative knowledge building has always been an essential practice of research communities, but the term has gained a new currency in relation to the activities of online communities, and is increasingly also applied to learning activities in formal settings that involve group work. Benfield and De Laat situate the debate about knowledge building in the context of a networked learning framework, and distinguish collaboration 'on task' from collaboration 'around the task' as having different social meanings for learners. In particular, they explore the influence of surveillance in the 'academic pantopticon' of institutional learning environments, and learner perceptions of fairness. Drawing on insights from learners themselves, they consider how issues of surveillance and fairness can be addressed in group work situations, and conclude that learners will make use of their own technologies and social networks to share know-how, however formal learning tasks are constructed.

### Introduction

Over at least the last two decades collaborative knowledge building has grown in use and importance in higher education. The 2008 Horizon Report identified 'renewed emphasis on collaborative learning' as a key challenge, 'pushing the educational community to develop new forms of interaction and assessment' (Educause 2008: 5). This coincides with the impact of educational technology, especially over the last decade. Salaway et al. (2007: 5) found that US undergraduate students are 'immersed in technology ownership and use'. Access to learning resources via the institutional virtual learning environment (VLE) is now deeply embedded in the undergraduate student experience and is highly valued by learners (Sharpe et al. 2006). Along with VLE communication tools like asynchronous discussion boards and synchronous chat rooms, recently there has been an explosive growth of Web 2.0 technologies. Social networking like Facebook, instant messaging like MSN, audio-visual file sharing like Flickr and YouTube are pervasive; personal devices like laptops and mobile phones are ubiquitous. As a result 'all learning is potentially technology-enabled' (JISC 2009: 1).

## Networked Learning

In this chapter we use a networked learning framework to understand the role of technology in students' collaborative learning and knowledge building. We are mindful that a distinction can be made between cooperative and collaborative learning. 'The primary difference between the two is whether tasks are divided up and completed individually (cooperative) or completed together through dialogue (collaborative)' (Paulus 2005). Our emphasis in this chapter is on the latter form, although there is little in the discussion that follows that does not apply equally to cooperative learning.

Technology-enhanced collaborative learning gained serious interest around the 1980s, notably with Scardamelia et al's (1989) groundbreaking work on Computer-Supported Intentional Learning Environments (CSILE). They explored the added value of discussion forums for collaborative knowledge building in groups. The focus was on discussing, challenging and extending (building on) each other's knowledge through group work. The field of Computer Supported Collaborative Learning (CSCL) has developed and researched tools like these ever since. One critique of CSCL, however, is its narrow focus on the micro level of collaborative learning in isolated small groups. We agree with Jones et al. (2006), who argue that a broader perspective on collaborative learning is needed, including research at the meso (institutional/organisational) and macro (national, global) level.

Networked learning is an alternative approach to technology-enhanced learning (McConnell 2000; De Laat and Lally 2003; Goodyear et al. 2004; Siemens 2004). Its relation to the networked society (Castells 2000), with its ever-growing use of information and communication technologies (ICT) and social networking on the Internet, makes it a relevant framework for professional development and lifelong learning. Research shows that having an extended network is crucial for personal and professional development (Granovetter 1973; Levin and Cross 2004). We prefer the term networked learning over CSCL a) because computer supported learning focuses, in our view, too much on the role of the computer, as against (technology-supported) networks; b) because instead of concentrating on collaborative learning only, we prefer a broader perspective open to both individual and collective learning and ranging from micro through meso to the macro level; and c) because we believe that networked learning fits better into post-compulsory and work-related learning than CSCL, which is thus far mostly connected to formal education.

By networked learning we mean the use of ICT to promote collaborative or cooperative connections between learners, their tutors and learning resources (Steeples and Jones 2002) and to enhance the efficacy of learning among its members. Early networked learning research mostly focused on exploring the affordances of technology to support learning (Goodyear et al. 2004; Conole and Dyke 2004). Interest now has turned to the social learning aspects of networked learning, with a focus on building and cultivating social networks and seeing technology as a part of this rather than as an end in itself (De Laat 2008).

From the perspective of networked learning it is important to explore how students fit technology in their day-to-day learning. Dalsgaard (2006) argues that the institutional VLE should play only a minor role in learning, with students relying on social software tools to manage their collaborative learning. In the same vein, Anderson (2005: 4) argues that social software like social bookmarking, weblogs and social networking are examples of 'networked tools that support and encourage individuals to learn together while retaining individual control over time, space, presence, activity, identity and relationship'.

Students spontaneously and strategically draw on and expand contacts within their networks to create social structures that support them during their studies, whether it is learning to live on their own, exploring student culture or managing learning activities. Contacts cultivated in their networks can range from very loosely coupled acquaintances to long-lasting friendships and community memberships. Both these weak and strong ties in their networks are important for learning. Granovetter (1973) showed the importance of weak ties to gain access (often called bridging) to new knowledge, while strong ties with peers close to you are needed to deepen and embed knowledge closely related to day-to-day shared practice. Levin and Cross (2004) studied the nature of these weak ties, looking at knowledge sharing in companies. They found that for informal learning and professional development people, rely for new knowledge on weak ties with competent people they can trust. De Laat et al. (2007) showed how in networked learning communities of eight to ten participants the strength of ties impacted collaborative learning. Analysis showed how people use their networks over time to develop and improve their own learning and their ability to become a more involved group member.

Other studies show that having or building a network will be beneficial to lifelong learning and professional development. In the field of teacher development for example, some key studies show the added value teacher networks have for the implementation of innovations, teacher development, school leadership and improved teaching practices (Lieberman and Wood 2002a, 2002b; Dresner and Starvel 2004; Dresner and Worley 2006; Earl and Katz 2007; Katz and Hands 2007). Thus, social networking supported by technology is an increasingly important field of study for understanding and improving the way people learn and create opportunities to develop their potential.

The networked learning framework allows us to approach collaborative learning from two perspectives. The first perspective is where collaborative learning is formally designed. Here students build knowledge together to complete a learning task. Typically the technology used to support this process is a VLE, wiki, website, etc. These networked learning activities can be seen as collaborative learning *on the task*. The second perspective takes the student point of view and looks at how students use technology to draw on social contacts for their learning assignments. These activities can be seen as collaborative learning *around the task*. Besides communication tools like mobile phones and Voice over Internet Protocol, this kind of collaboration involves networking tools such as social software. In this chapter we will present empirical data from both perspectives.

### The Benefits and Some Problems With Group Work

The research findings on cooperative learning show higher achievement, better long-term retention of learning, improved critical thinking, more positive interpersonal relationships and better social support, than do competitive or individualistic efforts (Johnson et al. 2007).

We also have to acknowledge that students experience difficulties in group work. Some of these include: lack of time to gel into an effective group; lack of teamwork skills; inappropriate group size and/or lack of sufficient heterogeneity in the group; and group think, or avoiding conflict (Johnson and Johnson 1999). Perhaps the most complaints are about social loafing, where individuals hold back or hide without the other members really realising it, and free riding (Johnson and Johnson 1999; Gottschall and García-Bayonas 2008), where some individuals get all the reward for little or no effort. A consequent effect is loss of motivation in the group due to perceived inequity (Johnson and Johnson 1999).

To this we can add that there is a contradiction that bedevils the application of cooperative and collaborative learning pedagogies in higher education: asking students to cooperate when in assessment terms their peers are their rivals (Cartney and Rouse 2006). Networked learning, with its perspective of multiple communities, including 'opportunities for groups to form, dissolve or re-form' (Hodgson and Reynolds 2005: 20), might offer a more participative and less hierarchical pedagogy than traditional models (Simons and De Laat 2006). However, an assessed group activity of limited duration severely restricts the opportunity for this pedagogy to gain a hold. Grades loom over groups as sources of coercion and possible division. And this situation is entrenched: 'Using competitive evaluation practices, such as grading on the normal curve has dominated postsecondary classes for the past 70 years. Despite the considerable research indicating that these practices should change, the status quo continues' (Johnson et al. 2007: 27).

Most of the work on cooperative and collaborative learning has been carried out in face-to-face, low technology contexts. We know from the rich vein of research on online distance learning that trust is especially important in online collaborative groups (McConnell 2006; Smith 2008: 325). But there has been very little investigation of the impact of time, distance and technology on virtual teams (Johnson et al. 2002; De Laat 2006) or the impact of these factors on group work carried out in technology-rich, on-campus environments. Yet virtual teams are increasingly important in organisations, enabling them to carry out complex processes despite geographic and organisational dispersion (Greenberg et al. 2007). And it is probably fair to say that virtually all student group work is now heavily mediated by technology. The mere requirement for two or more learners to produce a digital artefact of some kind, whether a PowerPoint presentation or a report in Word, will typically lead to a complex set of technology-mediated communications between participants involving face-to-face meetings sitting around a computer screen; continuing communications using email, mobile phones and Internet chat; and a flurry of exchanges of digital files via email and USB storage devices (Conole et al. 2006).

To complicate matters, the evidence is that engaging on-campus students with online communication and collaboration activities is problematic, with this area of VLE use frequently criticised by students (Sharpe et al. 2006). So we have a paradox: while communication technologies are readily available and massively used *around the task*, often the results of their formal use *on the task* falls well below our expectations.

### The Academic Panopticon

Increasingly learners are expected to carry out their learning in a public way. They leave digital traces of their interactions – discussion posts, wiki page edits, chat logs, blog posts or comments, SMS messages – that can be used to monitor quality and/or quantity of their contributions. In this sense the electronic learning environments our students use – especially the ubiquitous VLE, with its in-built tracking systems – resemble an *academic panopticon*. Jeremy Bentham's 1785 panopticon was a design for a circular prison, in which the prisoners' uncertainty over whether or not they were being watched at any given time meant that all could be kept under surveillance by just one warder. Time spent *on task* in institutional learning environments is time when students are aware of being potentially viewed and judged.

From a networked learning perspective, Dalsgaard and Paulsen (2009: 7) argue that the transparency afforded by digital environments, especially social networking environments, is vital:

Total seclusion is undesirable. Students should be stimulated to be visible as potential partners and resources for others. Transparent information could be a huge cooperative resource. The dilemma is that students who do not contribute to the community cannot be perceived as learning resources for others.

Of course in assessed group work situations, being transparent to other members of the group means also being visible for judgement. We shall see that some learners may use technology to seclude themselves and subgroups or to avoid surveillance.

As with the 'surveillance society' (Wood 2006) and its attendant erosion of trust and feelings of security in the people, the *academic panopticon* disturbs what Entwistle (2003) refers to as the 'sense of fairness and moral order' that is usually present in collaborative learning environments. The academic panopticon affects behaviours and feelings of trust of its inhabitants in various ways, depending on their awareness of it, their relative experience within it and their expectations about its use.

In the discussion that follows we draw on empirical data to illustrate both the potential for technology to enhance communication and collaboration in post-compulsory learning contexts and also to confound and complicate our existing understandings of how effective group work takes place. First we explore *on task* collaborative learning using a case study that illustrates how students use technology to organise their group learning tasks. Then we present data primarily concerned with *around the task* collaborative learning to illustrate how students draw on technology to work together on individual learning tasks.

## Case 1: On Task Collaborative Learning

This example draws on data taken across four consecutive semesters comprising approximately 400 survey responses and individual and group interviews with participants in a Business module at Oxford Brookes University (see Benfield and Prior 2007).

Team Challenges is a first year, undergraduate module run by Oxford Brookes University's Business School. It aims to develop students' theoretical and practical understanding of team working in a business context and to develop collaborative e-learning skills. Cohorts are large, usually just over 200 each semester, and diverse, with 25–30 per cent international students.

Team Challenges runs in on-campus mode and includes a fully online, collaborative activity called the 'Virtual Task'. Students are randomly allocated to teams of six that work online for five weeks in the institutional VLE to produce an electronic presentation. Overall the task is considered to be successful and sustainable. Over one hundred teams successfully completed the first four runs of the Virtual Task and none failed to do so. It has run ten times now in the hands of three different module leaders.

A key aim of the task is to promote student independence. Another is to make it feasible for just one module leader to supervise the activity of the 200+ students involved. It is impractical in such a large cohort to provide dedicated in-class 'training' in how to use the VLE. So the learning model is experiential and after just a few weeks of immersion in a tightly focused online collaborative task most students develop their online communication skills appreciably. Online scaffolds such as 'how to' guides and advice on effective team organisation, communication protocols and tactics provide support. Email support is also available to students who need it. That is now rare. There is a high level of student acceptance of the task and few requests for help.

Despite advice to rely primarily on the asynchronous discussion board, each semester very high proportions of students used synchronous modes of communication – online chat, face-to-face meetings and mobile phones. But such preferences were at times misplaced. Numerous students commented that it was nigh on impossible for everyone in their team to meet at once, either face-to-face or online. Where teams did so, some members could be disempowered or excluded totally. One participant explained:

> If most of the group meet up online at one point then they can decide virtually everything. And then whoever couldn't meet up at that time is just left with whatever they've decided.
>
> (James, first year Business)

Questions of advantage and disadvantage manifest themselves in different ways for online teamwork than in more traditional group activities. Some aspects of the challenge of cultural difference (Palloff and Pratt 2005), for example, may be heightened. Thus, students in online group tasks need to accommodate members whose first language is not English, for example by using simple language, devoid of slang and colloquialisms, devoting time to 'unpacking' unclear messages (Ryan 2000), and allocating appropriate roles that utilise individual strengths and minimise weaknesses (e.g. non-native speakers researching and drafting but not final editing). Correspondingly, tutors need to encourage inclusivity in groups by visibly supporting such processes.

Asynchronous communication can 'level the playing field' for some individuals in group activities. Those with poor computer or Internet access or low IT skills have time to overcome these barriers; those whose first language is not English have time to reflect for understanding and to draft and correct their contributions. Consequently, over time, in response to research findings, the Team Challenges module leader moved from a reluctance to either proscribe or promote specific methods of communication to overtly recommending the VLE discussion board as the most appropriate communication tool.

Peer review is frequently involved in online collaboration (Macdonald 2003; Clouder and Deepwell 2004; Brindley et al. 2009). It is a skill that designers often assume learners can carry out effectively when in fact they have little experience of it and need training in how to do it (Macdonald 2003). Even before the Virtual Task began, students were anxious about this. One said:

> I can see that editing stuff has got to be a bit of a sensitive spot for a lot of people, especially because I'm in the role of putting it all together and stuff. I may need to delete bits and edit and maybe reword stuff so it makes sense as a whole. And some people may be a bit weird about that or it might cause conflict.

(David, first year Business)

While the Virtual Task confirms that students can quite quickly acquire peer review skills, they will do so more efficiently and effectively when they are given structured support.

The academic panopticon was an active feature of the Virtual Task. Some expected the tracking features of the VLE to be used to prevent social loafing and freeloading, the behaviours most likely to undermine a sense of moral order. But in a large cohort it may not be practical for tutors to monitor each participant. More importantly, it is undesirable to do so when the task is intended to encourage learner independence. However, it is important that students know there are mechanisms for preventing or responding to freeloading. In the Virtual Task this is achieved not with intrusive or extensive monitoring, but with a formative assessment submission that includes the sanction of withdrawing inactive members from teams in the middle of the task and their recomposition into 'second chance' teams (Benfield and Prior 2007). There is a one time only, limited use of VLE tracking at this formative assessment stage to identify students who have not yet engaged in the task.

Assessment always signposts the actual curriculum for students (Ramsden 1992). The strategic use of assessment – summative, to reward participation and formative, to provide timely feedback and support students in structuring their activities – are key techniques in the success of the Virtual Task (Benfield and Prior 2007). Our data clearly show that the most effective teams allocated roles and responsibilities. It is equally clear that that would not have happened anything like as frequently as it did without the leverage of a formative assessment submission that requires groups to document their organisational decisions.

Some students responded to the academic panopticon by seeking to withdraw themselves and their groups from the possible surveillance of tutors. Designers of group tasks need to be sensitive to how some students feel threatened and exposed by learning in public. If they, like Dalsgaard and Paulsen (2009), value the transparency that electronic learning environments offer, hoping that students will see themselves as learning resources for others, they need to be explicit about this and work hard to inculcate these values in all aspects of their programmes.

## Case 2: Around the Task Collaborative Learning

We turn now to collaborative learning *around the task*. 'Peers play an important and often unacknowledged role in the learning experience' (JISC 2009: 3), using personal communication devices and services to seek help from each other and to cultivate support networks. Social networking sites, like Facebook (http://www.facebook.com/), Hyves (http://www.hyves.nl/) and LinkedIn (http://www.linkedin.com/) are popular examples. Creanor et al. paint a picture of rich, dynamic, networking, involving a largely unexplored ' "underworld" of digital communication among learners' (2006: 27). Conole et al. (2006: 4) found that in this 'underworld' 'technologies are used extensively to communicate with fellow peers and tutors, with students demonstrating use of a variety of tools (email, MSN chat, Skype, mobile phones, etc.) to support a range of communicative acts'.

The JISC-funded Learner Experiences Project (LXP) investigated how students fit technology into their day-to-day learning activities and explored possible subject differences in the use of technology (Conole et al. 2006). The LXP project collected eighty-five audio logs (voice messages delivered by phone rather then written diaries) by twenty students demonstrating how they used technology. Twelve students' audio logs were followed up with semi-structured interviews to help contextualise and extend the findings from the audio logs. In the following discussion we use representative samples of this data to illustrate the points.

If we focus on the use of technology for communication in support of learning, the most commonly reported communication technology was the mobile phone. Students in all subjects phoned and texted each other frequently, most commonly in connection with learning assignments that they were working on. Mobile phones were preferred for communication between students, family/friends and to some extent with teachers where an immediate response is required.

I use my mobile phone to communicate with class mates.

[W56]

Mobile phone messages are generally picked up quicker than emails, so better for urgent messages.

[X74]

Students also indicated that they use mobile phones a lot while planning and working on learning tasks.

Arrange meetings by text message on mobile phones.

[W74]

Share projects and information through email and mobile phone.

[W172]

Mobile phone and e-mail to contact friends to discuss work.

[X198]

One learner described how he and his colleagues support each other in their course work via their mobile phones:

Today I have used a number of technologies. The first tool I used was my mobile phone to text members of my class to find out examination hints that were given as I was not able to attend. This helped me greatly as now I know what to revise for my exams.

(Finbar, Computer Sciences)

Later Finbar noted that by talking to others about his coursework he gains a much better insight into how his peers are approaching things. So, as well as working on course material, peers share expertise, confide in each other, check in on each other's progress and update each other with course information (deadlines, hand-in dates, etc.).

However, there were a number of criticisms of mobile phones, chiefly their cost.

The use of mobile phone is expensive, and as computers are becoming able to do more, I am using mobile less and less.

[AO23]

Low cost communication technologies such as Skype, Microsoft's MSN and email were frequently used in preference, and there was evidence of them being used in a variety of ways (student–student, student–friends/ family, student–tutor). Skype, software that allows students to call people for free or at a low cost via the Internet, and MSN Messenger and other instant messaging software were specifically mentioned by international students and those who lived in halls of residences as a cheap and easy way to keep in touch with friends, colleagues and family.

To some extent instant messaging is also used by students to plan and carry out group learning tasks:

Instant messenger, free to use, ease of use to speak to people with fast response, ability to share files across it, ability to work on group projects with it, and ability to video conference.

[X53]

All students used email, which was the main technology for communicating with university staff. Students expected and received quick responses to their emails to their tutors and appreciated the channel of communication email provided.

Email – To contact others, predominantly lecturers and coursemates around assignment deadlines. I also use Gmail to back up work.

[X402]

In addition to the obvious use of email as a means of communicating with fellow students and tutors it was also used to set up meetings and submit assignments. This student demonstrates how essential email is to her communications with other students, her tutors and the department:

Almost all our communications with the university are through email... which is almost invaluable because we're all off site so much, from 3rd year onwards. Just posting things on the notice board wouldn't work.... We also have something quite useful, as a medical student, I can email any other medical student in my medical school, using a list server. This has been really useful this year, for my work as a rep and for advertising spare rooms in my house.

(Ann Marie, Medicine)

Several students had set up blogs and others reported reading blogs. None of these were hosted by the student's university.

In addition to that I used blogs today. I used a blog as part of a personal reflection on various happenings in the computer industry to increase my knowledge on what is going on in this industry as a whole and record personal opinions on what is going on.

(Finbar, Computer Sciences)

Overall the LXP study showed that students had no difficulties with any of the technologies and applications that they had selected for themselves. A broad review of the findings suggest that new forms of collaboration are emerging both with peers and via new 'smart' and adaptive technologies, suggesting a shift towards Salomon's (1993) notion of 'distributed cognition' and shared enterprise with tools.

They [technologies] help to display ideas and are a quick way to gather and collaborate info, improvements would be a conference setting on a mobile.

[X247]

I use these because it's easy [to] organise my life, thoughts and work. The biggest thing that would allow me to use them more effectively is if more students were aware of what the possibilities of using group collaboration tools such as citeulike and del.icio.us.

[X252]

## Discussion and Conclusions

Clearly students make creative use of technologies in support of their networked learning. Whether engaged in on-task collaborative learning and knowledge building, or making strategic use of social contacts within their network to support individual learning around the task, many students are advanced social learners. They use technology within networks of peers, sharing ideas and resources, exchanging draft reports, providing mutual support.

In both cases we have seen that students mainly prefer synchronous communication tools. Although Case 1 was set up for mainly asynchronous collaboration, students frequently used chat, face-to-face and mobile phones. For some this was just their preferred mode of communication, offering immediacy of response. For some it provided shelter from the academic panopticon. From Case 2 we have learned that students use this type of communication mainly to organise around the task and, because it is in real time, to get an instant reply on questions of urgency and for just in time learning (van Merrienboer et al. 2003).

An interesting paradox emerges from this chapter. On the one hand we see that students creatively fit preferred technology around their activities to support their networked learning, while on the other hand their choice of tools – particularly their preference for synchronous communication – does not always maximise the collaborative learning experience. One reason for this paradox is the need to learn new skills and competencies for the technologies that can support networked learning. Another is the personal and social meanings learners attach to different technologies. New forms of collaboration are emerging due to the use of technology, and learners have to develop strategies for engaging in them. Educationalists are also being challenged to develop the right kind of pedagogies, support processes, designs and assessments for these new forms of social learning networks.

During collaborative learning, students may encounter complex decision making. Effective networked learning presupposes that students have been given the opportunities to develop the technical and learning skills they need to carry out their learning activities. These include collaboration skills, the skills of peer review and of teamwork, including managing cultural difference, all of which need to be taught just as much as other academic skills like research and communication. For as Johnson et al. (2007: 24) comment, 'asking unskilled individuals to cooperate is somewhat futile'.

We have seen that effective collaboration requires a sense of moral order, a perception of fairness and equity in the academic environments that learners are expected to collaborate in. Language and cultural differences and differential access to or skills with technology need to be accounted for through inclusive designs and supports for collaborative tasks. Cases 1 and 2 both show, each in their own way, that the role of the academic panopticon should be explicitly acknowledged and negotiated with learners. *On the task* designs should acknowledge the reality of *around the task* networking and technology use. Which aspects of the surveillance and monitoring capabilities of digital learning environments will be used and which will not, how they will be used and why, need to be made explicit to avoid a clash of beliefs and expectations among participants.

From both cases we learn that there is a need for an extended dialogue with students about the various roles and responsibilities of tutors and peers. A review by De Laat, Simons and Wenger (2006) indicated that in networked learning communities the traditional teacher–student relationship is under tension and role confusion might occur. Values such as willingness to share and make one's learning 'transparent' to peers and tutors, seeing oneself as a learning resource for others, need to be nurtured against a weight of tradition and practice in higher education that favours individuality and competitiveness.

At the course, institutional and national level, networked learning demands assessment practices that promote interdependence and value both individual responsibility and contribution to group learning. At an institutional level we are left with questions about which (software) tools can best be used to support collaborative learning. Dalsgaard (2006) argues for the integration of social software with VLEs to allow students to have more active control over their own preferred way of learning. Social software tools allow for a better sense of social presence (Kreijns et al. 2004) and transparency (Dalsgaard 2006; Dalsgaard and Paulsen 2009) and therefore facilitate the extension of networks in support of learning. More careful thought needs to be given to how social networking software can enhance the student experience (Conole et al. 2006).

In conclusion, courses need to be designed with the recognition that students will use their own technologies to work collaboratively around set tasks, and will ascribe their own meanings to the institutional technologies set up for collaborating on task. Perceptions of fairness and surveillance are particularly significant, and must be addressed openly. Students empowered with their own technologies and social structures to support collaboration will appropriate and adapt the courses they are offered, to meet their personal needs.

## References

Anderson, T. (2005). Distance learning – social software's killer ap? Paper presented at ODLAA 2005 Conference, Adelaide, November. Retrieved 27 August, 2009, from http://www.odlaa.org/events/2005conf/nonref/odlaa2005Anderson.pdf.

Benfield, G. & Prior, J. (2007). Virtual teamwork within a campus based team skills module. In Proceedings of the Second International Blended Learning Conference: Supporting the Net Generation Learner, Hatfield: University of Hertfordshire Press.

Brindley, J., Blaschke, L.M. & Walti, C. (2009). Creating effective collaborative learning groups in an online environment, *The International Review of Research in Open and Distance Learning*, *10*(3), Retrieved 19 June, 2009, from http://www.irrodl.org/index.php/irrodl/issue/view/36.

Cartney, P. & Rouse, A. (2006). The emotional impact of learning in small groups: highlighting the impact on student progression and retention, *Teaching in Higher Education, 11*(1): 79–91.

Castells, M. (2000). *Rise of the network society, 2nd Edition,* Oxford: Blackwell Publishers, Inc.

Clouder, L. and Deepwell, F. (2004). Reflections on unexpected outcomes: learning from student collaboration in an online discussion forum. Networked Learning Conference 2004, April 2004, Lancaster University. Retrieved 5 April, 2007, from www.networkedlearningconference.org.uk/past/nlc2004/proceedings/individual_papers/clouderanddeepwell.htm.

Conole, G. & Dyke, M. (2004). What are the inherent affordances of information and communication technologies? *ALT-J, 12*(2): 113–124.

Conole, G., de Laat, M., Dillon, T. & Darby, J. (2006). LXP: student experiences of technologies – final report. Retrieved 19 June, 2009, from http://jisc.ac.uk/media/documents/programmes/elearningpedagogy/lxp_project_final_report_nov_06.pdf.

Creanor, L., Trinder, K., Gowan, D. & Howells, C. (2006). *LEX: the learner experience of e-learning. Final report* (report under the JISC e-pedagogy 'Understanding my learner' programme). Glasgow: Glasgow Caledonian University. Retrieved 20 August, 2009, from http://www.jisc.ac.uk/whatwedo/programmes/elearning_pedagogy/elp_learneroutcomes.aspx.

Dalsgaard, C. (2006). Social software: e-learning beyond learning management systems, *European Journal of Open, Distance and E-Learning (EURODL), 2006* (II). Retrieved 12 August, 2009, from http://www.eurodl.org/materials/contrib/2006/Christian_Dalsgaard.htm.

Dalsgaard, C. & Paulsen, M.F. (2009). Transparency in cooperative online education, *The International Review of Research in Open and Distance Learning, 10*(3).

De Laat, M. (2006). *Networked learning,* Apeldoorn: Politieacademie.

De Laat, M. (2008). *Netwerkleren, een haalbaarheidsstudie naar de kansen voor netwerkleren als vorm van professionalisering voor leraren,* RdMC: Heerlen.

De Laat, M. & Lally, V. (2003). Complexity, theory and praxis: researching collaborative learning and tutoring processes in a networked learning community, *Instructional Science, 31*(1&2): 7–39.

De Laat, M. F., Lally, V., Simons, P.R.J. & Wenger, E. (2006). A selective analysis of empirical findings in networked learning research in higher education: questing for coherence, *Educational Research Review, 1*(2): 99–111.

De Laat, M.F., Lally, V., Lipponen, L. & Simons, P.R.J. (2007). Investigating patterns of interaction in networked learning and computer-supported collaborative learning: a role for social network analysis, *International Journal of Computer-Supported Collaborative Learning, 2*(1): 87–103.

Dresner, M. & Starvel, E. (2004). Mutual benefits of scientist/teacher partnerships, *Academic Exchange Quarterly, 8*: 252–256.

Dresner, M. & Worley, E. (2006). Teacher research experiences, partnerships with scientists, and teacher networks sustaining factors from professional development, *Journal of Science Teacher Education, 17*: 1–14.

Earl, L. & Katz, S. (2007). Leadership in networked learning communities, *School Leadership and Management, 27*(3): 239–258.

Educause (2008). 2008 Horizon Report. Boulder, CO: Educause. Retrieved 30 January, 2009, from http://connect.educause.edu/Library/ELI/2008HorizonReport/45926?time=1233319370.

Entwistle, N. (2003). Concepts and conceptual frameworks underpinning the ETL Project. Retrieved 29 June, 2006, from http://www.ed.ac.uk/etl/publications.html.

Goodyear, P., Banks, S., Hodgson, V. & McConnell, D. (2004). *Advances in research on networked learning,* Norwell, MA: Kluwer Academic Publishers.

Gottschall, H. & García-Bayonas, M. (2008). Student attitudes towards group work among undergraduates in business administration, education and mathematics, *Educational Research Quarterly, 32*(1): 3–28.

Granovetter, M. (1973). The strength of weak ties, *American Journal of Sociology, 78*: 1360–1380.

Greenberg, P.S., Greenberg, R.H. & Antonucci, Y.L. (2007). Creating and sustaining trust in virtual teams, *Business Horizons, 50*(4): 325–333.

Hodgson, V. & Reynolds, M. (2005). Consensus, difference and 'multiple communities' in networked learning, *Studies in Higher Education, 30*(1): 11–24.

JISC (2009). Responding to learners: a guide for practitioners. Retrieved 8 June, 2009, from https://mw.brookes.ac.uk/display/JISCle2g/Guides.

Johnson, D.W. & Johnson, R.T. (1999). *Learning together and alone: cooperative, competitive and individualistic learning,* (Fifth Edition), Needham Heights, MA: Allyn and BaconJohnson, S. D., Suriya, C., Won Yoon, S., Berrett, J.V. & La Fleur, J. (2002). Team development and group processes of virtual learning teams, *Computers & Education, 39*(4): 379–393.

Johnson, D., Johnson, R. & Smith, K. (2007). The state of cooperative learning in postsecondary and professional settings, *Educational Psychology Review, 19*(1): 15–29.

Jones, C., Dirckinck-Holmfeld, L. & Lindström, B. (2006). A relational, indirect, meso-level approach to CSCL design in the next decade, *International Journal of Computer-Supported Collaborative Learning, 1*(1): 35–56.

Katz, S. & Hands, C. (2007). *Scaling up from one network to many: the establishment of networked learning communities within the district*, York: Region District School Board.

Kreijns, K., Kirschner, P., Jochems, W. & van Buuren, H. (2004). Determining sociability, social space, and social presence in (a) synchronous collaborative groups, *CyberPsychology & Behavior, 7*(2): 155–172.

Levin, D.Z. & Cross, R. (2004). The strength of weak ties you can trust: the mediating role of trust in effective knowledge transfer, *Management Science, 50*(11): 1477–1490.

Lieberman, A. & Wood, D. (2002a). From network learning to classroom teaching, *Journal of Educational Change, 3*: 315–337.

Lieberman, A. & Wood, D. (2002b). Untangling the threads: networks, community and teacher learning in the National Writing Project, *Teachers and Teaching: Theory and Practice, 8*(3/4): 295–302.

Macdonald, J. (2003). Assessing online collaborative learning: process and product, *Computers & Education, 40*: 377–391.

McConnell, D. (2000). *Implementing computer supported cooperative learning*, London: Kogan Page.

McConnell, D. (2006). *E-learning groups and communities of practice*, Maidenhead: The Society for Research into Higher Education & Open University Press.

Palloff, R.M. & Pratt, K. (2005). *Collaborating online: learning together in community*, San Francisco, CA: Jossey-Bass.

Paulus, T.M. (2005). Collaborative and cooperative approaches to online group work: the impact of task type, *Distance Education, 26*(1): 111–125.

Ramsden, P. (1992). *Learning to teach in higher education*, London: Routledge.

Ryan, J. (2000). *A guide to teaching international students*, Oxford: Oxford Centre for Staff and Learning Development.

Salaway, G., Caruso, J.B. & Nelson, M.R. (2007). The ECAR study of undergraduate students and information technology, 2007. Retrieved 9 October, 2007, from http://www.educause.edu/ir/library/pdf/ers0706/rs/ERS0706w.pdf.

Salomon, G. (Ed.) (1993). *Distributed cognitions: psychological and educational considerations*, Cambridge: Cambridge University Press.

Scardamelia, M., Bereiter, C., McLean, R., Swallow, J. & Woodruff, E. (1989). Computer supported intentional learning environments, *Journal of Educational Computing Research, 5*: 51–68.

Sharpe, R., Benfield, G., Roberts, G. & Francis, R. (2006). The undergraduate experience of blended e-learning: a review of UK literature and practice undertaken for the Higher Education Academy. Retrieved 3 October, 2006, from http://www.heacademy.ac.uk/assets/York/documents/ourwork/research/literature_reviews/blended_elearning_full_review.pdf.

Siemens, G. (2009). Connectivism: a learning theory for the digital age, *International Journal of Instructional Technology and Distance Learning*. Retrieved 12 November, 2009, from http://www.itdl.org/Journal/Jan_05/article01.htm.

Simons, P.R.J. & de Laat, M. (2006). E-pedagogies for networked learning. In L. Verschaffel, F. Dochy, M. Boekaerts and S. Vosniadou (Eds.) *Instructional psychology past, present, and future trends – sixteen essays in honour of Erik De Corte*, (pp. 239–255), Dordrecht, The Netherlands: Kluwer.

Smith, R.O. (2008). The paradox of trust in online collaborative groups, *Distance Education, 29*(3): 325–340.

Steeples, C. & Jones, C. (Eds.) (2002). *Networked learning: perspectives and issues*, London: Springer.

van Merrienboer, J.J.G., Kirschner, P.A. & Kester, L. (2003). Taking the load off a learner's mind: instructional design for complex learning, *Educational Psychologist, 38*(1): 5–13.

Wood, D.M. (2006). A report on the surveillance society for the information commissioner by the Surveillance Studies Network. Retrieved 15 June, 2009, from http://www.ico.gov.uk/upload/documents/library/data_protection/practical_application/surveillance_society_full_report_2006.pdf.

# 14

# 'But It's Not Just Developing Like a Learner, It's Developing as a Person'

## Reflections on E-portfolio-based Learning

### JULIE HUGHES

## Editors' Introduction

Some of the methods that have been used recently to study learners' experiences of e-learning – such as narratives, logs and personal reflections – have a longer history as tools for researching and supporting personal development. For several years, Julie Hughes has been using these and other participative techniques to explore e-portfolio-based learning. E-portfolios, described here as a 'domain', a 'genre', and a 'set of practices' rather than a single technology, have significantly shifted the locus of attention towards learners' own sense-making practices, because their content and the processes of their production are managed by learners. Hughes argues that a collaborative pedagogy supports the risk-taking required for personal development, and she builds on learners' own reflections to make her case for e-portfolio-based learning as identity work, on both a professional and a personal level.

## Introduction

In relation to learning, ontology trumps epistemology. That is to say, the student's being in the world is more important for her learning than her interests in developing knowledge and understanding in a particular field.

(Barnett 2007: 6)

... through reflection, we understand curriculum pluralized: as lived, as delivered, as experienced: it is in the intersection of these curricula that identities are formed: students exert the most authority in that intersection since they are the ones who inhabit the place; learning more about that place is a goal of reflection used for educational purposes.

(Yancey 1998: 202)

This chapter will explore how the use of e-portfolio tools within a specific conceptual and contextual pedagogic approach can support important transformative identity work, which encourages learners to use and inhabit the space, make sense and meaning of their situatedness and narrate and reflect upon their experiences over time, supporting conscious shifts within a developmental trajectory. Underpinning this pursuit is a personal desire as a practitioner and researcher to explore how to 're-think' and 're-do' pedagogy (Beetham and Sharpe 2007: 3), to support and illustrate what Mayes and de Freitas (2007: 13) claim as an emergent, 'new model of education' that is iterative, social, situated and mediated through relationships. Bolton (2001: 32) offers the foundations for a 'through the looking glass model' of reflective learning whose conditions are: 'certain uncertainty, serious playfulness and unquestioning questioning'. This pedagogy stresses the contingent and dynamic nature of professional reflection and learning, which must be driven by process rather than mapped as product. Bolton also carefully identifies that community members, 'may need time and gentle encouragement towards gaining the confidence required to create their own structure of appropriate and stretching enquiry...to people willing to 'not know' all the time, all sorts of things are possible' (Bolton 2001: 33). Within this framework, the use of e-portfolio may be explored as a 'trojan mouse' (Sharpe and Oliver 2007: 49), which requires teachers to:

> rethink not just how they use particular hardware or software, but all of what they do...to incorporate technology successfully requires the purpose of the course to be negotiated and made explicit. This process prompts reflection, negotiation and adaption to what has, traditionally, been a private and tacit area of work.

### A Personal Context – Beginning to 'Re-think' and 'Re-do'

I have been working with e-portfolios since 2004 in the School of Education at the University of Wolverhampton, predominantly in professional courses such as the full-time Postgraduate Certificate in Education (PGCE) for the post-compulsory sector and part-time foundation degrees (FDs) in Early Years and Supporting Inclusive Practices. The university is a widening participation institution. Sixty-seven per cent of its students are drawn from the Black Country boroughs and Birmingham; 36 per cent of students are part-time and 60 per cent of the student population are over 21 (QAA 2008). The student narratives (data) drawn upon in this chapter were gathered through individual and shared blogs, through webfolios and their artefacts presented for formative and summative assessment and from more traditional data gathering formats such as questionnaires, interviews (including an interview-plus approach) and focus groups.

Before engaging with e-portfolios I had used technology in my teaching as Laurillard (2007: xv–xvi) describes, simply and uncritically to 'support traditional modes of teaching which were nowhere near being transformational'. Initially my intention was to 'test' the potential in the e-portfolio technology to see if it could support and extend the dialogic feedback practices that informed my face-to-face pedagogy. I wanted my learners to inhabit and experience the e-portfolio space, as part of a repertoire of learning experiences, as a place for talking and not as a place for telling. To achieve this blend I had to learn how to create, exploit and enjoy the spaces to encourage engagement in extended reflective dialogue. The e-portfolio talk and talkback space became a dynamic source for data collection and conversation where I was able to pose reflexive questions to myself, students and colleagues about their experiences of learning and teaching in this environment, and their developing sense of self as education professionals. The movement from the private and tacit to the sharing of richly subjective narratives within communities has allowed an exploration of the experiences of transition points in higher education (HE), particularly to notions of becoming and belonging to higher education communities (Hulme and Hughes 2006; Hughes 2009) *and* then to related education professions (Hughes et al. 2008). Underpinning this pursuit is a focus upon the journey (the process) rather than upon arrival (the end product) as Richardson and St. Pierre (2005: 966–967) identify that, 'in the story (or stories) of becoming, we have a good chance of deconstructing the underlying academic ideology – that *being* a something… is better than becoming'.

Simultaneously I have explored the joys and the tensions of being the insider-researcher (Hughes 2007) trying out different ways of being. I settle for now within Lather's vision of catalytic validity, which:

> [r]epresents the degree to which the research process re-orients, focuses and energizes participants towards knowing reality in order to transform it, a process Freire (1973) terms conscientization…it flies in the face of positivist demands for researcher neutrality. The argument for catalytic validity lies not only within recognition of the reality-altering impact of the research process, but also in the desire to consciously channel this impact so that respondents gain self-understanding, and, ultimately, self-determination through research participation.
>
> (Lather 1991: 11)

Underpinning this work is a commitment to social justice and an emphasis upon the individual student's 'being in the world' (Barnett 2007: 6).

Inevitably as practitioner/researcher I am deeply embedded in the data that is deliberatively participative and so perhaps limited to its specific contexts.

The development of e-portfolios has been well documented elsewhere (Beetham 2005; Ward and Richardson 2005; Richardson and Ward 2005; Hartnell-Young et al. 2007). However, an interesting conceptual shift has emerged recently. In the UK, the Centre for Recording Achievement (CRA) has defined the e-portfolio domain as a broad one that is, or that might be, 'a repository, a means of presenting oneself and ones skills, qualities and achievements, a guidance tool, a means of sharing and collaborating and a means of encouraging a sense of personal identity' (2008). In the USA, Cambridge (2008) is theorizing that e-portfolio is, 'a genre and a set of practices supported by a set of technologies'. This genre of representation involves 'collecting evidence in authentic activity, reflecting upon that evidence and interacting with feedback, re-contextualising and reassembling this within an interpretative framework and a set of tools' (Cambridge 2008). Re-conceptualizing e-portfolio as a way of being and of interacting, as well as an artefact, allows us to rethink the possibilities for learner-directed reassembly, bricolage and identity negotiation. These are exciting possibilities which this chapter will endeavour to explore.

## What Are Learners Saying About Their Own Uses of Technology and the Impact it Has on Their Learning?

> Gave me the confidence to 'mess' with computers, i.e. press buttons I'm not used to.
>
> (Anon, FD student)

> Well to be honest I think it does break down the barriers, definitely, and people start getting to know each other.
>
> (Tracey, FD student)

Over the past five academic years I have seen and felt a shift when I introduce e-portfolio-based learning to groups of students. In part, this attributed to my own growing confidence and commitment to a reflective and collaborative approach – a set of practices supported by a set of tools. However, it is also due to more practical issues such as access to a computer for all students at induction and the provision of a large and friendly social learning space at the Walsall campus that hosts banks of computers and a café. Until January 2008 there were only two bookable IT suites on campus for School of Education students and supporting innovation often meant occupying lunchtime, twilight and evening sessions. Routine, informal access, lending the confidence to 'mess' with computers, is for many of my part-time learners a vital starting point.

Foundation degree students who are working full-time, and PGCE students on a one-year programme, do not have the time to 'mess with computers' and the learning of these skills has to be embedded in their curriculum for successful e-portfolio-based learning:

> well I'd got no skills in computers so when they said portfolios were going to be done online and not on paperwork, and I'd only done them on paperwork, it was panic, absolute panic but then when Julie had started going straight into it, it just went in like that…I got it, immediately.…I didn't have to panic. In fact I ended up showing nearly everybody in the class what I had been shown… it just seemed easy … I don't want to patronise anyone who didn't find it easy. I just found it simple.
>
> (Carole, PGCE student)

This was a particularly poignant experience for Carole, a dyslexic learner as:

> Having struggled for years as a dyslexic student, I feel the Pebble-pad has allowed me to be at the same level as everyone else and in some cases ahead of them. I'm sure you can imagine what this does to my confidence and self-esteem, (being at the top of the class instead of the bottom).
>
> (Carole, PGCE student)

Rohan, one of the group members that Carole supported, offers a different novice account:

> As a self-confessed novice in the use of IT, the prospect of using the e-portfolio frightened the hell out of me. However, several months of use and a portfolio full of positive and negative experiences…I am glad that I was required to use this facility. Feeling a lot more comfortable with the package.
>
> (Rohan, PGCE student)

Rohan's comment that he was required to use the 'facility/package' is an important one to consider for several reasons. At this stage (2005–6 PGCE group) the use of e-portfolio was not compulsory. It was not embedded in the PGCE as a whole until 2007. My group was encouraged/cajoled to use the system with the promise of engaged reflection and feedback and collaborative learning opportunities. Rohan's later point, 'I have increasingly used it not just as a form of information storage but as a means of expressing and sharing my personal thoughts with other "bloggers" in my group', evidences the potential multiple uses by students and a movement away from the earlier preferred digital storage mode. The organizational opportunities afforded by this digital environment are also very important to some students. Jenny, a PGCE student featured in the JISC *The Learner's Voice* publication (2007), describes her e-portfolio as 'an organised place to put everything … it's a filing cabinet online but its got a dialogue with it as well'.

Mary, an FD student and dyslexic learner, conceptualizes her e-portfolio as 'my pocket book – there all the time, full of assets, you know where things are…if you've got a spare five minutes, it's always there – can just log on'. However, it is also the scaffolding of the e-portfolio activities themselves which offer organizational control:

> when you initially set up a document you can…categorise all your pages … The first page was my introduction and then …my theory… so I could actually see in my mind's eye that I'd covered every base and they were all tabs down the side which was quite helpful…You could add pictures into it … you could change all your layout to make it more interesting.
>
> (Mary, FD student)

Embedding scaffolded reflective activities as individual blog entries offers the possibility for ongoing and iterative models of PDP (Personal Development Planning), a benefit Mary describes as 'having it all there, being able to see how far I've come – spatial and visual journey, capturing in the moment'. Reflective blogging – or writing in the moment – is not a comfortable experience for all students, however, as this comment demonstrates: 'I felt intimidated by other students who can type more quickly'. This is the dilemma faced when embedding practice opportunities into the curriculum, as the practice becomes very public and for some students this is intimidating rather than supportive. Differentiated sessions, detailed handouts and one-to-one support are vital to close the ability and confidence gaps. Supporting this requires rethinking and redoing of pedagogy across a curriculum team.

The emerging pedagogic opportunities were explored through an ongoing conversation, at a meta-cognitive level, with my students (Hughes 2007). Karen, when asked to describe what learning was like in this new environment, responded:

> It's like emptying a big jigsaw and building it slowly in pieces. Finding pieces of work that fit together and building from there and then maybe trying a different area afterwards. There's no logical, symmetrical or linear route but emphasis upon drawing out the best points and building upon them.
>
> (Karen, PGCE student)

These e-portfolio-based learning processes are described in a recent JISC (2008: 6) publication as, 'rich and complex processes of planning, synthesising, sharing, discussing, reflecting, giving, receiving and responding to feedback'. If we think about new models of education (Mayes and de Freitas 2007) emerging from these practices then Karen's comment is a fascinating and sophisticated starting point for what e-portfolio-based learning might feel like, and a challenge for e-portfolio educators. Karen's jigsaw analogy, which celebrates hypertext and non-linearity, became a powerful scaffold for my thinking and practice and by implication the thinking and practice of my students.

### What Meanings do Learners Ascribe to the Social–technical Practices They Engage in?

> Being an eportfolio learner gave me the opportunity not only to explore new ways of learning, but to become part of a community that has supported and encouraged each other throughout our journey to becoming new teachers. The blog tool within the eportfolio allowed us the safe space to share thoughts, feelings, anxieties, laughter and tears and because it was a shared space we could see the value in the perception of thoughts and opinions of others in the group...The ongoing dialogue with my peers and tutor was fundamental in my development as a reflective writer and new teacher. It was a creative collaborative learning space, a lifeline on what could sometimes be a bumpy road.
>
> (Hughes & Purnell 2008)

FD and PGCE students might appear to be at opposite ends of the undergraduate HE ladder – one group at entry level and one group completing a postgraduate professional qualification. However, as learners they share strikingly similar hopes, fears and expectations that are beautifully illustrated through their e-portfolio narratives. Dialogue-based PDP is intrinsic to both programmes, and students are required to reflect upon themselves and their development as learners and as (para)professionals throughout their programme of study. Students are encouraged to talk back (Lillis 2001) to their tutor and peers, and to theorize and integrate these new reflections into their shifting sense of self. These writing patches (including action planning narratives) build cumulatively into summative assessments. As Mary's earlier comment identifies, the spatial and visual journey is laid open through the use of an e-portfolio system and the individual can trace their reflective learning trajectory. As this anonymous FD student comments, 'it helped me reflect. Writing in this manner can uncover aspects of your thoughts that you might not be aware of.' Laura, a PGCE student, comments specifically on the role of her peers in this developing reflexivity:

> Not only has the writing of the reflective journal been instrumental in the process of self-reflection, as too has the ability and confidence to share my journals with the rest of the group. In the 'Reflective Cycle' suggested by Gibbs (1998), the process of self-reflection is considered in a very neat and circular way, which I have come to find, is not how the process always evolves and fails to take into account the non-linear movement between stages. In the past, I tended to reflect upon incidents

by jumping straight in and thinking what I could have and should have done when things have gone wrong, completely missing out the beginning three stages of the cycle: feelings, evaluation and analysis.

I feel that the process of sharing my journals has allowed me to learn from my peers and explore the three stages of the model that I have frequently missed out. Sharing my journals in an electronic format via Pebble Pad has also facilitated my ease at being able to share feelings with peers that I probably would not do face-to-face. The thoughts and comments from others also aid my evaluation and analysis of situations, importantly helping me to draw upon the incident and find the best way to move forward.

(Laura, PGCE student)

Sarah, an FD student, comments specifically on the community reflections and the role it has had in her transition into the university:

using blogging has helped me develop as a learner. I think by writing it down and knowing that there is someone at the other end willing to listen and offer advice has been a huge factor in my learning journey. To know that I am not alone in this experience is a boost to my confidence.

(Sarah, FD student)

Reflection on self-development can be a traumatic and testing experience, as Tom indicates:

The PGCE has brought about the following feelings and experiences. I have been stretched mentally. I have also experienced anxiety, disappointment, frustration and at times I have felt blind. The e-portfolio for me has been a sort of picture frame where I can look and retain my thought electronically.

(Tom, PGCE student)

The picture fame metaphor is a useful one to consider when reflecting upon the development of new teachers. Tom's articulation of the need to sometimes contain and control (frame) thoughts and reflections is an important one. Reflection, a contested term, 'is difficult' (Clegg, 2004: 292), and

[r]eflection is not, by definition, critical…reflection becomes critical when it has two distinctive purposes. The first is to understand how considerations of power undergrid, frame and distort educational processes and interactions. The second is to question assumptions and practices that make our teaching lives easier but actually work against our own best long-term interests.

(Brookfield 1995: 8)

Pete, a PGCE student, illustrates just how uncomfortable this journey can be when he shares his experience of failing a lesson observation with his peers:

Others have made this journey before but I was prepared to travel uncomfortably and prepared to go the distance with the risk taking. I was going make the journey of self reflection an opportunity that I have always been looking for and have now been given another chance to explore and take those leaps into the unknown. I was going to grab it with both hands. If I was complacent then others should know, let's make the voyage an experience and something to be shared and I did agonise whether to put myself out there all open and vulnerable, but shared I did, making a dreadfully painful experience into something which changed me and maybe others. My shared reflective journal was such a rewarding experience for me personally, I grew in confidence and as a practitioner.

(Pete, PGCE student)

Zoe, a PGCE student, offers an important reminder about discomfort, which offers a critique of the assumptions we may make about face-to-face learning episodes:

In the second semester we began to share our critical incidents via Pebble Pad. This has proved much more beneficial to me because it meant that I could compose myself, think about the incident and then tell my story. I found the distance to be liberating because I could subdue the feelings of inferiority I had when listening to my peers. I could write down my experiences in my own time, set at my own pace, rather than at the set time given in the face-to-face discussions.

(Zoe, PGCE student)

The safe but simultaneously risky space provided by the use of an e-portfolio system offers the opportunity for students to 'come into a felt relationship with uncertainty' (Barnett 2007: 34), a space that supports a 'will to learn' (Barnett 2007: 1). Barnett's (2007: 126) guidance on a pedagogy for uncertain times in HE states its main pedagogic task as 'simple to state and near impossible to achieve. It is that of releasing students that they come into themselves, in relation to their curricula challenges. They become beings-for-themselves… They have their own will to learn.' Barnett's vision (2007: 7) for HE for the contemporary world insists upon the need for a vocabulary of 'excitement, passion, self-confidence, journey, travel, will, energy, being and becoming'. The following anonymous reflections from FD students upon the perceived benefits of e-portfolio-based learning offer an indication of their will to learn.

I feel empowered and far more positive for the future and not so daunted. I don't feel as scared as learning will be less stressfull now and will therefore minimise my threats and it's great to read back and think – "did that really worry me?"

(Anon FD student)

As an H.E student – confidence grew tremendously because I had no idea what I was letting myself in for initially! Found that I really enjoyed the challenge & stimulation of university life. (In truth, I would rather be a full time student, I enjoy it so much!!). My experience at uni has strengthened my belief in myself at work – I am much more confident and happy to try out new strategies with children. Absolutely love writing. Always have. Academic writing is a challenge, especially the referencing but found the experience very satisfying. I especially enjoy reflective writing – it helps me put a perspective on what I do.

(Anon FD student)

## Shifting Identities – How Do Learners Inhabit the Place?

I'm only a Teaching Assistant – me, going to University?

(Anon FD student)

I had been told as a teenager that I was not intelligent enough to achieve my ambition of becoming a teacher.

(Anon FD student)

…the person that started back in September is not the person I recognise now and as I unwrap this part of myself I come to realise I see others as well as myself with different eyes.

(Anon FD student)

I belong here.

(Anon FD student)

It seems that within this environment no longer am I (the student) the passive listener. The learning involves a shift from surface to deep learning in which I need to be an active participant.

(Mary, FD student)

Becoming teacher, for this student, is like learning to swim:

I have managed to download or upload whatever a video (thanks Em) to my blog and I'm so proud. It is of my youngest learning how to swim. But it is so much more than that. In it he jumps in at the deep end and I know that this scares him a lot. He struggles at the deep end and has a float for support even though he can swim quite well without it. He bumps into an obstacle and the teacher taps him on his way. I mean how symbolic of my journey is this? I have somewhat cautiously, eventually taken the plunge in the deep end and despite knowing in my heart of hearts that I can do it I hold onto my old habits and lack of confidence like a float in the hope that they will support me in some way when actually I don't need them anymore because I CAN SWIM!! I just have to keep reminding myself of this when my shadows loom. Despite the obstacles he keeps going and eventually having almost drowned and looking exhausted he succeeds. Like mother like son.

(Chloe, PGCE student)

Yancey's (1998: 200) assertion that, 'through the talk we become' offers a reading of e-portfolio-based learning in which the writer/reflecter is able to invent 'repeatedly and recursively, a composing self'. Reflection 'woven into curriculum' (ibid: 17), supported by ongoing feedback from peers and tutors, can support what Yancey describes as enacted reflection where students 'conjoin inside and outside lives, move to synthesize, reveal gaps, make some sense of the world, show us how it means' (ibid: 188). The reflective comments from FD and PGCE students reveal this as they struggle with the disconnects and connects of their learning. However, without their ongoing reflective blogging, much of this would be rendered invisible both to the individual and to the audiences they are writing for. The ability to map the journey from disbelief ('*me going to University?*') through the adoption of new and challenging perspectives ('*taking the plunge*') to belonging and beyond ('*swimming*') demonstrates how 'it is just possible that the student may come into a new mode of being' (Barnett 2007: 1).

Barnett's assertion that an ontological turn is urgently needed, and that space and risk are critical factors for successful study, must be tempered by his acknowledgement that 'the pedagogical being is fragile ... it is brittle, liable to shatter suddenly' (Barnett 2007: 29). E-portfolio-based learning offers space to the interplay of the pluralized curriculum (Yancey 1998) but the fragility of the pedagogy and the participants must be recognized: 'care and passion together are called for in bringing about a continuing pedagogy of air' (Barnett 2007: 170). As Karen the PGCE student identified, learning in this new space requires an 'emphasis upon drawing out the best points and building upon them...within no logical, symmetrical or linear route'.

In contrast with many contemporary approaches to the curriculum, this integrated, non-modular learning experience, rooted within a dialogic and collaborative framework, can support risk-taking. What Barnett calls pedagogical bungee jumping is a reciprocal experience: 'out of the giving comes more giving, out of the daring comes more daring' (Barnett 2007: 133). As Pete and Chloe's reflections demonstrate, jumping in at the deep end and making their vulnerability a part of their learning experience was crucial to their personal and professional development.

One size does not fit all. But the past five years as an e-portfolio teacher have convinced me that there is the potential for powerful transformational learning through the use of e-portfolio technologies if the conditions are created for ownership, reciprocity, dialogic reflection and a focus on the journey – the distance travelled. Adopting and modelling dialogic practices as conceptual tools for course design and delivery can play a critical role in supporting learners, who are future educators, to self-consciously narrate and reflect upon their ongoing development as a trajectory that offers spaces for identity work.

## References

Barnett, R. (2007). *A will to learn. Being a student in an age of uncertainty*, Berkshire: Open University Press.
Beetham, H. (2005). *Eportfolios in post-16 learning in the UK: developments, issues and opportunities. Report to the JISC e-learning and pedagogy programme*. Retrieved 15 August, 2005, from http://jisc.ac.uk/uploaded_documents/eportfolio_ped.doc.
Beetham, H. & Sharpe, R. (Eds.) (2007). *Rethinking pedagogy for a digital age. Designing and delivering e-learning*, London: Routledge.
Bolton, G. (2001). *Reflective practice. Writing and professional development*, London: Paul Chapman.
Brookfield, S.D. (1995). *Becoming a critically reflective teacher*, San Francisco, CA: Jossey-Bass.
Cambridge, D. (2008). *Models of ePortfolio practice*. TLT Workshop. Retrieved 13 July, 2008, from https://admin.acrobat.com/_a738382050/p87097382/.
Clegg, S. (2004). Critical readings: progress files and the production of the autonomous learner, *Teaching in Higher Education*, 9(3), 287–298.
CRA (2008). *E-portfolios/introduction*. Retrieved 25 June, 2008, from http://www.recordingachievement.org/eportfolios/default.asp.
Hartnell-Young, E., Harrison, C., Crook, C., Pemberton, R., Ioves, G., Fisher, T. & Davies, L. (2007). *Impact study of e-portfolios on learning*, Becta, Retrieved 19 October, 2009, from http://partners.becta.org.uk/index.php?section=rh&catcode=_re_rp_02&rid=14007.
Hughes, J. (2007). Possibilities for patchwork eportfolios? Critical dialogues and reflexivity as strategic acts of interruption. Unpublished Masters' dissertation. Retrieved 2 January, 2009, from http://wlv.openrepository.com/wlv/handle/2436/64614.
Hughes, J. (2009). Becoming an eportfolio teacher. In: D. Cambridge, B. Cambridge and K. Yancey (Eds.) *Electronic portfolios 2.0: emergent findings and shared questions*, Washington, DC: Stylus Publishing.
Hughes, J. and Purnell, E. (2008). Blogging for beginners? Using blogs and eportfolios in teacher education. *Sixth International Networked Learning Conference Proceedings*, Halkidiki, Greece.
Hughes, J., Lacey, C. & Wise, D. (2008). Beyond projects and piloting – embedding an eportfolio in a Post Graduate Certificate in eEducation (PGCE) – an innovation too far? In H.J. Miller & A.L. Jefferies (Eds.) *Enhancing the student experience. Proceedings of the Third International Blended Learning Conference (pp. 54–62)*, Hertfordshire: University of Hertfordshire Press.
Hulme, M. & Hughes, J. (2006). Patchwork e-dialogues in the professional development of new teachers. In J. O'Donoghue (Ed.) *Technology supported learning and teaching: a staff perspective (pp. 192–209)*, Hershey, PA: Idea Group Inc.
JISC (2007). *The learner's voice*. Retrieved 1 September, 2007, from http://www.jisc.ac.uk/whatwedo/programmes/elearningpedagogy/learneroutcomes/learnervoices.
JISC (2008). *Effective practice with e-portfolios. Supporting 21st century learning*. Retrieved 10 September, 2008, from http://www.jisc.ac.uk/media/documents/publications/effectivepracticeeportfolios.pdf.
Lather, P. (1991). *Getting smart. Feminist research and pedagogy with/in the postmodern*, New York: Routledge.
Laurillard, D. (2007). Foreword. In H. Beetham and R. Sharpe (Eds.) *Rethinking pedagogy for a digital age: designing and delivering e-learning (pp. xv–xvii)*, London: Routledge.
Lillis, T.M. (2001). *Student writing. Access, regulation, desire*, London: Routledge.
Mayes, T. & de Freitas, S. (2007). Learning and e-learning: the role of theory. In H. Beetham and R. Sharpe (Eds.) *Rethinking pedagogy for a digital age: designing and delivering e-learning (pp. 13–25)*, London: Routledge.
QAA (2008). *Institutional Audit. University of Wolverhampton*. Retrieved 28 November, 2008, from http://www.qaa.ac.uk/reviews/reports/institutional/Wolverhampton09/RG410Wolverhampton.pdf.

Richardson, H.C. & Ward, R. (2005). *Developing and implementing a methodology for reviewing eportfolio products*, The Centre for Recording Achievement. Retrieved 5 September, 2005, from http://www.jisc.ac.uk/uploaded_documents/epfr.doc.

Richardson, L. & St. Pierre, E.A. (2005). Writing: a method of inquiry. In N.K. Denzin and Y.S. Lincoln (Eds.) *The Sage handbook of qualitative research* (3rd Ed.), Thousand Oaks, CA: Sage.

Sharpe, R. & Oliver, M. (2007). Designing courses for e-learning. In H. Beetham and R. Sharpe (Eds.) *Rethinking pedagogy for a digital age: designing and delivering e-learning* (pp. 41–51), London: Routledge.

Ward, R. & Richardson, H.C. (2005). *Getting what you want: implementing personal development planning through e-portfolio*. Retrieved 28 September, 2005, from http://www.recordingachievement.org/downloads/0504AugGettingWhatYouWant.pdf.

Yancey, K.B. (1998). *Reflection in the writing classroom*, Logan, UT: Utah State University Press.

# 15
# Skills and Strategies for E-learning in a Participatory Culture

SIMON WALKER, JILL JAMESON AND MALCOLM RYAN

## Editors' Introduction

This chapter argues that the skills acquired through participation in Web 2.0 spaces – what Jenkins (2006) refers to as *participatory skills* – can be harnessed in support of academic development. Participatory skills considered in this light include play, performance, simulation, appropriation, multitasking, judgement, transmedia navigation, networking and negotiation. The authors note that their relationship to more traditional academic skills is rarely recognized by educational organizations or by learners themselves. Based on practical teaching experience, the authors outline developmental strategies for helping learners to bridge the gap between informal, participatory learning and the expectations of academic study. At the same time they suggest that a deeper engagement is required of educators, both in recognizing the contribution that participatory cultures make to lifelong learning skills, and in convincing young people of the relevance of traditional literacies in their networked lives.

## Introduction

> Every problem contains within itself the seeds of its own solution.
>
> (Stanley Arnold)

In 2006, the Leitch report propelled an increasingly centralized government-led agenda for skills reform into further and higher education (Leitch 2006). Questions concerning the appropriateness – or not – of academic and vocational skills have seeded a debate about the relevance and types of skills that graduates should possess to enable them to take a full and active role in a democratic learning and earning society.

This chapter considers the changing nature of knowledge acquisition in an ever more digitized era, whilst recognizing the problematic nature of government-driven agendas for skills development (Wolf 2007), and the complexity of determining what, precisely, the fuzzily deterministic concept 'skills' actually means. It examines the types of skills and literacies learners need to take full advantage of through the formal *and* informal learning opportunities that now exist. Regardless of the aims of government or their teachers, learners are using their own tools and technologies to tap into communities and networks to fulfil their own needs and in doing so are, to a variable extent, participating in the development of valuable skills for use in later life. These same learners are also engaged in formal learning situations where their skill sets and approaches to acquiring knowledge may be largely unacknowledged, unappreciated and under-exploited. In their turn, as Graff (2003) points out, these learners often fail to recognize the relevance of traditional academic skills that will enable them to connect at deeper levels with the new media, and contribute more fully to their own development and to society as a whole.

This is not to say that participative online activity is the same as participative online *learning* activity. Most learners struggle to transfer skills effectively from informal to formal learning contexts without explicit guidance: they not only need targeted support in their personal development but also exposure to new learning and teaching approaches that foreground digital scholarship and information strategies.

To fully engage students, the authors identify the need for revised models of academic practice that draw upon emerging learning theories for a digital age.

## The Changing Significances of Literacy

Since its inception, compulsory formal education has been orientated towards the development of language, predominantly the cultivation of interactions through the activities of reading and writing linear text. This may be changing as we move into a digital age characterized by a wide range of broadcast and interactive media. Digital media offer new modes of representation and expression, which stretch the term 'literacy' to include representational fluency in a variety of forms, not limited to the printed word. We should be mindful, however, of the danger that the orthodoxy of 'literacies', emerging as a field of study in its own right, may become over-theorized and appropriated by institutions in what Beetham et al. (2009: 10) describe as 'a set of terms to be laid over existing policies and institutional practices without any real changes to how learners experience their relationships with knowledge, learning and technology.'

If learners are to make appropriate intellectual judgements about the quality and reliability of information relating to the concepts and frameworks comprising their subject knowledge base, it is crucial to provide opportunities to develop critical literacies. Although students' social use of Web 2.0 tools is increasing, this does not in itself provide them with the skills for collaborative learning or engagement in professional or scholarly communities of practice. At the same time, while most institutions provide 'information' skills training, and an awareness of the characteristics of digital information, there is little focus on the personal and social skills that allow learners to share information effectively or operate in group situations, and which have been identified as important for future employment (Pea 2008). Academics acknowledge the need for a cultural shift, but they express anxiety and concern over a lack of coherent, tried and tested, pedagogic models driven by clear institutional strategies (Armstrong and Franklin 2008).

## Models to Support Changing Practices

It is clear that institutions in all educational sectors are struggling to keep pace with developments in technology, and proliferating opportunities for informal learning in virtual environments beyond the control of any educational organization. Learners are venturing into places that formal educators may never go, absorbing new kinds of knowledge, creating their own interactive learning arenas, and joining 24/7 global dialogues in affinity spaces such as Wikipedia, Facebook, Twitter, YouTube, Wetpaint, Flickr and 3D multi-user environments. How are these rapidly expanding digital environments affecting learning? How can institutions keep up with these new ways in which students are increasingly collaborating in interactive knowledge creation?

Whereas previously students learned through the formal absorption of authoritative knowledge transmitted didactically in lectures, John Seeley Brown (2002) suggests that student learning is beginning to be more 'discovery based', linked to the ready availability of 'infotainment' in masses of web-based information and entertainment resources. George Siemens (2005) has argued that learning theories are evolving to accommodate and frame new ways in which we may now be learning as a result of the rapid explosion in e-learning technological developments in the twenty-first century. He contends that behaviourism, cognitivism, and constructivism, which he classifies as 'the three broad learning theories most often utilized in the creation of instructional environments', are now giving way to a new learning theory: 'connectivism'. Siemens states that 'connectivism presents a model of learning that acknowledges the tectonic shifts in a society where learning is no longer an internal, individualistic activity', and argues that new kinds of group learning are evolving, in which skills of connecting with other people in digital networks are increasingly important.

To test these theories about learning and e-learning in practical situations, it is useful to consider how students have previously responded to the use of e-learning for specific study skills development. Between May 2005 and March 2007, the JISC-funded eLISA (e-Learning Independent Study Award) project explored the potential of Moodle and LAMS e-learning systems to deliver study skills. Evaluation studies of both the eLISA and the follow-on eLIDA CAMEL project revealed that learning activities mediated through these systems did enhance learner participation, performance and motivation (Jameson et al. 2006a, 2006b, 2008; Jameson 2007).

Students themselves rated the effectiveness of the online study skills materials more highly than reading a book or visiting a website, while many teachers involved in the study reported that the materials were 'very effective' at enhancing both the learning experience and the achievement of outcomes (Masterman 2006). It is significant, however, that the strengths of this approach were considered to be features of the learning materials and activities on offer, rather than properties of the online environment itself (ibid: 40).

The eLISA work demonstrated that appropriately designed learning activities can invigorate students' learning capabilities. It targeted study skills particularly suited to computer-mediated environments, such as information searching, time management, revision and exam techniques, careers research and writing a CV or personal statement. In this context, skills that teachers considered less suitable for online support included reading, note taking, essay and report writing, and presentation techniques.

The research also revealed just how quickly new technologies were changing attitudes and approaches to formal education, as well as theories of knowledge acquisition. In 2006, learning designs were influenced by the prevailing learning theory of social constructivism. In 2009, theories of connectivism are in the ascent, as learners use their own digital devices to access their chosen global networks. Educational organizations must consider new ways to support learners' development within this digitally networked environment (Bradwell 2009).

### Participatory Culture and Formal Learning

Effective learning now needs to encompass digital literacies: the capacity for critical engagement and active participation in both the new media culture and traditional academia. The relationship between learning in formal settings and the development of strategies for informal digitally mediated learning – what Jenkins (2006) refers to as 'participatory culture' – is still relatively under-examined. Jenkins describes features of this culture as being 'relatively low barriers to artistic expression and civic engagement, strong support for creating and sharing one's creations, and some type of informal mentorship whereby what is known by the most experienced is passed along to novices' (ibid: 3).

Participants in this emergent culture, which include many millions of people in online communities across the world, use digital media to create collective forms of expression such as mash-ups, zines and video productions, and shape the flow of information through activities such as blogging and

**Table 15.1** Table of Jenkins' (2006) Participatory Skills (Reproduced With Permission From The MIT Press and Funded By the John D. and Catherine T. MacArthur Foundation)

| | |
|---|---|
| Play | The capacity to experiment with and explore your surroundings as a form of problem-solving. |
| Performance | The ability to adopt alternative identities for the purpose of improvisation and discovery. |
| Simulation | The ability to interpret and construct dynamic models of real world processes. |
| Appropriation | The ability to meaningfully sample and remix media content. |
| Multitasking | The ability to scan one's environment and shift focus as needed to salient details. |
| Distributed Cognition | The ability to interact meaningfully with tools that expand mental capacities. |
| Collective Intelligence | The ability to pool knowledge and compare notes with others toward a common goal. |
| Judgement | The ability to evaluate the reliability and credibility of different information sources. |
| Transmedia Navigation | The ability to follow the flow of stories and information across multiple modalities. |
| Networking | The ability to search for, synthesize, and disseminate information. |
| Negotiation | The ability to travel across diverse communities, discerning and respecting multiple perspectives, and grasping and following alternative norms. |

podcasting. Jenkins (ibid.) proposes a range of skills required and fostered by active skills listed in Table 15.1.

These are skills that, outside the participatory culture itself, may not yet be highly prized but should be viewed as potentially supportive of high-value academic skills. At face value, the ability to contribute to social networking sites, upload videos, blogs and podcasts, to follow and be followed on microblogging sites, to take part in 3D multiuser virtual environments, to add to a wiki, or create mash-ups and zines, do not appear closely related to formal study skills. They have an air of superficiality about them. Indeed, they are often condemned as part of the shallowness of modern youth culture, and are reported by the media as evidence that, in a traditional academic sense, students have become less literate than they were (Mehegan 2007). Attempts by educational organizations to engage with social technologies are often viewed with disapproval in media reporting (Curtis 2009). We suggest that these 'participatory skills' are, in fact, examples of highly relevant social and cognitive competences, that could be harnessed and further developed in formal settings to support lifelong and life-wide learning.

There are elements of crossover between the traditional and the new literacies that are obvious and require little or no explanation. For example, the importance in formal educational settings of play (as experimentation and exploration) and performance (as testing roles and identities in different settings) has been long established (Huizinga 1950; Bruner et al. 1976; Gagne 1985). While Garvey (1990) suggests that play is inherently unproductive, the practice of 'wilfing' (what was I looking for) may in fact become highly productive in an intensively interconnected environment, in which necessary knowledge is often only a few clicks away.

Academics frequently bemoan their students' lack of time-management skills, yet these same students are able, in the context of their social and virtual worlds, to multitask with ease: they can shift focus between various applications on their desktop, text on their phone and listen to music. It is not beyond imagination to develop this capacity for multitasking into a more rigorous sense of prioritization, so the learner understands that while following multiple trains of thought can lead to happy discoveries, at the same time there need to be periods of summary and focus in an academic or work environment in which deadlines have to be met.

Play as simulation is an equally important tool for learning, and academics in many disciplines have employed computer models to create powerful simulations. Learners are using many of the same skills to navigate the educationally motivated world of an academic simulation (for example, a business studies simulation of a commercial start-up project) as they are using to progress in the entertaining world of a computer game (for example Zoo Tycoon).

Other skills that learners have intuited in new media environments are more subtly, but no less significantly, connected. The combined skills of appropriation and editing, for example, are second nature to many young learners. Material on the web is constantly mashed up, sampled, reworked, adapted and re-presented for personal and social ends. In doing this, learners exhibit many of the same skills that are required to search out, paraphrase, manipulate and represent data or source material for academic ends. Written, audio and image-based media are all available for creative re-appropriation on the web. There is significant value in learners bringing to their academic studies these habits of selecting and appropriating materials, seeing and creating new patterns of meaning, and sharing information in creative ways. If they could take back to their virtual worlds an increased respect for intellectual property and more critical appreciation of different modes of representation, then the depth and quality of their appropriations would be enhanced.

Likewise, skills of judgement and decision making, which students continually employ in online activities, are demanded in the academic environment. Perhaps without realizing it, learners display judgement when they filter and aggregate data sources, when they decide whether to believe this person's comment, accept that person's friendship request, tag that entry, link to this video, trust a wiki reference or write on someone's wall. A similar set of cognitive processes is involved in choosing, filtering and judging sources of scholarly evidence, and registering professional or academic opinions, though the criteria for judgement may differ. So in an informal setting, students are already exhibiting skills relevant to the construction of academic argument: analysis of the claims of others, weighing evidence, spotting and identifying contradictions and being critical. Graff (2003) makes a similar case for recognizing the ability of young people to argue in a normal day-to-day context, while developing their critical reasoning skills in an academic environment.

Jenkins, building on earlier work by Salomon et al. (1991) and Salomon (1993), uses the phrase 'distributed cognition' to refer to tools and practices that effectively externalize and expand human intelligence (Jenkins 2006). Obvious examples are word-processing or GPS driven applications, although Jenkins is keen to stress that 'distributed cognition is not just about technologies; it is also about tapping social institutions... or connecting with remote experts' (ibid: 37). More and more learners are entering university with the expectation that they will rely on digital tools and networks to deal with information, to advance thought and to test ideas. Combined with students' fluency in the skills of aggregation (the ability to assimilate related information from a range of web sources), practices of distributed cognition achieve relevance both as a participatory and as an academic skill.

By the time these young digital experts reach higher or further education, most will have experienced in one form or another what Levy (2000) calls 'collective intelligence' (quoted in Jenkins 2006: 39), perhaps through contributing to a wiki, or to a forum discussion thread, or simply to an online news site, whereby knowledge is shared in common. The question of how to make effective use of this powerful phenomenon is of interest not just to academics, but also to policy makers and corporate executives. Educational institutions have already started to pool their knowledge – broadening access to their research libraries, establishing communities of practice, building partnerships and generally blurring their traditional boundaries – and increasingly it will be these models of the 'edgeless university' (Bradwell 2009) that become familiar to students of the digital age.

One of the major problems that students face in the information-rich, multimodal but anarchic Web 2.0 world is organizing the vast amount of information and opinion that exists, largely without peer review or quality control. The emergence of a qualitatively different information environment, coupled with a new communication environment, challenges learners' information skills. Rowlands (2007) identifies learners born and brought up in the Internet age as the most web-literate generation ever, yet in searching the web for information, experience difficulty in evaluating information for its relevance, accuracy or authority (Rowlands et al. 2008: 303).

Even well designed 'webquests' rarely take advantage of technologies that encourage socially constructive methods of learning, such as social bookmarking or citation tools, or encourage students to communicate their own conclusions as new sources of knowledge and meaning. If through formal learning, students can become more effective, discriminating networkers, better judges of information they receive and more credible communicators, they have the potential to be key participants in the knowledge economy. For, as Mason and Rennie point out, 'the shelf life of information is now so short that knowing where to find information is more valuable than knowing any particular piece of information' (2008: 10).

Another new, and allied, skill is that of transmedia navigation, or the ability to track information across various platforms. Again, digital experts are well-versed in a multimodal approach, switching with ease between text, video, screen-based information, micro-blogging, podcasts, virtual worlds or game-play culture. Perhaps unknowingly, they understand the syntax and semiotics of each arena in which they participate, and the particular etiquettes that apply. This offers a good grounding for understanding the syntax, semiotics and etiquette of academic communication, particularly as it advances out of the print age. Drawing on a study at the University of Portsmouth, Roy Williams notes that 'multi-modal possibilities allow for the linking and integration of cognitive, tacit, affective, cultural, personal, graphic and photographic ways of exploring, articulating, expressing and representing sense-making about learning and identity' (Williams et al. 2009).

In the process of contributing to the collective intelligence of Web 2.0, of navigating its myriad modalities, and of networking, learners will also have displayed enhanced capacities for negotiation as they encounter diverse online communities, learn to respect multiple perspectives and the importance of 'difference'. These skills in negotiation will prove invaluable in the context of college or university life, as students find themselves thrust, perhaps for the first time, into a social and international melting pot. They are skills that can be harnessed to hone students' powers of academic argument: skills of persuasion, assertion, of understanding alternative viewpoints, bridging and debating. They are also skills that can be honed in more strategic ways, for example by negotiating terms in 'contract cheating', a method by which one student can employ another to produce original assignments without fear of plagiarism detection (Clarke 2008).

The reflective skills that digital learners exhibit – attending to their peers' input, reflecting on their own output, responding to feedback – are also vital to make them fully rounded, competent members of the higher education community. Once honed, these reflective skills will enable students to adapt and develop their academic output, experimenting with when and how to take risks.

Finally, among the new literacies that students bring to higher and further education, there is the skill of concept building. Digital learners no longer need advanced web-building or programming skills in order to construct simple websites, profile pages, blogs and twitter streams. Every time a learner puts together a personal profile, for example, by amalgamating text, pictures, links, favourites, friends, they are constructing a representation of themselves as a conceptual entity. Often, too, when they are contributing to the collective intelligence of the web, they will be exercising their concept-building skills, however unlikely they are to think of it in these terms.

In summary, the authors propose the following categories to locate participatory skills within valued academic skills:

- Enquiry – the ability to locate multiple sources of information from established institutions and nomadic communities.
- Decision making – the ability to determine the relevance of information to make informed decisions to the best of one's judgement.
- Aggregation – the ability to assimilate related information from a range of web sources.
- Concept building – the ability to construct websites, profile pages, blogs, etc. that define and /or build concepts or identities.
- Editing – the ability to check over, revise and correct written and image-based information, amending, re-hashing and improving production outputs.
- Reflection – the ability to evaluate and critique one's own ideas, to attend to peers' input, to consider the merits of different outputs, respond to feedback, collate evidence of performance, and set new goals.

## Strategies for Building Academic Skills

If institutions were to place explicit value on these new participatory skills they would, in effect, raise their learners' awareness of the new-found media literacies in their possession. At the same time, they would be building on these skills, using a range of developmental interventions to support more traditional academic learning skills. In learning theory terms, institutions could use a constructivist approach to develop connectivist skills.

We believe that by valuing their students' existing skills, developed through participatory cultural activities, universities and colleges can create a mutually respectful, virtuous learning circle. If the recognition and further development of participatory skills – such as negotiation, enquiry, reflection, appropriation and concept building – were embedded across the curriculum, we believe this would help address many areas of perceived academic weakness, such as shorter attention spans, a lack of reflection, poor text literacy and inappropriate source use (Oblinger and Oblinger 2005).

The authors are aware that some assumptions are being made in claiming the relevance of participatory skills to formal learning: that learners already possess participatory skills; that these are easily transferable to academic contexts and affinity spaces; and that both learners and teachers can be convinced of their value. There is evidence that may support both assumptions. In the IBEL project, which explored digital interventions in traditional learning situations between 2007 and 2008, many learners expressed a range of positive views regarding the potential for integrating participatory skills in formal learning situations. For example, one student found the discussion forum useful 'because it's similar to other chat room sites' (Walker 2008: 26). Others commented on the importance of sharing ideas with peers and the ability to collaborate with others during periods of independent study.

So how can institutions bring about the changes in practice necessary for this new paradigm? The institutional response must be holistic in nature, embedding literacies into the heart of learning rather than attempting to bolt-on additional skills. Evidence now suggests that the provision of separate skills modules can undermine motivation (Beetham et al. 2009: 71) and that there may be difficulty in applying skills learned in one context to another (Canning 2007). Yet the strong tendency in formal education is to provide training to meet a perceived skills gap, rather than developing academic practice to incorporate skills development, and defining authentic tasks that lead to engagement and deep understanding. The following strategies are proposed as examples of developmental interventions, designed to support key academic skills in technology-mediated learning environments.

1. Concept building (induction activity): the transition from school to university may be eased by building discipline-related concepts through the construction of profiles, an activity most learners are familiar with. For example, a lecturer might set a task for individuals or small groups to research the impact of a well known academic scholar in their discipline. By creating a social network profile page for this figure, learners can exhibit concept-building skills in a familiar virtual environment. Extending this with role-play activities can further enrich understanding. The results can be connected together as a knowledge sphere, linking groups of learners together with external resources.

2. HE level 1 literature research: social bookmarking and citation sites can be used by novice learners as they begin to review the literature and evaluate the sources of relevance to their discipline. By using cognitive tools within a social context that comprises an audience of peers, as well as – potentially – researchers and lecturers, learners tap into existing practices of collaborative knowledge building. The tools can be used to share information flexibly, support commentary and peer feedback, and provide materials for class discussion. Support for information

searching and critical feedback can be offered to develop metacognitive skills. Social bookmarking and annotation engage learners in the development of critical enquiry skills, and can be used as an opportunity to reflect critically on the learning process, their role within it, and their relationship to valued knowledge.

3. Increasing student participation: the use of a personal response system (PRS) as part of the lecture experience can engage students collaboratively in answering problems posed by the lecturer. Learners need to be able to read the problem appropriately, assess their current knowledge, use judgement to select a response, use technology to make the response, and assess the results. They must then compare their results with others in their vicinity, and try to persuade them of their point of view. The lecture theatre is turned into a theatre for social learning, connecting groups of learners together and demonstrating vividly the advantages of collaborative knowledge building.

4. Critical evaluation through role play: learning activities that use 3D multiuser virtual environments, such as Second Life, can support the development of formal academic skills on the basis of participatory skills such as the use of avatars. The externalization of a particular identity as an avatar allows students to practice communication and lifelike interactions with a community of other Second Life users. In a project at the University of Greenwich, Youth and Community students were encouraged to explore diversity and taboos in a safe Second Life environment, explorations that led to some fascinating insights into representation and social acceptance. Through enactment, learners were able to test out critical and theoretical concepts and apply them in practical workplace scenarios.

5. Building academic community: peer support is a hugely influential factor in students' retention and motivation to study, and social networking sites such as Facebook are now routinely used to help students meet others and share concerns. Peer group networks can be enhanced by the use of peer mentoring schemes, which pair second years with new students, or third years with alumni. Social networking sites can also be used as virtual communities of practice in which undergraduates discuss real problems of their discipline or profession alongside researchers and lecturers. These can be deeply engaging to learners.

## Conclusion

Digital skills for learning are now recognized as globally important. Indeed, as a recent report for the UN, UNESCO and the EU asserted, media education is the 'defining option' for the future and demands 'strategies that can be shared, tested and adopted in a spirit of social change that goes beyond [institutional] reform' (Frau-Meigs and Torrent 2009: 16).

Bandura and Schunk (1981) suggest that self-motivation and self-efficacy are key signs of an effective learner. As the REAP (*Re-engineering Assessment Practices)* project has shown in Scotland, strategic uses of technology within a clear pedagogical rationale can lead to real benefits in terms of student self-regulation (Nicol 2009). The institutional challenge is to bridge the gap for students between learning – or playing, or performing, or negotiating or networking – in an informal context, to carrying out these activities in a formal, academic context.

The shift in learning context and paradigm is not an easy one, involving recognition of skills acquired outside of formal learning, and their development in scholarly and professional tasks. Once there is an intention to bridge the gap, the educational institution is already better placed to meet the needs of its students. If the curriculum succeeds in developing learners' self-confidence and their capacity for creativity (Selwyn 2008), then their engagement, commitment and attainments can only be enhanced.

## References

Armstrong, J. & Franklin, T. (2008). *A review of current and developing international practice in the use of social networking (Web 2.0) in higher education.* Franklin Consulting. Retrieved 15 October, 2009, from http://clex.org.uk/8.%20Franklin%20Consulting%20Intnl%20Review-%20final%20report.doc.

Bandura, A. & Schunk, D.H. (1981). Cultivating competence, self-efficacy, and intrinsic interest through proximal motivation. *Journal of Personality and Social Psychology, 41,* 586–598.

Beetham, H., McGill, L. & Littlejohn, A. (2009). *Thriving in the 21st C: learning literacies for the digital age* (LLida project), JISC. Retrieved 22 June, 2009, from http://www.jisc.ac.uk/media/documents/projects/llidareportjune2009.pdf.

Bradwell, P. (2009). *The edgeless university: Why higher education must embrace technology.* DEMOS. Retrieved 28 June, 2009, from http://www.demos.co.uk/publications/the-edgeless-university.

Bruner, J., Jolly, A. & Sylva, K. (1976). *Play – its role in development and evolution.* New York: Basic Books, Inc.

Canning, R. (2007). Reconceptualising core skills. *Journal of Education and Work, 20*(1), 17–26.

Clarke, B. (2008). *Contract cheating … and sold to the student at the back.* Presentation 20 November 2008. University of Greenwich. Retrieved 2 June, 2009, from http://web-dev-csc.gre.ac.uk/conference/conf45/index.php?p=426.

Curtis, P. (2009). Pupils to study Twitter and blogs in primary shake-up. *Guardian Newspaper,* 25 March 2009. Retrieved 2 September, 2009, from http://www.guardian.co.uk/education/2009/mar/25/primary-schools-twitter-curriculum.

Frau-Meigs, D. & Torrent, J. (Eds.) (2009). *Mapping media education policies in the world: visions, programmes and challenges.* United Nations, Alliance of Civilizations, UNESCO, European Commission and Grupo Comunicar. Retrieved 4 July, 2009, from http://www.unaoc.org/images//mapping_media_education_book_final_version.pdf.

Gagne, R. (1985). *The conditions of learning.* Retrieved 16 November, 2008, from http://tip.psychology.org/gagne.html.

Garvey, C. (1990). *Play.* Cambridge, MA: Harvard University Press.

Graff, G. (2003). *Clueless in academe: how schooling obscures the life of the mind.* New Haven, CT and London: Yale University Press.

Huizinga, J. (1950). *Homo Ludens: a study of the play element in culture.* New York: Roy Publishers.

Jameson, J. (2007). *Final report of the JISC eLISA Project.* Retrieved 11 July, 2009, from http://www.jisc.ac.uk/whatwedo/programmes/edistributed/elisa.aspx.

Jameson, J., Ferrell, G., Kelly, J., Walker, S. & Ryan, M. (2006a). Building trust and shared knowledge in communities of e-learning practice: collaborative leadership in the JISC eLISA and CAMEL lifelong learning projects. *British Journal of Educational Technology,* 37(6): 949–968.

Jameson, J., Walker, S., Ryan, M., Masterman, E., Lee, S., Noble, H., Dastbaz, M. & Noakes, P. (2006b, September). *Designing learning for eLISA,* Paper presented at *Association for Learning Technology Conference,* Heriot-Watt University, Edinburgh, Scotland. Retrieved 11 July, 2009, from http://works.bepress.com/jill_jameson/14/.

Jameson, J., Walker, S., Riachi, R., Kelly, J., Stiles, M. & Masterman, E. (2008). *Final report of the eLIDA CAMEL Project.* Retrieved 11 July, 2009, from http://www.jisc.ac.uk/media/documents/programmes/elearningpedagogy/elidacamelfinal.pdf.

Jenkins, H (2006). *Confronting the challenges of participatory culture: media education for the 21st century.* MacArthur Foundation. Retrieved 12 December, 2008, from http://www.digitallearning.macfound.org/atf/cf/%7B7E45C7E0-A3E0-4B89-AC9C-E807E1B0AE4E%7D/JENKINS_WHITE_PAPER.PDF.

Leitch, S. (2006). *Prosperity for all in the global economy – world class skills: final report of the Leitch review of skills.* London: HMSO/HM Treasury. Retrieved 11 July, 2009, from http://www.hm-treasury.gov.uk/leitch.

Mason, R. & Rennie, F. (2008). *E-learning and social networking handbook: resources for higher education.* New York: Routledge.

Masterman, E. (2006). *Distributed e-learning regional pilot projects: JISC eLISA independent lifelong learning project evaluation report.* University of Oxford Learning Technologies Group unpublished report.

Mehegan, D. (2007). *Young people reading a lot less.* Boston Globe Newspaper. Retrieved 30 July, 2009, from http://www.boston.com/news/education/k_12/articles/2007/11/19/young_people_reading_a_lot_less/.

Nicol, D. (2009). Transforming assessment and feedback: enhancing integration and empowerment in the first year. *Quality Enhancement Themes: The First Year Experience.* Quality Assurance Agency for Higher Education. Retrieved 12 July, 2009, from, http://www.enhancementthemes.ac.uk/documents/firstyear/First_Year_Transforming_Assess.pdf.

Oblinger, D.G. & Oblinger, J.L. (Eds.) (2005) *Educating the Net Generation.* Boulder, CO: Educause. Retrieved 10 June, 2009, from http://www.educause.edu/educatingthenetgen.

Pea, R. (2008, November). *Fostering learning in the networked world.* Paper presented at Exploring Technology-enabled Change in Education, Sheffield. Retrieved 7 November, 2008, from http://events.becta.org.uk/display.cfm?resID=38800.

Rowlands, I., Nicholas, D., Williams, P., Huntington, P., Fieldhouse, M., Gunter, B., Withey, R., Jamali, H., Dobrowolski, T. & Tenopir, C. (2008). *The Google generation: the information behaviour of the researcher of the future.* Aslib Proceedings, 60, 4.

Salomon, G. (1993). *Distributed cognitions: psychological and educational considerations.* New York: Cambridge University Press.

Salomon, G., Perkins, D. N. & Globerson, T. (1991). Partners in cognition: extending human intelligence with intelligent technologies. *Educational Researcher, 20*(3), 2–9.

Seely Brown, J. (2002). *Growing up digital: how the web changes work, education, and the ways people learn.* United States Distance Learning Association. Retrieved 29 June, 2009, from http://www.usdla.org/html/journal/FEB02_Issue/article01.html.

Selwyn, N. (2008). *Education 2.0? Designing the web for teaching and learning.* TLRP. Institute of Education. Retrieved 15 May, 2009, from http://www.tlrp.org/pub/documents/TELcomm.pdf.

Siemens, G. (2005). Connectivism: a learning theory for the digital age. *eLearnSpace article,* 2004, updated 2005. Retrieved 29 June, 2009, from http://www.elearnspace.org/Articles/connectivism.htm.

Walker, S. (2008). *BECTA International Baccalaureate E-Learning Laboratory.* Becta Evaluation Report. Retrieved 22 February, 2009, from http://partners.becta.org.uk/index.php?section=rh&catcode=_re_rp_02&rid=15656.

Williams, R., Gumtau, S. & Karousou, R. (2009). Nested narratives at Greenwich. In S. Walker, M. Ryan and R. Teed (Eds.) *Learning from the learners' experience. Proceedings of the Greenwich E-learning Conference.* Retrieved 3 July, 2009, from http://web-dev-csc.gre.ac.uk/conference/conf37/docs/Learning%20from%20the%20Learners%20Experience2008.pdf.

Wolf, A. (2007). Round and round the houses: the Leitch review of skills. *Local Economy, 22*(2), 111–117.

# Index